DISCONTINUITIES:
NEW ESSAYS ON RENAISSANCE LITERATURE AND CRITICISM

Over the past two decades there has been a perceived paradigm shift in the study of English Renaissance literature. Scholarly attention has moved from the individual to the social as the agent of literary production and the principal site of discussion. Genius is now far less likely to be invoked than discourse, culture, or ideology. The intellectual shift, routinely associated with new historicism, feminism, and cultural materialism, has been neither uncontested nor simple and uniform. The essays in the present volume set out to identify, examine, and respond to these discontinuities, and in so doing attest to the extraordinary vitality of contemporary Renaissance studies.

VIVIANA COMENSOLI is a professor in the Department of English at Wilfrid Laurier University. She is the author of 'Household Business': Domestic Plays of Early Modern England (U of Toronto P, 1996).
PAUL STEVENS is an associate professor in the Department of English at Queen's University. He is the author of Imagination and the Presence of Shakespeare in 'Paradise Lost' (U of Wisconsin P, 1985).

THEORY/CULTURE

General Editors:
Linda Hutcheon, Gary Leonard,
Janet Paterson, Paul Perron, and Jill Matus

EDITED BY
VIVIANA COMENSOLI AND PAUL STEVENS

Discontinuities:

New Essays on Renaissance Literature
and Criticism

UNIVERSITY OF TORONTO PRESS
Toronto Buffalo London

© University of Toronto Press Incorporated 1998
Toronto Buffalo London
Printed in Canada

ISBN 0-8020-0436-9 (cloth)
ISBN 0-8020-7225-9 (paper)

Printed on acid-free paper

Canadian Cataloguing in Publication Data

Main entry under title:

Discontinuities: new essays on Renaissance literature and criticism

(Theory/culture)
Includes index
ISBN 0-8020-0436-9 (bound) ISBN 0-8020-7225-9 (pbk.)

1. English literature – Early modern, 1500–1700 – History and criticism.
I. Comensoli, Viviana.   II. Stevens, Paul, 1946–   .   III. Series.

PR411.D57 1998   820.9'003   c98-931123-6

University of Toronto Press acknowledges the financial assistance to its publishing program of the Canada Council for the Arts and the Ontario Arts
Council.

Contents

PART III: RETHINKING SUBJECTIVITY: THE TURN TO LACAN

PART IV: POLITICAL ENGAGEMENT AND PROFESSIONAL DISCONTINUITIES

Acknowledgments

We wish to acknowledge the generous assistance given us by colleagues and friends, in particular Achsah Guibbory, Richard Helgerson, Barbara Lewalski, Sara Deats, Anne Russell, Jean Metcalfe, Ted McGee, Lynne Magnusson, Edward Pechter, and Valerie Traub. We are also grateful to the general editors of the series, especially to Linda Hutcheon for encouraging the project at its inception, and to the superb editorial staff – Suzanne Rancourt, Barb Porter, Kristen Pederson, and Darlene Money. The anonymous readers of the Press offered perceptive and illuminating readings of the volume. We extend special thanks to Elaine Auerbach, who prepared the index, and to our research assistants, Viona Falk and Robert Parker. Joanne Buehler-Buchan, Karen Donnelly, and Kathy Goodfriend provided invaluable secretarial assistance. We are also grateful for the financial support we received from Queen's University and from the Office of Research and the Academic Development Fund of Wilfrid Laurier University. Our editorial collaboration on the volume was a very agreeable one, and we extend our greatest thanks to the contributors.

VIVIANA COMENSOLI AND PAUL STEVENS

Introduction

VIVIANA COMENSOLI AND PAUL STEVENS

Over the past two decades there has been what many have called, using Thomas Kuhn's well-worn but still useful vocabulary, a 'paradigm shift' in the study of English Renaissance literature. Attention has moved from the individual to the social as the agent of literary production and the principal site of discussion. Genius is now far less likely to be invoked than discourse, culture, ideology, or *habitus*. Even the term *Renaissance* has increasingly given way to the less celebratory, more muted *early modern*. Louis Montrose, in the 1989 collection of essays *The New Historicism*, describes the shift this way: 'There has recently emerged within Renaissance studies, as in Anglo-American literary studies generally, a renewed concern with the historical, social, and political conditions and consequences of literary production and reproduction: The writing and reading of texts, as well as the processes by which they are circulated and categorized, analyzed and taught, are being reconstructed as historically determined and determining modes of cultural work' (15). So familiar are these claims that it is now possible to detect signs of weariness in responses to them. 'The last thing we need to hear more of,' writes Annabel Patterson, 'is the ascendency of various forms of historicism, and the differences between them' (432). Even more disillusioned is Jonathan Crewe, who believes that the passing of the recent moment of triumph for Renaissance studies in effecting this paradigm shift has left it enfeebled – 'in a state akin to slow imperial decline' (346). Such pessimism is, we feel, somewhat premature. The intellectual shift under discussion, routinely associated, as in Montrose, with new historicism, feminism, and cultural materialism, as in Dollimore and Sinfield's *Political Shakespeare* (1985), has been neither uncontested nor simple and uniform. Apart from a pervasive and often unreflective agreement that literature does political work, no clear-cut consensus or new 'normal science' has emerged. The changes we have experienced as a profession are neither fully understood nor complete. They have in fact produced a complex variety not simply of 'ongoing or emergent concerns' (Crewe 347) but of contradictions, unresolved discontinuities, new problems and new issues inadvertently created in the process of analysing old ones. The essays in the present volume, in very different ways, all set out to identify, examine, and respond to these discontinuities, while at the same time offering new possibilities. In so doing, they indicate something of the extraordinary vitality of contemporary Renaissance studies.

As a pointed example of what we mean by the discontinuous state of English Renaissance studies, the second section of the volume – 'What to Do with Shakespeare?' – comprises essays by two scholars who share similar theoretical interests, both influenced by the more sophisticated forms of economism associated with writers like Pierre Bourdieu, Jean-Joseph Goux, and most recently John Guillory, both convinced of the contingent value of canonical authors, but both deeply at odds over the desirability of keeping Shakespeare at the centre. For Elizabeth Hanson, in 'Against a Synecdochic Shakespeare,' one of the many inadvertent effects of Renaissance critics' appeal to Derridean textuality and then Foucaultian discourse has been the reinforcement of certain synecdochic habits of thought. In a way that was reassuringly familiar, Shakespeare became a synecdoche for an almost exhaustive range of common cultural and discursive patterns – convenient evidence of the culture as a whole. In her incisive analysis of *The Merchant of Venice* and *Eastward Ho!*, an analysis that attends to the social conditions or 'banalities' of the playwrights' 'professional practice and local ideological investments' (83), Hanson demonstrates in illuminating detail how Shakespeare's drama is not the ideological centre, the representative case, but just one of many competing articulations of mercantile aspiration and anxiety made for and by different social groups. In this she shows just how much is to be gained in understanding the discursive heterogeneity of early modern England by situating Shakespeare 'in relation to his contemporaries, rather than letting him simply stand for them' (77).

For Karen Newman, in 'Cultural Capital's Gold Standard,' on the other hand, such decentring of Shakespeare is a wasted opportunity. Both Hanson and Newman are, or so it would seem, thoroughgoing historicists, but whereas Hanson's gaze is firmly fixed on early modern culture as a historical object of study, Newman has her eye on the historicity of her own practice. While the one seems to stand outside of or above history, the other seems to revel in being immersed in it. Looking at Guillory's map of the history of literary studies, Newman sees a radical transformation in what constitutes cultural capital: just as the exchange value of the classics was superseded by that of the vernacular literatures, and that of poetry by that of the novel, so now the exchange value of literature itself is about to be replaced by that of mass cultural, multimedia forms. Shakespeare is certainly a synecdoche but most importantly not so much for early modern culture as for the canonical literature now under threat. It is crucial to keep Shakespeare at the centre, Newman argues, because he 'allows the contemporary critic working in the early modern period to be read' (100). Thus for Newman, synecdochic Shakespeare, far from being an impediment, is an opportunity. Since there is no gold standard, no absolute measure of intrinsic worth, Shakespeare's exchange value, and with him all that he represents, whether it be early modern culture or canonical literature, may actually be inflated by deliberately rereading him in terms of contemporary cultural interests. Following the example of the commercial theatre, that is exactly what Newman sets out to do in reading *Timon of Athens* as an example of early modern sexuality, apostrophizing the play in terms of its much neglected but insistent homoeroticism.

To the extent that Hanson feels constrained by the need to respect the integrity of the object of study, namely the 'text' of early modern culture, she is what Richard Rorty would ironically call a weak textualist; to the extent that Newman feels free to inflate the value of *Timon*, to describe the text in such a way as to make it do what she considers desirable, she is a strong textualist (Rorty 153). While there are several ways of characterizing the differences between Hanson's and Newman's essays, emphasizing the difference between historicist obligation on the one hand and textualist freedom on the other epitomizes one of the central discontinuities we aim to foreground.

From its inception, the one abiding discontinuity that has shaped the discourse of English literary studies has been the tension between science and poetry, fact and imagination, scholarship and criticism, and most recently criticism and theory. In the early 1980s the triumph of poststructuralist theory was compromised by a dramatic resurgence of history, especially history understood as a means of calling attention to theory's apparent indifference to politics (Attridge et al. 1–9). De-construction in particular, it was claimed, lacked 'a coherent politi-cal agenda, let alone the pragmatic means to carry an agenda out' (Rapaport 98). In North America, resurgent history and hegemonic theory, mediated through some of the more enduring forms of New Criticism, gave birth to new historicism (see Liu 721–71). The degree to which this movement was a new formulation of the old discontinuity between fact and imagination is captured in Montrose's now famous chiasmus that the function of criticism was to do equal and simultaneous justice to 'the historicity of texts and the textuality of history' (20). The enormous difficulty of this task is indicated in the divergence between Hanson and Newman, the one feeling bound by the first part of the chiasmus, the other liberated by the second. As Stanley Fish explains in defining the main problem of new historicism, the real difficulty lies in keeping the two parts together, in reconciling 'the assertion of "wall to wall" textuality – the denial that the writing of history could find its foundation in a substratum of unmediated fact – with the desire to say something specific and normative' (303). While all of the essays in this volume struggle with this central discontinuity, those in the opening section – 'Recovering Women's Writing: Historicism vs. Textualism' – do so most immediately.

The emergence of the new historicist and cultural materialist strains of political criticism in Renaissance studies coincided with the emergence of a complex array of feminist approaches, whose practitioners felt the need to say something specific and normative far more urgently than did the writers of many of the more mannerist articulations of early new historicism, articulations that often seemed to take pleasure in their own powerless paradoxicality (Lentricchia 241; Stevens 467). While many feminist scholars set about their tasks by unearthing an extraordinary range of archival material, others concentrated on re-interpretation, and, stimulated by the fertility of poststructuralist theory, espoused it as an especially effective means of producing new knowledge about gender relations. As Derrida himself explained, the programs of deconstruction and feminism initially had much in common, especially in terms of the institutional resistance they encountered (Showalter in Todd 128). But discomfort about the degree to which poststructuralism's valorization of endless, impersonal textuality might compromise the feminist need to recover something of the particularity of Renaissance women's lives and their complex and wide-ranging responses to the category of gender was apparent from the beginning (Todd 125–9). This discomfort is taken up and turned into a forceful argument by Sylvia Brown in 'Over Her Dead Body: Feminism, Poststructuralism, and the Mother's Legacy,' the opening essay of the volume.

Brown differs from Hanson in suggesting that the irrepressible textuality of poststructuralism is not just occasionally or inadvertently occlusive, but irredeemably so. Through a careful analysis of the criticism of Mothers' Legacies, books of religious advice written by a mother for her children's use after her death, Brown argues that 'deconstruction is a "false friend," falsely congenial to the extraordinary circumstances of [the Legacies'] female authors who write under, and out of, the threat of death. Deconstruction ultimately undermines these authors' experience and extraordinariness' (13). As a result of deconstruction's extreme rhetoricity, its insistence that finally 'knowledge can only be self-referential knowledge about language' (14), all extra-linguistic distinctions collapse, rendering the political agenda of feminism meaningless. Most disturbing for Brown, in collapsing the distinction between actual and rhetorical violence, deconstruction, she argues, has the capacity 'to trivialize empirical instances of oppression and exploitation' (14). In its refusal to come to an easy or comforting rapprochement between theory and history, and between poststructuralism and feminism, Brown's essay exemplifies one of the central aims of the present volume in not downplaying or finessing the difficulties of the discontinuities it identifies.

Brown concludes her essay by urging us 'to learn from historians' (22–3), but it is precisely this exhortation and its confidence in contemporary historiography that worry the two other contributors to this section. Linda Woodbridge, whose *Women and the English Renaissance* (1984) is generally considered to be one of the most effective works in unearthing new materials for a fresh historical study of women in the period (Cohen 25), draws attention to the failure of literary critics to question 'the solid sea floor of History' (56). In 'Dark Ladies,' Woodbridge argues that while literary texts and the culture they are believed to produce are routinely ironized, social history, especially in the form of standard works like Lawrence Stone's *Family, Sex, and Marriage in England 1500–1800*, has been silently treated as a stable point of reference. When we selectively ignore the rhetoricity of contemporary academic historiography, what we know of women, a social group symbolized for Woodbridge by the nameless 'dark' ladies of so many sonnet sequences, grows more obscure. In 'The Modernity of the Early Modern,' Katherine Osler Acheson takes Woodbridge's concerns a stage further. Implicit in Acheson's argument is the suspicion that contemporary historiography is incapable of affording us access both to what most precisely makes the 'early modern' modern and to the distinctiveness of Renaissance women and men, an access desired by Brown. Specifically, conventional historiography's lack of self-reflection or interest in its own rhetorical constitution, especially as it is reflected even in some of the most textualist literary criticism, condemns scholars to oscillate between overestimating and underestimating our proximity to the past – 'between glib conflations of then and now, and anxious disavowals of similarity' (31). It is in this discontinuity itself that Acheson sees the most compelling explanation for the modernity of the early modern. For the same rhetorical complex that produces this discontinuity – the metonymic patterns by which we break with the past and establish our authority over it, together with the metaphoric moves by which we submit and acknowledge our subjection to it – is remarkably evident in the literary remains of a seventeenth-century woman like Anne Clifford. Acheson's Clifford emerges as a paradoxical figure, a woman who is simultaneously remote and familiar. The paradox is explained in the irony that the particular trope, the metonymy, that enables Clifford to stand outside of history and to articulate effectively her remoteness from us is a part of the same rhetorical complex, the same metonymy-metaphor oscillation, that makes her familiar to us, that makes both us and her 'modern.'

Acheson's use of rhetorical analysis to produce a theoretically coherent form of historical knowledge is not meant to respond directly to Brown, but in effect it does. Acheson's model enables those who might want to do so to characterize Brown's tough historicist stance as a function of the metonymic desire to stand outside of or above history – to 'reconstruct the past in order to authorise the future' (Pocock in Acheson 33). The question with which Acheson's formulation is not concerned, however, is that of desire. Why exactly would Lady Clifford or anybody else *want* to authorize the future? Why would such a desire be so strong in some women and not in others? Opposed as they are in many ways, both Brown and Acheson consider their work political, particular, and contingent; as such, their essays are antithetical to the apolitical, universalist, and essentialist claims that have been made for traditional psychoanalysis. In this they are not alone; much recent Renaissance criticism, whether historicist or textualist in emphasis, has treated Freudian psychoanalysis with suspicion if not open contempt. The irony is, however, that we are so embedded in psychoanalytic habits of thought that attempts to explain desire or to rewrite subjectivity without recourse to the vocabulary and resources of psychoanalysis have proved extremely difficult. This discontinuity is central to the third group of essays, 'Rethinking Subjectivity: The Turn to Lacan.'

The *locus classicus* in Renaissance studies for the case against psychoanalysis is Stephen Greenblatt's 1986 article 'Psychoanalysis and Renaissance Culture,' and it is to that article that the opening essay of this section, Tracey Sedinger's 'Historicism and Renaissance Culture,' most directly writes back. For Greenblatt, the universalist claims of psychoanalysis are naïvely anachronistic. Freudian psychoanalysis, he argues, is unaware that the inalienable selfhood, the 'primal, creatural individuation' (214) that it imagines as a universal category is in fact a cultural artefact, an invention of the Renaissance: 'psychoanalysis,' he writes, 'is at once the fulfilment and effacement of specifically Renaissance insights' (210). For Greenblatt, identity is anything but inalienable; it is a product of a complex set of historically contingent cultural and material relations, that is, social relations.

In her trenchant critique, Sedinger makes three principal points. First, Greenblatt's historicism treats history, even when recast as 'histories,' as its inalienable ground or foundation, and in its routine appeals to the particular and material 'evidence' of histories it represents a thinly disguised, although inadvertent, return to stone-kicking empiricism. 'In the final analysis,' historicism effectively insists on 'the priority (and the purity) of facts over theory' (123). Second, the emphasis on the historical contingency of the subject's social construction encourages the kind of relativism that renders historicism's own claims to transhistorical political (in the sense of moral) judgment incoherent. Third and most important, the social constructivism that determines Greenblatt's understanding of identity assumes a direct and immediately effective relationship between the subject and the social. In the vocabulary of Althusser's deeply influential appropriation of Lacan, social constructivism assumes that interpellation always works, that individuals are always already subjects, mirror-images of the cultural discourses or ideology in which they find themselves. Sedinger's most radical move, following Slavoj Žižek, is to suggest that the reverse is the case. Interpellation always fails: 'the subject is not the product of interpellation,' but is itself 'occasioned by the *failure* of interpellation' (130). Emphasizing this failure, or discontinuity, between the subject and the social enables Sedinger to indicate the stubborn reality of a psychic life independent of the subject's 'particular socio-historical moment' (132), and to recover the loss or lack that explains desire as the defining characteristic of that psychic life. In this, Sedinger points to renewed possibilities for psychoanalytic criticism.

Something of the range and explanatory force of those possibilities is indicated in the two other essays in this section. While Susan Zimmerman focuses on the intensity of horror in early modern tragedy, Nate Johnson analyses the function of the abject in the process of canon-formation. Zimmerman begins her essay 'Marginal Man' not with reference to the failure of historicist or textualist criticism but to the failure of anthropology. The recurrent question – how exactly are we to explain desire? – anthropology, argues Zimmerman, also leaves unanswered. While the richly evocative work of Georges Bataille and Mary Douglas locates desire and its antithesis, horror, 'in the subject's recognition of interstitial being,' it 'fails to account for the psychic mechanisms that *construct* the interstitial as that which the subject both dreads and desires' (160, emphasis added). To understand this process, Zimmerman, openly defying, like Sedinger, historicism's objections to the 'transhistorical legitimacy' of psychoanalysis (160), turns to Lacan and his conception of primordial loss. The enduring sense of loss that the subject suffers on entering consciousness, language, or the 'symbolic order,' becomes the occasion of both dread and desire – desire to the extent that the interstice or split responsible for this sense of loss may be overcome, and dread to the extent that it presages some kind of final dissolution. In patriarchal societies 'woman' plays a key figurative role; 'she' is overdetermined, figuring the interstitial or marginal in both its dreadful and desirable senses. What Zimmerman discovers, however, when she applies this theory to the representation of horror in such early modern dramas as *The Revenger's Tragedy* and *The Duchess of Malfi* is that men as much as women function as figures of the marginal at its most repulsive. In other words, the psychoanalytic interrogation of horror in these plays reveals a new way of plotting the instability of sexual boundaries in the early modern theatre.

In 'Donne's Odious Comparison,' Nate Johnson also turns to Lacan. In his careful analysis of the textual history of 'The Comparison,' he suggests that history might serve as a synecdoche for the Levitical quality of the process by which editors and critics feel compelled to maintain the integrity and purity of the canon. But just as Johnson imaginatively points to the Lacanian drive behind the imperatives of Leviticus and of our own canon-making, he concedes the counter-attraction of Guillory's sociological account of canon-formation. At this point one is forcefully reminded once again of just how discontinuous are contemporary Renaissance studies.

The one element that most of the essays in the collection refuse to question is the need for political engagement. But this refusal in itself is intensely problematic. The two essays in part four, 'Political Engagement and Professional Discontinuities,' address some of the tensions and contradictions produced by the commitment to political criticism. In 'Academic Exchange: Text, Politics, and the Construction of English and American Identities in Contemporary Renaissance Criticism,' Barry Taylor examines the claim of British cultural materialism to practise a more authentic politics than its North American counterpart, while Sharon O'Dair responds with an essay on the blindness of North American criticism to the categories of class and status. For Taylor, the myth of an impassive cultural materialism overshadowed by a flashy and vulgar new historicism stems from the long-established 'binary tropology' (183) of Englishness vs. Americanness. As in many narratives of *presence*, this binary grounds professionalization in the continuity of a monolithic history that insists upon a 'containment' model of ideology, a model that new historicists are accused of having fabricated in response to their own political complacency. The gravest implication of the 'containment' model, argues Taylor, is that if it is not untenable, then the practice of a dissident criticism is impossible. In 'The Status of Class in Shakespeare: or, Why Critics Love to Hate Capitalism,' O'Dair also argues in favour of a more radical critical practice, but one in which as readers we are more critically self-conscious about the complex relations between class, status, and interpretation. O'Dair contends that the inability of contemporary Renaissance criticism to theorize adequately the politics of inequality is part of a general unwillingness within the profession to acknowledge how we participate in and promote a contemporary system of 'inequality rooted in status differentiation' (220). To take up O'Dair's challenge would mean to acknowledge 'the power of our own contemporary political allegiances' and 'to confront our own awkward relationship to capitalism' (220). For O'Dair, Renaissance criticism's blindness to inequality is crystallized in the tendency to view a play like *Timon of Athens* as sharing Shakespeare's critique of a money society in defence of a 'parasitic, self-indulgent élite' ruled by

Timon, an élite whose dominance depended upon the brutal exploitation of 'the masses of people' (213). O'Dair offers a bold critique of
what she sees as a complementary tendency on the part of critics to
oppose capitalism, a tendency that serves 'to protect their own prerogative of judgment over the people, to de-legitimize the voices of the
people, voices expressed in the marketplace for literature and culture'
(219).

If the experience of reading these essays as a collection is that of
constantly having the ground from underneath one cut away, then the
volume has succeeded in its principal aim: not to acquiesce in a facile
syncretism and represent Renaissance studies as a cohesive union of
various new methodologies, but to represent it, as we feel it is, as a
dramatically discontinuous but vital field of intellectual enquiry. We
take our cue from Milton's wonderful image of London in the English
Civil War: 'that then the people, or the greater part, more then at other
times, [were] wholly tak'n up with the study of highest and most important matters to be reform'd ... disputing, reasoning, reading, inventing,
discoursing, ev'n to a rarity, and admiration' (*Areopagitica* II.557). But
lest we become complacent in this thought, Marta Straznicky in the
Afterword provides the final jolt, emphasizing the discontinuity we
cannot afford to allow to remain unresolved, namely the discontinuity
between research and teaching.

WORKS CITED

Althusser, Louis. *Lenin and Philosophy and Other Essays.* Trans. Ben Brewster.
New York: Monthly Review P, 1971.
Attridge, Derek, et al. *Poststructuralism and the Question of History.* Cambridge:
Cambridge UP, 1987.
Bataille, Georges. *Erotism: Death and Sensuality.* Trans. Mary Dalwood. San Fran-
cisco: City Lights Books, 1957.
Bourdieu, Pierre. *Outline of a Theory of Practice.* Trans. Richard Nice. Cambridge:
Cambridge UP, 1977.
– *Distinction: A Social Critique of the Judgment of Taste.* Trans. Richard Nice. Cam-
bridge, MA: Harvard UP, 1984.
– *The Logic of Practice.* Trans. Richard Nice. Stanford: Stanford UP, 1990.
Cohen, Walter. 'Political Criticism of Shakespeare.' *Shakespeare Reproduced.* Ed.
Jean E. Howard and Marion F. O'Connor. 18–46.
Crewe, Jonathan. 'The State of Renaissance Studies; Or, A Future for *ELR*?'
English Literary Renaissance 25.3 (1995): 341–71.

Dollimore, Jonathan, and Alan Sinfield, eds. *Political Shakespeare: New Essays in Cultural Materialism*. Manchester: Manchester UP, 1985.

Douglas, Mary. *Purity and Danger: An Analysis of the Concepts of Pollution and Taboo*. London: Routledge & Kegan Paul, 1966.

Fish, Stanley. 'Commentary: The Young and the Restless.' *The New Historicism*. Ed. H. Aram Veeser. 303–16.

Goux, Jean-Joseph. *Symbolic Economies: After Marx and Freud*. Trans. Jennifer Curtiss Gage. Ithaca: Cornell UP, 1990.

Greenblatt, Stephen. 'Psychoanalysis and Renaissance Culture.' *Literary Theory/Renaissance Texts*. Ed. Patricia Parker and David Quint. 210–24.

Guillory, John. *Cultural Capital: The Problem of Literary Canon Formation*. Chicago: U of Chicago P, 1993.

Howard, Jean E., and Marion F. O'Connor, eds. *Shakespeare Reproduced: The Text in History and Ideology*. New York: Methuen, 1987.

Kuhn, Thomas S. *The Structure of Scientific Revolutions*. Chicago: U of Chicago P, 1962.

Lentricchia, Frank. 'Foucault's Legacy: A New Historicism.' *The New Historicism*. Ed. H. Aram Veeser. 231–42.

Liu, Alan. 'The Power of Formalism: The New Historicism.' *ELH* 56.1 (Winter 1989): 721–71.

Milton, John. *Complete Prose Works of John Milton*. Ed. Don M. Wolfe et al. 8 vols. New Haven: Yale UP, 1953–82.

Montrose, Louis A. 'Professing the Renaissance: The Poetics and Politics of Culture.' *The New Historicism*. Ed. H. Aram Veeser. 15–36.

Parker, Patricia, and David Quint, eds. *Literary Theory/Renaissance Texts*. Baltimore: Johns Hopkins UP, 1986.

Patterson, Annabel. 'Still Reading Spenser After All These Years?' *English Literary Renaissance* 25.3 (1995): 432–44.

Pocock, J.G.A. 'Time, Institutions and Action: An Essay on Traditions and Their Understanding.' *Politics, Language and Time: Essays on Political Thought and History*. New York: Atheneum, 1973. 233–72.

Rapaport, Herman. 'Deconstruction's Other: Trinh t. Minh-ha and Jacques Derrida.' *diacritics* 25.2 (1995): 98–113.

Rorty, Richard. *The Consequences of Pragmatism*. Minneapolis: U of Minnesota P, 1983.

Stevens, Paul. 'Tudor England's Postmodern Colonialists.' *University of Toronto Quarterly* 63.3 (1994): 464–7.

Stone, Lawrence. *The Family, Sex, and Marriage in England 1500–1800*. London: Weidenfeld & Nicholson, 1977.

Todd, Janet. *Feminist Literary History*. New York: Routledge, 1988.

Veeser, H. Aram, ed. *The New Historicism*. New York: Routledge, 1989.

Woodbridge, Linda. *Women and the English Renaissance: Literature and the Nature of Womankind, 1540–1620*. Urbana and Chicago: U of Illinois P, 1984.

Žižek, Slavoj. *The Sublime Object of Ideology*. London: Verso, 1989.

PART ONE
RECOVERING WOMEN'S WRITING:
HISTORICISM VS. TEXTUALISM

1

'Over Her Dead Body': Feminism, Post-structuralism, and the Mother's Legacy

SYLVIA BROWN

The program of gynocritics is to construct a female framework for the analysis of women's literature, to develop new models based on the study of female experience, rather than to adapt male models and theories.

Elaine Showalter, 'Toward a Feminist Poetics,' 1979

In its extreme forms this point of view *could* lead to the conclusion that the study of female-authored texts makes no difference ...

Jean E. Howard, Address, Interdisciplinary Forum, MLA Convention, 1989

The difference between my two epigraphs is a decade of feminism and the 'point of view' to which Jean Howard refers: the poststructuralist critique of language and subjectivity. The critique, which in Howard's words has 'put paid to the idea of a subjectivity unproblematically in possession of its "own experience" or speaking and writing outside always already patriarchally inflected discourses,' has been co-opted by feminist as well as new historicist approaches to early modern texts ('Feminism and the Question of History' 152). Despite the brief qualification recorded in the epigraph, Howard welcomes this shared

I would like to thank Victoria Kahn, as well as the anonymous readers and the editors of *Discontinuities: New Essays on Renaissance Literature and Criticism* for their helpful comments. Where possible, I have retained original spellings from early modern texts, but have normalized *u* and *v*.

'point of view.'[1] She sees it as a means of strengthening feminism by healing an enduring 'split' between those who work on female-authored texts and those who critique male discourse, and as a means of forging an alliance between feminism and new historicism against 'those who want to install great literature above politics and ideology' (152, 150).

My aim is to investigate what this 'point of view' means for the study of early modern women's writing. Since 1979, critics working on early women writers have increasingly adopted deconstructive techniques and poststructuralist assumptions about the instability of language and subjectivity. They have sought both to update Showalter's program in order to keep pace with the rise of critical theory in the 1980s, and to move in tandem with new historicist approaches. Yet, far from healing a 'split' between (to recall Showalter's terms) gynocritics and feminist critique, I contend that the logic of poststructuralism works to undermine the study of female-authored texts and, more generally, the feminist aims and concerns that initiated the serious study of women's writing in the first place. Under the deconstructive rubric of poststructuralism, the study of female-authored texts ultimately *does not make a difference.* Furthermore, as poststructuralism detaches language and subjectivity from a material context, gender as a historically specific category of analysis, and even historical analysis itself, drops into insignificance.[2]

My points of reference for this investigation are, on the one hand, Elaine Showalter's definition of 'gynocritics,' which provides a control (in the experimental sense) in the form of an original itinerary for the study of women's writing, and, on the other, the mother's legacy book, a genre appropriated by women in the sixteenth and seventeenth centuries and a test case for the combination of poststructuralist approaches with feminist aims. For a number of recent studies of early modern

1 Howard's address to the MLA was later published as 'Feminism and the Question of History: Resituating the Debate,' *Women's Studies* (Special Issue: *Women in the Renaissance*) 19.2 (1991): 149–57.
2 The centrality of gender to the practice of feminist history has been forcefully articulated by Joan Wallach Scott in an influential address given to the American Historical Association in December 1985. The address was published one year later as 'Gender: A Useful Category of Historical Analysis' in *The American Historical Review,* and is reprinted in *Coming To Terms: Feminism, Theory, Politics,* ed. Elizabeth Weed (New York: Routledge, 1989). Scott herself, however, comes to look to poststructuralism to supply an epistemology for radical feminist politics (see *Gender and the Politics of History,* passim; and Bryan Palmer's critique of Scott's later work [Palmer 172–86]).

women's writing, the alliance of poststructuralism and feminism has produced a theoretically sophisticated gynocritics, in which deconstructive analysis ideally recovers women's voices and histories that have been elided or pushed to the margins, and finds prized moments of resistance in the interstices. The mothers' legacies in particular seem to invite a critical alliance between deconstruction and feminism. The authors of mothers' legacies wrote in the voice of an already dead mother; this self-deconstruction, however, was deliberate and served to liberate them from silence. Anne Bradstreet's verse introduction to a collection of prose meditations, poems, and aphorisms, which she bequeathed as a manuscript legacy to her family, suggests the paradox of authorial absence and presence:

> This book by any yet unread,
> I leave for you when I am dead,
> That being gone, here you may find
> What was your living mother's mind. (240, 1–4)

In *The Mothers Blessing* Dorothy Leigh uses the paradox to exonerate herself from the unwomanly activity of writing, 'a thing so unusuall among us' (4). Leigh addresses her three sons: 'Neither must you, my sonnes, when you come to bee of judgement, blame me for writing to you, since Nature telleth me, that I cannot long bee here to speake unto you, and this my mind will continue long after mee in writing ...' (12). It is not merely death but a combination of death and maternity – the paradoxical dissolution and simultaneous emphasis on sexual difference – that Bradstreet, Leigh, and others invoke to authorize their writing. 'Therefore,' Leigh writes, 'let no man blame a mother, though she something exceed in writing to her children, since every man knowes, that the love of a mother to her children, is hardly contained within the bounds of reason' (12). As Mary Beth Rose has observed, the authors of mothers' legacies effect a reversal of the pattern found in Protestant moral and religious writings about the family. Household tracts first opened the door for the possible empowerment of women by emphasizing and politicizing the family and, implicitly, women in their accepted familial roles. In practice, however, these tracts shut the door as soon as it was opened, erasing the initial differentiation of the role of the mother through a constant reversion to the terms 'parents' and 'father' (307–8). Women who wrote mothers' legacies simultaneously used and resisted the discourses of the tracts, 'reversing' those discourses by first erasing and then asserting themselves as mothers and authoritative agents (Rose 313), as in the example of Anne Bradstreet's verses.

Rose's argument gives both discourse and women authors power over the text of the mother's legacy, and is in this sense both a poststructuralist and feminist argument. Other critics writing on the mother's legacy, such as Teresa Feroli and Wendy Wall, move metonymically from the self-deconstructive strategies of the authors to their own deconstructive readings. As I shall argue, deconstructive feminism continues to find its moral horizon in the ideals that Showalter first articulated in 1979; however, with poststructuralism added to the toolbox, the reproduction of the patriarchal past is forestalled by deconstruction. Yet delight in eclecticism has perhaps too readily succeeded a wariness of adapting 'male models and theories.' Remembering how and why feminism began, not rising above but recalling its politics, we must ask whether poststructuralist approaches do in fact serve feminism's aims of challenging all manifestations of patriarchy, including those beyond the text, and making women's voices heard. How far have we travelled from the original itinerary? Are reading women's texts and reconstructing women's lives now less powerful because less credited activities for literary feminism? If so, we must ask whether feminism itself, under the influence of poststructuralism, is losing ground as a hermeneutic and political movement.[3]

In evaluating developments in feminism over the past thirty years, Maggie Humm writes of the 'fundamental aim of any feminist cultural work.' Addressing literary critics and theorists in particular, she asserts that their guiding question must be 'what contribution can literary criticism make to *feminist* projects?' (20). Or, how can readings be related to social activity, to women's material experiences? (26). Frances Mascia-Lees, Patricia Sharpe, and Colleen Ballerino Cohen draw out the implications of postmodernist practices in contemporary anthropology, and especially those that crowd out feminism as well as ethical and

3 Maggie Humm makes the point, valid for both North America and Britain, that students are drawn to women's studies and readers to women's writing and feminist criticism because they seek the 'woman-centered perspective.' The primarily professional academics who teach, edit, and write for such audiences have not altogether abandoned this perspective; and it cannot be abandoned altogether, unless at the cost of an effective feminist politics. None the less, as Humm points out, 'it might appear that feminist thinking has fractured into a poststructuralist rejection of the "essentialism" in such a perspective' (26).

political content; 'feminist theory,' they write, 'is an intellectual system that knows its politics' (8). Feminists can argue with one another in their many voices because they know themselves as an interest group: 'Feminist politics provide an explicit structure that frames our research questions and moderates the interactions in which we engage with other women. Where there is no such political structure, the danger of veiled agendas is great' (22). But, one might ask, would a feminism based on a thoroughly poststructuralist epistemology necessarily know its own politics?[4] My own critique assumes and addresses what I believe is still a point of consensus within the plurality of 'feminisms': the need to relate feminist work to actual political, institutional, and social change. Jean Howard acknowledges this need in her articulation of the 'present goal' of feminism: 'the amelioration of oppression and exploitation based on gender and sexuality' ('Feminism and the Question of History' 151). Poststructuralism does not necessarily help us to reach this goal, for the poststructuralist critique of language and subjectivity undermines the concepts of agency that are crucial for the possibility of social change. For a politically effective literary feminism, moreover, intimately connected to and drawing strength from women's texts and the material contexts of those texts, the poststructuralist point of view might prove fatal.

II

Mothers' legacies were books of religious advice written by mothers for their children's use after the mothers' death. If we may judge by the numbers of editions in England, they were the 'best-sellers' of early modern women's writing.[5] Their popularity immediately suggests complicity with the dominant ideology: they received widespread approval and were read because they reproduced culturally acceptable representations of female virtue as passive, private, and self-effacing. Elizabeth Jocelin's *Mothers Legacie* is prefaced by the 'Approbation' of the divine Thomas Goad, who obtained Jocelin's manuscript after her death and edited it for publication, making substantive alterations to

4 For a sceptical response see Appleby, Hunt, and Jacob (226–30).
5 Dorothy Leigh's *The Mothers Blessing* was the most popular of the mothers' legacies, with twenty-three editions printed between 1616 and 1674. Elizabeth Jocelin's *The Mothers Legacie* was close behind with eight editions printed between 1624 and 1684.

her text. Goad writes approvingly of Jocelin's pious resignation: 'she secretly tooke order for the buying a new winding-sheet' as soon as she felt herself to be 'quicke with child' (sig. a5^r). 'And about that time,' Goad writes, 'undauntedly looking death in the face, privatly in her Closet between God and her, she wrote these pious Meditations; whereof her selfe strangely speaketh to her owne bowels in this manner, *It may seeme strange to thee to receive these lines from a mother that died when thou wert borne*' (sigs. a5^r–a5^v). Yet these private, self-effacing, strange texts were printed and reprinted. And, although Elizabeth Jocelin and Anne Bradstreet intended their manuscript legacies for a familial audience, Dorothy Leigh had hers printed. As Leigh herself states, she 'sent abroad' *The Mothers Blessing* in order to ensure that her eldest son would not hoard it, thereby imaginatively circumventing the patriarchal law of primogeniture as well as restrictions on women's writing (sig. A7^r). Mothers' legacies, printed or not, could function as vehicles both of godly zeal and political criticism. Leigh, for example, took the occasion of advising her sons to make strong, public statements about companionate marriage and the need for the continuing reformation of the church (55, 233). And Jocelin, the most self-effacing author of a mother's legacy, used the didactic occasion of her text to present a normative portrait of the ideal preacher, which at the time could be read as coded political criticism (5–8), while the most outspoken, like Leigh, readily admitted that men occupy 'the first and chiefe place' and that wives should be subject to their husbands (16–17, 38).

Presented with such contradictions, both within the genre and within individual texts, deconstructive feminism offers a means of undoing enmeshed resistances and complicities, and, perhaps paradoxically, of *constructing* a liberationist tradition of women's writing. By deliberately reading for ideological contradictions, particularly for moments when patriarchy generates its own critique, deconstruction simultaneously acknowledges what is 'always already patriarchally inflected' as well as its erased other – the women's stories, voices, and experiences that have been submerged and silenced. Thus, Elizabeth Jocelin overplays in her legacy the self-abnegation of feminine virtue by such dramatic gestures of resignation as calling for her winding sheet to be laid upon her immediately after giving birth (sig. a5^v), and by analogous rhetorical gestures that show, as she puts it in the dedicatory epistle to her husband, that she is 'religiously prepared to die' (sig. B10^r). Contrary to Goad's description of Jocelin as an exceptionally learned woman for her time,[6] she writes to her husband (who presumably knew as much as Goad knew): 'My deare, thou knowest me so well, I shall not need to tell thee, I have written honest thoughts in a disordered fashion, not observing method. For thou knowest how short I am of learning & natural endowments to take such a course in writing ...' (sigs. B10^v–B11^r). She continues in this vein, beyond the requirements of the conventional modesty topos. The rhetorical gestures of self-abnegation and excessive female modesty paradoxically enable Jocelin not only to write, but to write with a secure moral authority. (It is perhaps no accident that she signs the epistle to her husband, 'Thine Inviolable.') By resisting complicity with the discourses of patriarchy and piety – a resistance that is uncovered by a reading at once feminist and deconstructive – Jocelin wins her own version of immortal fame.

Yet the same method of reading for instances of patriarchy's undoing applies to male-authored texts, and this is the point at which the study of female-authored texts could, as Howard intimates, cease to make a difference. Deconstruction involves the feminist literary historian in a contradiction between methodologies and aims. With respect to the mother's legacy, deconstruction is often used to the implicit end of reconstructing as far as possible the authentic female selves, that is, the voices or strategies behind the patriarchal strictures of the genre. Whether we are offered glimpses of victimization or rebellion or both, feminist historical investigation is motivated by the desire to connect in some way with women's lives and experiences.[7] The logic of deconstruction and the philosophical basis of poststructuralism do not,

6 In his 'Approbation,' Goad writes that Jocelin was 'carefully nurtured' in the household of her grandfather, William Chaderton, professor of divinity at Cambridge and later bishop successively of Chester and Lincoln, 'as in those accomplishments of knowledge in Language, History, and some Arts, so principally in studies of piety' (sig. a1^v). When Jocelin married, in addition to 'the domestique cares pertaining to a wife,' she employed herself 'in the studies of morality and history, the better by the helpe of forraine languages'; she was, moreover, 'not without a taste and faculty in Poetry' (sig. a3^r).

7 It is a measure of how far poststructuralist assumptions police critical language that we can no longer say that this desire to connect is a desire for historical truth, even when we acknowledge that the desire can never be satisfied, that historical truth is always partial, that sources are limited and our interpretations distorted by cultural and chronological distance. Appleby, Hunt, and Jacob, however, do come close to saying this in *Telling the Truth about History*.

however, sanction such motives: 'authenticity,' 'experience,' 'truth' are not valid categories of analysis. Poststructuralist critiques of language and subjectivity break down all such 'claims.'[8]

Still, Teresa Feroli in her recent study of Elizabeth Jocelin employs deconstruction to 'reveal' Jocelin's true psychological state, namely, pathological despair. Feroli's lexicon is itself revealing: 'By reading her legacy as an autobiography of a lost self, we can begin to *deconstruct* Goad's "monument" to maternal devotion *to reveal* Jocelin's text as *a testimony* to the troubling despair of a mother who calls to her child from the grave' (91, emphasis added). Significantly, it seems here that only Goad's masculine textual overlay will be deconstructed, while Jocelin's text will remain intact, to be revealed, to give testimony to female truth and experience. Yet in writing her legacy, and in authorizing it through an excess of 'motherly zeale' (sig. B3^r), Jocelin participates in the creation of her own 'monument to maternal devotion,' so that Jocelin herself does not escape Feroli's deconstruction. It is interesting, however, that Feroli's statement of her argument should imply that Jocelin does escape such an approach. Feroli can thus maintain at least a surface distinction between feminist critique and gynocritics.

While a feminist critique can afford deconstruction in its task of dethroning patriarchal figures like Goad, the rigorous application of deconstruction to women authors undermines the rationale for investigating them *as* women authors by a radical destabilization of the categories 'woman' and 'author.' The drive to linguistic and conceptual destabilization has its origins in the more general postmodernist attack on Enlightenment *Man*. Appleby, Hunt, and Jacob point out that Foucault and Derrida, as the successors of Nietzsche and Heidegger, 'leveled their sights on Western Man, defined as rational, capable of objectivity, and in possession of knowledge that corresponds to the truth of nature and society. In short, they attacked the entire Enlightenment project' (208). The demise of the author is a consequence of the fall of Western Man, for the author 'was the creation of the same discourses of the seventeenth and eighteenth century that insisted more generally on personal responsibility' (216). Applied to *woman* – who historically

8 See Appleby, Hunt, and Jacob on the representative views of Foucault and Derrida, both of whom, they argue, 'aimed to decenter the subject, that is, question his or her primacy as a location for making judgments and seeking truth ... their critiques of the subject and of language fostered a deeper skepticism about the (disappearing) self and truth' (212).

did not share in the Enlightenment benefits of autonomy, agency, and rationality – and more specifically to the early women writers who struggled to enjoy the authority, the possession of self and text, which Foucault and Derrida dismiss as illusory, the consequence of the demise of the author is once more to write women out of the story.[9]

Invoking the word 'testimony,' Feroli echoes the legal language of the mother's legacy, with which Goad also plays in the opening lines of his 'Approbation.' Goad's playfulness, however, underlines the social fact that, under the law of coverture in early modern England, married women were not ordinarily permitted to write their own wills: 'Our lawes disable those, that are under *Covert-baron*, from disposing by Will and Testament any temporall estate. But no law prohibiteth any possessor of morall and sprirituall riches, to impart them unto others, either in life by communicating, or in death by bequeathing' (sig. A3[r]). Goad's apology actually emphasizes the precarious legitimacy of Jocelin's enterprise. His acquisition, alteration, and framing of her manuscript for publication further exemplifies the fragile authority of female writers over their own texts.[10] These women do not ask for the kind of treatment accorded the Enlightenment Author. Moreover, if one aspect of feminist literary history is to affirm women's possession of their own texts and experiences, and to acknowledge their creative

9 See, for example, Derrida writing on Nietzsche's 'styles.' For both men, 'woman' is an elusive rhetorical and philosophical device, and an opportunity for virtuoso linguistic performance:

> Woman (truth) will not be pinned down.
> In truth woman, truth will not be pinned down.
> That which will not be pinned down by truth is, in truth *feminine*. This should not, however, be hast[i]ly mistaken for a woman's femininity, for female sexuality, or for any other of those essentializing fetishes ...   (Derrida 55)

10 Another case, involving the posthumous writings of a godly woman, Jane Ratcliffe, is discussed by Peter Lake. Although we know that Ratcliffe left voluminous commentaries on scripture, impressing her spiritual advisor John Ley with their insight, we have only Ley's edited selections in his printed funeral sermon on Ratcliffe, *Pattern of Piety or the Religious Life and Death of That Grave and Gracious Matron Mrs Jane Ratcliffe* (1640). Lake reads Ley's sermon for signs of possible feminist elements in Ratcliffe's godliness. His conclusions are judiciously expressed and convincing, but he is admittedly hampered by the fact that Ratcliffe's godliness is accessible only through Ley. According to Ley, Ratcliffe herself facilitated the mediation, for she consented to record her scriptural observations only when Ley promised to correct them (Lake 154).

strategies of resistance to patriarchal language and culture, the other equally important aspect is to identify cases of dispossession. A decon-structive view of the authorship of the *Mothers Legacie* erases Goad's act of piracy,[11] together with the act's significance in and for a patriarchal culture, in that Goad and Jocelin both become mere functions of the text. With the poststructuralist removal of responsibility from language, both gynocriticism and feminist critique are on shaky ground.[12]

Wendy Wall, in her essay 'Isabella Whitney and the Female Legacy,' combines, like Feroli, the aims of a feminist literary history that de-pends upon some degree of agency, with the methods and technical vocabulary of deconstruction. Wall, however, sees the mother's legacy not as testimony of maternal despair, but as a genre strategically used by women who wish to break into print. In a neat paradox, however, the women's strategy is self-deconstruction. Writing about one of the earliest mothers' legacies, Elizabeth Grymeston's *Miscelanea. Meditations. Memoratives*, Wall describes the form of the mother's legacy as inherently deconstructive but manipulable: 'Grymeston labors to fashion ... the true portrait of her mind, the visible sign of herself as a speaking subject. The form dictates that she create, of course, a riven subjec-tivity: a "true portrait" predicated on erasure' (39). Wall works with two notions of agency at once. One belongs to the feminist project of rehabilitating women as subjects who speak and act with intent. Accordingly, Grymeston is a creator; she 'labors to fashion' a true por-trait of her mind in her legacy. More generally, Wall writes of women actively using the mother's legacy 'to assume control ... to articulate desire ... to display mastery ... to claim the power to show publicly ...' (44). The second deconstructive notion of agency defines the text as

---

11 For the substantive changes that Goad made to Jocelin's manuscript, see below, section IV.

12 Again, this has implications for political agency beyond feminist literary history. Reflecting on the close relations between 'academics and activists,' which are characteristic of both ethnic studies and feminism, Nancy Hartsock asks with some justified annoyance: 'Why is it, exactly at the moment when so many of us who have been silenced begin to demand the right to name ourselves, to act as subjects rather than objects of history, that just then the concept of subjecthood becomes "problematic"?' (196). The result is, in the worst case, to 'recapitulate the effects of Enlightenment theories' – which, ironically, constitute the very conceptual system being problematized – 'theories that deny marginalized people [non-Westerners as well as women] the right to participate in defining the terms of their interaction with people in the mainstream' (191). For a similar argument see Mascia-Lees, Sharpe, and Ballerino Cohen (below, n14).

the protagonist, the 'form' of the mother's legacy 'dictat[ing]' what Grymeston creates. When the text alone acts, sexual difference begins not to matter, and Wall can write of the mother's legacy that it is 'a form not crucial for its feminine difference, or for its marking of a female consciousness, but for its provision of a [rhetorical] stance' (46). Wall returns several times to the idea of a 'cultural script' that the mothers' legacies rehearse; yet women use this cultural script 'for empowerment' (44). Despite the poststructuralist vocabulary, the main argument of the essay rests on the feminist notion of agency with intent to resist. Arguing that the authors of mothers' legacies set out to create erasure, 'deploy[ing]' their riven subjectivity 'as a rhetorical strategy' (40), Wall ultimately uses deconstruction more as analogy than methodology.

In both Feroli's and Wall's analyses of the mothers' legacies, the ostensible use of deconstruction to reveal underlying despair or resistance is guaranteed by circular argument. Taking the true woman behind the text to be either a 'lost self' or a self-deconstructing subject, these deconstructive readings, which seize upon anxieties about identity, self-possession, and agency, and resolve them in a fundamentally illusory subjectivity, will surely yield the expected result. This model of reading, moreover, is slippery on the question of how much conscious control early modern women authors may have had over their rhetorical practices – perhaps necessarily, for the next step is that they should cease to matter as authors at all. In the case of the mothers' legacies, deconstruction is a 'false friend,' falsely congenial to the extraordinary circumstances of female authors who write under, and out of, the threat of death. Deconstruction ultimately undermines these authors' experience and extraordinariness, and is for this reason a questionable ally in the feminist project of recovering and valuing women's lives and writing.

III

Feminists often casually invoke the term 'deconstruction' when challenging inequalities, criticizing patriarchal institutions, and in general questioning what has too long remained unquestioned. But the word carries its own program.[13] The adoption of a deconstructive vocabulary involves us in poststructuralist assumptions whose logic runs counter

13 In discussing the aspects of deconstruction found in postmodernism, Appleby, Hunt, and Jacob note its dubious descent from Nietzsche as well as its employment against

not only to feminist aims but also to historical approaches to early modern texts. This is evident in the work of critics who are more self-consciously 'rigorous' than eclectic in their deconstruction and feminism. Marguerite Waller, in her deconstructive feminist contribution to the 1986 anthology *Rewriting the Renaissance*, acknowledges the incompatibility of aims and methodology. Following Shoshana Felman, however, Waller sees the 'nonconfrontation' of deconstruction and feminism as productive. Her assertion that they supplement each other, working 'together fruitfully as demarcations of each other's explanatory limits,' promises critical richness and fullness of analysis (160). In fact, what Waller recommends amounts to linguistic solipsism: knowledge can only be self-referential knowledge about language, and self-referential knowledge constitutes our reality (161). In such a world, 'empirical' and rhetorical violence are one and the same. Indeed, Waller's article asserts that Richard, as well as Anne, is seduced in *Richard III*, that their seductions are ultimately only – rather, pre-eminently — rhetorical. Their common seduction is thus really a seduction into liberal humanist subjectivity and its confident use of language (167–74).

One can see how the rhetorical argument about violence and seduction could be used to trivialize empirical instances of oppression and exploitation, or to make any historical frame irrelevant. One can also see how, in Waller's analysis of Shakespeare's play, gender ceases to matter. Carol Neely cites Waller's article as one example among many of a persistent, insidious patriarchalism that pervades current theoretical discourses ('Constructing the Subject' 13). Neely's specific targets are new historicism and cultural materialism, whose practitioners she lumps together as 'cult-historicists'; but she also touches on the 'semio-deconstructive' critics. The latter's 'imperative to deconstruct,' she contends, does not in practice extend to gender: 'In this discourse woman has been always already subordinated' (10). Indeed, gender drops out of the discourse altogether, for it is most often read allegorically, that is, it is turned into something else (11). For Neely, the disappearance of gender is a consequence of the poststructuralist replacement of the subject with 'subject positions,' a strategy that calls into question gendered subjects, authors, and texts, and, by implication,

the Enlightenment Project (208ff.). Mascia-Lees and her co-authors speculate that the deconstructive style of much contemporary anthropology, together with its rejection of feminist approaches, may be mostly about staking first claim in a new territory, thereby preserving male jobs and dominance in the academy (16).

the basis for all feminist critique (13). Academic feminism's aim of reading and writing women out of subordination is critically hampered when it adopts the notion of 'subject positions': 'Denying the unitary subject, declaring the end of difference, does not do away with the difference between men and women or with the subordination of women; it merely conceals it' (13). With 'the end of difference,' the ground of opposition against patriarchy is removed.[14] Moreover, as agency and gender disappear into subject positions that are wholly determined by self-referential discourse, it no longer becomes possible to write about women who act, write, comply, and resist, at least not without hedging on some form of 'cancellation.' Ironically, problematizing subjectivity does not in practice problematize the traditional canon of 'male authors,' seeming instead to authorize a quiet return to 'great literature.'[15]

The tendency to undermine the rationale for the study of women's writing has become symptomatic of the more widespread loss of the ground that feminism has gained against patriarchy. Poststructuralists 'dematerialize' women, as Neely puts it (10), disregarding the material conditions of their lives and texts in what one social historian describes as a 'descent into discourse.'[16] This neglect has its own consequences for a *historical* feminist criticism. The conception of 'woman' as a deconstructable linguistic position removes women from the particularity of time and place, and takes them out of history and culture.[17] Here poststructuralism clashes with the historical imperatives of feminism:

14 In the words of Mascia-Lees, Sharpe, and Ballerino Cohen, the discipline of 'decentering the Cartesian subject' (that is, of deconstructing Enlightenment Man) is seen as potentially 'invigorating' to those who have been 'traditionally excluded from discourse' – women and non-Western peoples (28). But in practice, they conclude, by abolishing differences in the name of unsetting hierarchies, 'such readings ignore or obscure exploitation and power differential and, therefore, offer no ground to fight oppression and effect change' (29).

15 Humm notes the tendency of American feminist deconstructionists to focus on male writers (148). See also Spivak 206–23.

16 This is Palmer's governing phrase in *Descent into Discourse*.

17 Palmer cites Denise Riley's *'Am I That Name?' Feminism and the Category of 'Women' in History* as an example, in which 'there is no historically continuous "woman" or "women."' Instead, '"woman" is discursively constructed, and always relatively to other categories' that are themselves unstable, including the category of history (167). Riley, notes Palmer, is a useful polemicist against essentialism in that she is urging feminism to be 'not fixed, rigid, and "woman" bound, but moving, supple, versatile. Just what the politics of this would look like, and how effective they could be against the strong and persistent forces of an opposition that, whatever *its* fluctuations and

the when, how, and why of oppression as well as the struggle and
endurance. Once again, Marguerite Waller acknowledges the discontinuity of her deconstructive-feminist approach. If, on the one hand,
feminism asks when 'man' began to be the privileged term, the 'logic
of deconstruction,' on the other hand, 'suspends the conditions under which it makes sense to ask direct, historical, and epistemological questions' (160).[18] Waller resolves the discontinuity in favour of
the 'non-traditional epistemology' of deconstruction, in which the only
knowledge (and reality) is self-referential knowledge about language.
In this epistemology, rhetorical strategies become 'events,' the incompatibility of deconstructionist and feminist arguments being, for example,
itself an 'event,' and, as such, becoming 'accessible as a historical reality' (161). Waller's treatment here of 'events' and 'history' is similar
to her treatment of 'violence' and 'seduction,' terms that, even in their
'empirical' versions, are ultimately about the ways in which language
refers to itself.

But there is, paradoxically, a self-authorizing side to Waller's argument, which depends upon a more traditional epistemology for
the meanings of history and reality. Although as a deconstructionist
Waller rejects the moral, instrumental use of language, such as the
'self-aggrandizing' gesture of judging (166), she is moved to write of the
'commitment' that informs her argument (161); and she still makes value
judgments, particularly about the value of poststructuralist critical approaches over traditional criticism based on moral or aesthetic judgment
(162). Waller suggests that her own rhetorical moves of deconstructing
other rhetorical moves – the 'anti-seduction' that she performs through
her article – will make a difference to real oppression and real events;
for, if events are fundamentally rhetorical, rhetoric alone will make a
difference (161). There is still a right way at the end of it: for the critic,
for feminism, for the fictional characters of Anne and Richard, but it
lies in repudiating liberal-humanist ideas about autonomous selves and

---

instabilities, has a visible continuity and powerful, identifiable presences, remains to
be seen ...' (167).
18 In discussing the genealogy of the postmodernist project, which has grown out of
and supported poststructuralist approaches to texts, the social historians Appleby,
Hunt, and Jacob are most concerned about its attack on the concept of history. From
the beginning, 'Nietzsche and Heidegger attacked historicism and its central concern,
man.' Deconstructive historians, like deconstructive literary critics, have followed
Nietzsche and Heidegger in attacking ideas of linear development, causality, and
objectivity (211).

common language. 'Historical reality' seems to exist for Waller in more than one epistemological world, allowing her to accommodate rhetorical and empirical events, anti-moral and progressive stances, poststructuralist and feminist modes.

Ambivalent accommodation informs much contemporary criticism of early modern texts. It is characteristic, for instance, of the imperative to 'historicize.' What is meant by historicizing is usually unclear; thus the term 'insufficiently historicized,' like 'insufficiently theorized,' serves as an all-purpose condemnation. However, both poststructuralist and traditional ideas of history contribute to the notion of historicizing, and the resulting amalgam itself contributes to the contradictions of deconstructive-feminist readings. Jean Howard argues about the benefits of the encounter between new historicism and feminism in reconstituting 'what counts as historical knowledge of this field,' and suggests that feminist efforts to 'rewrite the Renaissance' have already benefited from the insights of poststructuralism via the new historicism ('Feminism and the Question of History' 151–2, and passim).[19] Poststructuralist notions about the free play of signifiers and the illusoriness of subjectivity inform much of new historicism in the same eclectic way as they do deconstructive feminism. In new historicism, however, cultural discourses rather than signifiers are in free play, and historical causality, together with agency, is 'problematized.' At best, new historicism offers a fluid model of social analysis – texts and culture shape and are shaped by one another – and therefore a flexible model of social change. At worst, new historicism does not provide for social change; in the very fluidity of its typical performances, it loses all ideas of motive, intent, or cause, presenting necessarily synchronic rather than diachronic accounts. The synchronic picture itself, moreover, often amounts to a static typology, with free-floating monolithic 'discourses' replacing authors, political actors, and historical agents. As a result, some of the 'historicizing' impressions of Greenblatt or Foucault are decidedly ahistorical; and feminist readings and rewritings of the Renaissance, in response, often themselves put aside history.

Wendy Wall's essay 'Isabella Whitney and the Female Legacy' provides one example of historicization tending toward the ahistorical. Wall begins by locating the mother's legacy in a 'female tradition.' As a liter-

19 The critical discourses of poststructuralism and new historicism, however, are involved in an agon of their own. See, for instance, Marguerite Waller's review of Stephen Greenblatt's *Renaissance Self-Fashioning*, in 'Academic Tootsie' (2–20).

ary form, the mother's legacy became recognizably female as more and more women wrote or published books of advice for their children and used approaching death as an organizing and authorizing topos. Elizabeth Grymeston's *Miscelanea. Meditations. Memoratives* (printed in 1604) was the first of such books. The 'Praiers' of Lady Frances Abergavenny in *The Monument of Matrones* (1582) might also be an early prototype, for the title states that Lady Frances committed the work to her only daughter at the hour of her death. Wall mentions both of these texts, as well as the principal mothers' legacies printed during the decade following the appearance of Dorothy Leigh's *The Mothers Blessing* in 1616, which was also the period when the form began to flourish.[20] Wall goes on to demonstrate how Isabella Whitney, who published in the late 1560s and early 1570s, strategically exploited the 'female tradition' of the mother's legacy to authorize her own writing. Wall argues that in using the conceit of a 'will' in the versified farewell to London that closes *A Sweet Nosgay* (1573), Whitney 'found it advantageous to draw from the authorizing strategies of those doomed mothers,' her 'fictional text ironically re-present[ing] and rehears[ing] the tradition from which mothers spoke from the grave' (49, 55–6). But is this strategy possible given that Whitney dates the dedication to *A Sweet Nosgay* October 1573, that is, nearly a decade before Frances Abergavenny's prayers were printed, thirty years before Grymeston's *Miscelanea*, and more than forty years before Leigh's *The Mothers Blessing*? Yes, if the text and not Whitney is assigned primary agency, if the poem is seen as 're-present[ing] and rehears[ing]' a tradition that operates not through historical time but only as a particular (or 'historicized') rhetorical stance. At the same time, however, Wall's historicizing argument enlists these poststructuralist moves to place the mother's legacy in a female literary tradition in which chronology and the strategic resistance of female authors still count. By the time Whitney 'draws from' the mother's legacy in the early 1570s, Wall suggests, 'the form had become part of a cultural script that was frequently linked to female expression' (56).[21] Wall's use

---

20 Mothers' legacies appear in significant numbers at around the time of or shortly after the publication of Leigh's and Jocelin's; these include 'M.R.'s' *The Mothers Counsell* (1642) and Elizabeth Richardson's *A Ladies Legacie to her Daughters* (1645). Elizabeth Clinton's *The Countess of Lincolnes Nurserie* (1622) can also, arguably, be included in this list.

21 The argument would be more convincing if Wall could discover written or printed legacies, or other cultural examples of mothers speaking from the grave before the 1570s.

of the past-perfect tense and her feminist argument assume and depend upon empirical, causally related, chronological events – the stuff of 'traditional history.' With respect to causality and agency, however, the poststructuralist indeterminacy behind the notion of a 'cultural script' elides the need to be traditionally historical. The contradictions in Wall's argument are symptomatic of a pervasive methodological discontinuity in the criticism of early modern literary texts. The poststructural dissociation of texts from authors, and of events from their empirical context, makes the causal and chronological questions of history seem unimportant – just when history, in the shape of historicization, is being called in to supplement literary study.

IV

Undermining both feminist and historical aims and methodologies, poststructuralism is doubly unfriendly to the study of early modern women's writing. Jean Howard acknowledges this problem, noting that the anthologies of such writing now available are 'often implicitly disparaged or overlooked by avant-garde critics' who prefer the practice, more deconstructive than feminist, of reading 'familiar texts *with a difference*' ('Feminism and the Question of History' 154). To re-affirm the importance of female-authored texts, we should not, surely, bind ourselves even more firmly to the assumptions and approaches of poststructuralism.[22] If we return to the mothers' legacies as a touchstone, we may begin to see what a genuinely historical, coherently feminist approach to early women's writing might require.

We need, first of all, to value women's experience, and to consider that experience in light of commonalities as well as differences across time, societies, and individuals. That is to say, we need a way of acknowledging the cultural and linguistic conventions that play into experience without also denying the material grounding of that experience. The disappearance of the category 'woman' in poststructuralism

---

22 Yet this is precisely what Howard recommends in urging feminism into an alliance with new historicism by reason of their common poststructuralist critiques of autonomous subjectivity and of language 'outside always already patriarchally inflected discourses.' On the other hand, Howard's constructive suggestion that male and female, literary and non-literary texts be read in view of one another in order to 'problematize' woman's 'voice' and the canon (154) need not be couched in poststructuralist terms, but could contribute to a genuinely historical (rather than historicizing) reconsideration of women's texts.

represents such a denial, with serious political consequences. We need the category 'woman' in order to speak meaningfully about women across time and cultures: of women as diverse, but also sharing common experiences of oppression – political, legal, economic, and social – and a common agenda to change such oppression. To deny all this by making self-referential discourse the only reality is to weaken rather than support an efficacious, broadly based feminist movement; or, perhaps, finally to remove academic feminism altogether from such a movement.[23]

The poststructuralist attack on the relevance of the material and the existence of the real also has serious consequences for the women who wrote the mothers' legacies, and for our responses to their texts. A rigorously poststructuralist approach has no use for one of the most compelling features of the mother's legacy: the material, bodily realities that inform the representation. Dorothy Leigh justifies her venture into the male sphere of book production by the authority of female reproduction, by an appeal straight from her woman's body. The eloquence of her appeal depends on the connection – which is not necessarily perfect, but is certainly meaningful – between her text and the lived experience of maternal suffering and maternal bonding: 'Is it possible, that shee, which hath carried her child within her, so neere her hart, and brought it forth into this world with so much bitter paine, so many grones and cries, can forget it? ... will she not blesse it every time it suckes on her breasts, when shee feeleth the bloud come from her heart to nourish it?' (9–10). If women's public speech is restricted because of the body, silence being associated with chastity, then the authors of the mothers' legacies answer with arguments from the body, and specifically the maternal body. While Leigh's words comment on a passage from the prophet Isaiah – 'Can a woman forget her sucking child, that she should not have compassion on the son of her wombe?' (King James Version 49: 15) – a patriarchal figure whom she quotes to support her maternal authority, and while her reference to mother's milk as a sublimation of blood from the heart is a culturally and historically specific belief, none the less there remain continuities and commonalities that make mothers' legacies written by women in the seventeenth century meaningful, relevant, and poignant for feminists in the 1990s. Poststructuralism downplays the experiences

---

23 In Maggie Humm's words, 'The poststructuralist love of decentring, deconstructing and open endings, seems to many feminists to threaten the legitimacy of a worldwide movement dedicated to creating a social space for constituencies of women' (145).

of the body in favour of the body as cultural construct, rather than recognizing the more complex ways in which cultural constructs shape but never completely determine lived experience. The poststructural-ist approach runs the risk of trivializing the material conditions of women outside of texts, such as the fact that a married woman in seventeenth-century England could realistically expect to end her life in childbed (see Dobbie 87–90). In enlisting the aid of poststructuralism in its own combat with essentialism and the fixed, repressive gender roles authorized by essentialist approaches, feminism runs the risk of repudiating both the facts and the dignity of women's historical ex-perience, as well as the texts that arise from and participate in that experience.

We need also to account for complex, conflicted authorship with-out dispossessing women authors. Elizabeth Jocelin's legacy presents complicated problems of authorship, but also offers a rich and rare glimpse into the processes of one woman's writing, and of the male editing of that writing. Although well known to those studying early modern women's writing, Jocelin's text is usually read and discussed in its printed – that is, in Thomas Goad's – version. Jocelin's autograph manuscript, however, survives in the British Library, complete with clear authorial revisions. Finding it in Jocelin's desk after her death, Goad prepared the manuscript for publication by writing the prefatory 'Approbation,' and by making changes to her manuscript, changes that, among other things, recast Jocelin's portrait of feminine virtue. Whereas Jocelin, for instance, writes of the exemplary woman as 'wise or learned or religious,' Goad emends the phrase to 'wise or honest, or religious' (f. 20^r, *Legacie* 38). Goad also omits one crucial passage in Jocelin's advice to a daughter: 'if thou beest a daughter thou hast a calling to wch thou must not dishonor [:] thou art a christian ...' (f. 31^v). Elsewhere in his version of the legacy, it is evident that Goad's occasional additions of the word 'calling' are restricted to ordained ministers, and therefore restricted by gender (6–7, 113). The effect of Goad's omission is to deny both Jocelin's daughter and most of her readers an acceptable, even hon-ourable, model of female activity and ambition through participation in the 'priesthood of all believers.'

Authorial revisions in the autograph manuscript clearly indicate that Jocelin herself struggles with the ideology of feminine modesty. She deletes the word 'eloquence' and replaces it with the phrase 'skill to write' in a statement of self-deprecation – 'if I had skill to write ...' – as if even a hypothetical claim to eloquence is too nearly a usurpation of male authority (f. 8^V). At the end of the epistle to her husband, Jocelin expresses the hope that the following treatise 'wil not be unprofitable,' then emends the phrase to 'altogether unprofitable,' thereby intensifying her modesty in line with a lengthy profession of ignorance that precedes the emendation (ff. 5^V–6^r). However, an acknowledgment of many-layered or conflicted authorship, or of the contradictions in sexual ideology that these texts dramatize, does not require the philosophical backing of a poststructuralist point of view that would dissociate Elizabeth Jocelin, a real historical woman, from her text. It is not only helpful to know that Jocelin was raised by a former Cambridge divinity professor and lived with her husband at Oakington in Cambridgeshire, the Cambridge connections signifying possible access to a centre of thriving godly and intellectual life; it is also necessary to see her as an author with agency, composing, revising, and writing passages that her male editor chose to omit or change, and leaving us with valuable evidence of the processes of female authorship.

Jocelin may have left us the traces of a struggle with patriarchal ideology – in her writing, and in the encounter of her posthumous manuscript with Goad and with publication – but this struggle does not annihilate her. On the contrary, through charting the struggle itself, we are able, however imperfectly, to recover something of the voice and experience of a seventeenth-century woman *who writes*. As with any palimpsest, and like the introduction to a Victorian reprint by the bishop of Rochester, who thought he could see approaching dissolution shaping the final words of the autograph manuscript (Roffen vi), the 'Approbation' and Goad's emendations overlie a text and an integrity of experience that still belong to Elizabeth Jocelin. To deny Jocelin's ownership is to participate in the inequity of the common law under which Jocelin and all seventeenth-century women lived, a position against both the spirit and the letter of the project of feminism.

V

The responsibility of feminists is to offer solutions, however provisional, and the luxury of deconstructionists to forgo the need for any. Carol Neely suggests several feminist responses to the implicit patriarchalism of the 'new Renaissance discourses,' including pushing those discourses even further toward eclecticism and 'genuine historicization' (18). If we want genuine historicization in the sense of a genuinely historical methodology, however, we ought to be prepared to learn from historians.[24] In an address delivered at the same MLA forum in which Jean Howard delivered hers, social historian Martha Howell challenges feminist literary critics to ask historians' questions: What are the social uses and effects of a given text? Who produces it, and with what resources? Who reads it, and with what results? The historians' questions are questions of causality, intentionality, and agency, categories that are invalid for poststructuralists. But Howell seeks no alliance with poststructuralism: 'Let me acknowledge at the outset that what I might wish you to do is illegitimate, that it would fall outside the terms of poststructural theory' (144). Howell calls instead for the study of early modern women's writing according to the practices of a feminist history that both affirms women's experience and assumes that it is knowable and recoverable, within the limits of evidence and interpretation acknowledged by contemporary historiography, and shaped by the goals of the feminist project itself. Both Jean Howard and Martha Howell are interested in historical and cultural specificity, but while the feminist history that Howell practises is interested in social change and in investigating social fact, the poststructuralism that Howard calls to her aid, if rigorously applied, constitutes a philosophical attack on causality, intention, agency, and fact. Not that Howell herself believes in unmediated access to past experience, or in absolute guarantees of what happened and why. However, she suggests a complex model of historical investigation that places women at the centre and does not sacrifice the political ideals that motivated the beginning of 'gynocritics,' ideals that still support feminist academic enterprise.[25]

24 Historians themselves are by no means in agreement about methodology. Palmer as well as Appleby, Hunt, and Jacob respond to historians practising postmodernist history, an endeavour that harbours some of the pitfalls of deconstructive feminism. Palmer writes of a 'descent into discourse unmindful of any material moorings and historical context,' which has accompanied the shift 'toward poststructuralism' (157, 163). Appleby and her co-authors similarly see the chief problem of postmodernist history as 'the problem of linguistic determinism or conflation, the reduction of the social and natural world to language and context to text' (230).

25 Appleby, Hunt, and Jacob take a stand against the 'ironic mode' of the postmodernist practice of history: relativistic, possibly cynical, allowing itself to be only fragmentary and partial. They emphasize instead the need for 'narrative coherence, causal analysis, and social contextualization' (227–8). And, although the historical narratives they envision are based partially on aesthetic or formal choices, they also stress that these choices have social and political content: 'we are highlighting the need for the most

When we apply this model to the mothers' legacies, we should ask why they appeared in a cluster around the 1620s, what place they had in the literature of devotion and in godly culture, and in what ways they were different from and similar to the greater body of household-government books by male authors. We should ask also how gender works together with the other identities of the authors of mothers' legacies: English, godly, of the middling sort. By what family, class, patronage, and clerical ties can we locate these women in the social, religious, and political life of their time?[26] We need the ability to make factual and moral judgments, even as we recognize their limits, in order to understand and challenge the patriarchal cultures that the authors of the mothers' legacies internalized and resisted. We need to recognize these authors as real women, making history as well as made by it. We need to ask whether the deconstructive techniques that we often bring to this work, and the poststructuralist thinking behind those techniques, get us to where we as feminists want to go.

WORKS CITED

Abergavenny, Frances. 'The Praiers Made by the Right Honourable Ladie Frances Aburgavennie, and Comited at the Hour of her Death to ... Her Only Daughter.' *The Monument of Matrones ... compiled ... by Thomas Bentley.* London, 1582. 139–213.
Appleby, Joyce, Lynn Hunt, and Margaret Jacob. *Telling the Truth about History.* New York and London: Norton, 1994.
Bradstreet, Anne. *The Works of Anne Bradstreet.* Ed. Jeannine Hensley. Cambridge, MA: Belknap, 1967.
Brown, Sylvia. 'Godly Household Government from Perkins to Milton: The Rhetoric and Politics of Œconomia, 1600–1645.' Diss. Princeton U, 1994.
Derrida, Jacques. *Spurs: Nietzsche's Styles.* Trans. Barbara Harlow. London and Chicago: U of Chicago P, 1978.
Dobbie, B.M. Willmott. 'An Attempt to Estimate the True Rate of Maternal Mortality, Sixteenth to Eighteenth Centuries.' *Medical History* 26 (1982): 79–90.

---

objective possible explanations as the only way to move forward ... toward a more intellectually alive, democratic community, toward the kind of society in which we would like to live' (228–9).
26 I have tried to address some of these questions in 'Godly Household Government from Perkins to Milton: The Rhetoric and Politics of Œconomia, 1600–1645,' diss., Princeton U, 1994, chap. 2.

Feroli, Teresa. '"*Infelix Simulacrum*": The Rewriting of Loss in Elizabeth Jocelin's *The Mothers Legacie*.' *ELH* 61.1 (1994): 89–102.

Grymeston, Elizabeth. *Miscelanea. Meditations. Memoratives*. London, 1604.

Hartsock, Nancy. 'Rethinking Modernism: Minority vs. Majority Theories.' *Cultural Critique [Special Issue: The Nature and Context of Minority Discourse II]*. Ed. Abdul R. Jan Mohamed and David Lloyd. 7 (Fall 1987): 187–206.

Howard, Jean E. 'Feminism and the Question of History: Resituating the Debate.' *Women's Studies (Special Issue: Women in the Renaissance, An Interdisciplinary Forum [Modern Language Association of America 1989])* 19.2 (1991): 149–57.

– Address. Interdisciplinary Forum. Modern Language Association of America Annual Convention. 1989.

Howell, Martha C. 'A Feminist Historian Looks at the New Historicism: What's So Historical About It?' *Women's Studies* 19.2 (1991): 139–47.

Humm, Maggie. *A Reader's Guide to Contemporary Feminist Literary Criticism*. London and Toronto: Harvester Wheatsheaf, 1994.

Jocelin, Elizabeth. *The Mothers Legacie, To her Unborne Childe*. London, 1624.

– *The Mothers Legacie*. Additional ms. 27, 467. British Library, London.

Lake, Peter. 'Feminine Piety and Personal Potency: The "Emancipation" of Mrs Jane Ratcliffe.' *Seventeenth Century* 2.2 (1987): 143–65.

Leigh, Dorothy. *The Mothers Blessing*. London, 1616.

Mascia-Lees, Frances E., Patricia Sharpe, and Colleen Ballerino Cohen. 'The Postmodernist Turn in Anthropology: Cautions from a Feminist Perspective.' *Signs: Journal of Women in Culture and Society* 15.1 (1989): 7–33.

Neely, Carol Thomas. 'Constructing the Subject: Feminist Practice and the New Renaissance Discourses.' *English Literary Renaissance* 18.1 (1988): 5–18.

Palmer, Bryan D. *Descent into Discourse: The Reification of Language and the Writing of Social History*. Philadelphia: Temple UP, 1990.

Riley, Denise. *'Am I That Name?' Feminism and the Category of 'Women' in History*. Basingstoke: Macmillan; Minneapolis: U of Minnesota P, 1988.

Roffen, Randall T. Introduction. *The Mother's Legacy to her Unborn Child by Elizabeth Jocelin Anno 1622* ... Rpt of 6th ed. London and New York: Macmillan, 1894.

Rose, Mary Beth. 'Where Are the Mothers in Shakespeare? Options for Gender Representation in the English Renaissance.' *Shakespeare Quarterly* 42.3 (1991): 291–314.

Scott, Joan Wallach. *Gender and the Politics of History*. New York: Columbia UP, 1988.

– 'Gender: A Useful Category of Historical Analysis.' *Coming To Terms: Feminism, Theory, Politics*. Ed. Elizabeth Weed. New York and London: Routledge, 1989. 81–100.

Showalter, Elaine. 'Toward a Feminist Poetics.' *The New Feminist Criticism: Essays on Women, Literature, and Theory.* Ed. Elaine Showalter. New York: Pantheon, 1985. 125–43. First published in *Women Writing and Writing About Women.* Ed. Mary Jacobus. London: Croom Helm with Oxford University Women's Studies Committee; New York: Barnes & Noble, 1979.

Spivak, Gayatri Chakravorty. 'Feminism and Deconstruction, Again: Negotiating with Unacknowledged Masculinism.' *Between Feminism and Psychoanalysis.* Ed. Teresa Brennan. London and New York: Routledge, 1989. 206–23.

Wall, Wendy. 'Isabella Whitney and the Female Legacy.' *ELH* 58.1–2 (1991): 35–62.

Waller, Marguerite. 'Academic Tootsie: The Denial of Difference and the Difference It Makes.' *diacritics* 17.1 (1987): 2–20.

– 'Usurpation, Seduction, and the Problematics of the Proper: A "Deconstructive," "Feminist" Rereading of the Seductions of Richard and Anne in Shakespeare's *Richard III.*' *Rewriting the Renaissance: The Discourses of Sexual Difference in Early Modern Europe.* Ed. Margaret W. Ferguson et al. Chicago: U of Chicago P, 1986. 159–74.

Whitney, Isabella. *A Sweet Nosgay; or Pleasant Posye: Contayning a Hundred and Ten Phylosophicall Flowers.* London, 1573.

2

The Modernity of the Early Modern: The Example of Anne Clifford

KATHERINE OSLER ACHESON

Imaginary time is indistinguishable from directions in space. If one can go north, one can turn around and head south; equally, if one can go forward in imaginary time, one ought to be able to turn round and go backward. This means there can be no important difference between the forward and the backward directions of imaginary time. On the other hand, when one looks at 'real' time, there's a very big difference between the forward and the backward directions, as we all know. Where does this difference between the past and the future come from? Why do we remember the past but not the future?

Stephen Hawking, *A Brief History of Time* 143–4

La modernité est un combat. Sans cesse recommençant. Parce qu'elle est un état naissant, indéfiniment naissant, du sujet, de son histoire, de son sens.

Henri Meschonnic, *Modernité, Modernité* 9

The modernity of the early modern is a hallmark of new historical and cultural materialist work of the past fifteen years, and a commonplace of feminist studies of the English literary Renaissance during this century. Stephen Greenblatt's personal excursion, at the conclusion of

I should like to express my gratitude to the marquess of Bath, Longleat House, for permission to cite from the Portland Papers, XXIII ff 80–119, and to the Abbot Hall Art Gallery for permission to reproduce *The Great Picture of the Clifford Family*. I should also like to thank Germaine Warkentin for her abiding assistance with my work on Anne

Renaissance Self-Fashioning, in which 'our culture' (257) signifies both then and now,[1] and his desire to 'speak with the dead,' which prefaces his essay collection published in 1988 (*Shakespearean Negotiations*), are paradigmatic of the conflation of the present and the past in these works. Leah S. Marcus sees the identification between the early modern and the postmodern as one of the key factors distinguishing the new historicism from the old: 'we are moving away from interpreting the period as a time of re-naissance, cultural rebirth, the reawakening of an earlier era conceived of as ... classic; we are coming to view the period more in terms of elements repeated thereafter, those features of the age that appear to us precursors of our own twentieth century, the modern, the postmodern' (41). In feminist criticism, the identity between the early modern and the modern, or postmodern, female subject was first articulated in Virginia Woolf's invocation of Judith Shakespeare, who 'lives in you and in me ... she lives; for great poets do not die; they are continuing presences ... the opportunity will come and the dead poet who was Shakespeare's sister will put on the body which she has so often laid down' (198–9).[2] Mary G. Mason reflected the predominant critical paradigm in feminist criticism of the 1980s when she wrote of women's autobiography from the fourteenth through the seventeenth centuries that 'we recognize them each and all as distinctively, radically, the story of a woman' (235). A more recent example reflecting Woolf's body-snatching trope is Sara Jayne Steen's statement of her desire for the laughing, writing body of the woman of the past, in this case Arbella Stuart, a statement that takes on necrophilic tones: 'Like most women's

---

Clifford; further thanks go to Marcie Frank, both for the books on the shelf behind her desk, and for her helpful comments on the paper.

1 'Epilogue' (255–7); see especially the closing statements: 'For the Renaissance figures we have considered understand that in *our* culture to abandon self-fashioning is to abandon the craving for freedom, and to let go of one's stubborn hold upon selfhood, even selfhood conceived as a fiction, is to die. As for myself, I have related this brief story of my encounter with the distraught father on the plane because I want to bear witness at the close to my overwhelming need to sustain the illusion that I am the principal maker of my own identity' (257, emphasis added).
2 Obviously, as time passes, there are more and more dead people for the living to identify with; Sandra M. Gilbert and Susan Gubar called the 1979 collection of essays on female poets that they edited *Shakespeare's Sisters*, paying tribute to Judith Shakespeare; in their preface to the *Norton Anthology of Writing by Women* they begin with a quotation from *A Room of One's Own*, thus invoking both Woolf and Judith Shakespeare as female voices made present in the anthology.

scholars, I feel a responsibility to a woman ... who once existed in bodily form, walked on rush mats, laughed, and put her pen to paper. I want her to speak as directly as possible across the cultural and linguistic barriers that separate us' (n. pag.).

Objections have, of course, been raised against the transparent identification of protomodern and postmodern identities that pervades these critical texts. Calls have been made, by feminists and new historicists, prompting attention to discontinuity and difference based upon Foucault's notion of genealogy ('Nietzsche, Genealogy, History' 139–40 and passim).[3] Carolyn Porter's words are representative in this respect: the new historicism, she writes, 'has generated forms of critical practice that continue to exhibit the force of a formalist legacy whose subtle denials of history – as the scene of heterogeneity, difference, contradiction, at least – persist' (253). Jonathan Dollimore writes simply that 'in English studies especially the modern and the early modern have been erroneously conflated' (*Sexual Dissidence* 279); Marilyn Butler's formulation could stand as a motto for these critiques: 'the past ... is *different* from the present' (25). It has recently become customary to preface collections, editions, and analyses with statements respecting the diversity, multivocality, and even fragmentation of the past, and to pay salutary tribute to what Foucault calls the 'disparity' and 'dissension' that lie at the origins of things (142). Susan Zimmerman's introduction to *Erotic Politics*, in which

---

3 The following list is representative rather than comprehensive: for critiques of the new historicism's tendencies to homogenize history, usually by reifying the individual subject and denying the complexity and diversity of the past, see Carol T. Neely, Carolyn Porter, Lee Patterson, as well as Marilyn Butler, Alan Liu, and more generally Kathy E. Ferguson. Neely's and Porter's concerns are indicative of the criticisms produced by feminists of the new historicism, which were simultaneous with criticisms produced within feminism of the ahistorical female subject that is the organizing principle of works by Betty S. Travitsky, Susan Gilbert and Sandra Gubar, Elaine Beilin, and, on women's autobiography, Mary G. Mason and Domna Stanton; these criticisms begin with works such as Linda Gordon's article and Denise Riley's book, and are represented in works by Catharine R. Stimpson, and in the introductions to Elizabeth D. Harvey's book, and to collections of essays edited by Diane Purkiss and Clare Brant, and Julia Epstein and Kristina Straub. The most influential work in recent feminist studies in this respect (as in others) is undoubtedly Judith Butler's *Gender Trouble*. Interest in the diversity of the textual past is illustrated in recent editions, including Hans Gabler's *Ulysses*, and particularly, for Renaissance or early modern scholars, of Shakespeare (Stanley Wells and Gary Taylor, Stephen Urkowitz) and theoretically articulated in historically inflected critiques of editing, beginning with Jerome McGann's *Critique*.

she lauds the ways in which cultural materialism 'eschews all totalizing narratives' and 'displace[s] the concept of history as a linear, diachronic continuum with the concept of culture-specific, synchronic, histor*ies*' (1) is typical; similarly, in the introduction to a volume of essays in the newer field of queer theory, *Queering the Renaissance*, Jonathan Goldberg writes that the essays try 'to locate a center without a center' (14).

Statements calling for decentred centres, disparate histories, and attention to fundamental difference, although easy to utter, are fraught with difficulties in practice, and the identification between the early modern and the postmodern has a tendency to reassert itself. Jonathan Dollimore is careful to acknowledge the problems of conflation, but at the same time draws upon identification between the early modern, the modern, and the postmodern (*Sexual Dissidence* 279–83 and passim). The first essay in the Goldberg collection suggests the same sort of strategic identification, beginning as follows: 'Historians queering the Renaissance occupy a particularly auspicious vantage point for probing the social fictions spun by the United States Supreme Court's notorious decision in *Bowers v. Hardwick*' (Halley 15). Susan Zimmerman's essay in *Erotic Politics*, which concerns the erotics of transvestism on the Jacobean stage, concludes with the following statement: 'Perhaps it is suitably ironic that in attempting to understand the sexual production of the Jacobean transvestite stage, we are caught in an historical trajectory that anticipates the repressions of our own future' ('Disruptive Desire' 56). Commentators on the recurrence of identification in these criticisms, when they do not call for attention to 'disparity,' and so on, tend to resign us to the inevitability of such identification, on the basis that our critical activity requires it. 'Interpretation,' writes Kathy E. Ferguson, 'is *all* there is' (335), and as such requires the operations of analogy, similitude, and other versions of identification; as Alan Liu writes specifically of the new historicism, 'though *we* would understand the historical *them* in all their strangeness, the forms of our understanding are fated at last to reveal that *they* are a remembrance or a prophecy of *us*' (733).

These approaches to the question of the modernity of the early modern focus on the extent to which particular forms of subjectivity are shared across time and cultures, and are therefore open to interminable, cyclical argument. If we consider the modern to mark, not a subjectivity but a rhetorical positioning of the writing subject in relation to the past and the future, we come closer to the denotative meaning of modernity. The *Oxford English Dictionary* defines modernity as a shifting marker of the present, 'characterized by a departure from or repudiation of accepted or traditional styles and values.' Henri Meschonnic captures the indeterminacy of the term when he states that modernity is 'un combat,' 'sans cesse recommençant,' 'indéfiniment naissant' (9). Modernity, therefore, is a marker of change or resistance within the present, which depends upon the positioning of the subject's relation to the past; it is, in other words, a mark of radicalism, as J.G.A. Pocock writes: 'the radical reconstructs the past in order to authorise the future; he historicises the present in order to deprive it of authority' (261). Modernity may be inscribed, in these terms, in states of subjectivity, or in material relations within the world, but it is most specifically inscribed in the rhetorical structures of historical forms of writing, including literary texts.

There are two main rhetorical structures in which the identification between the early modern and the modern is proposed in the critical writings discussed above. The first of these, in which the writing subject is conceived of as existing outside of history, is characterized by a metonymic relationship to the past. The second, in which the writing subject is conceived of as existing within history, is characterized by a metaphoric relationship with the past. These techniques of marking the modern are also to be found in Renaissance writing. This structural similarity suggests that the basis for our identification with the early modern lies in our common forms of positing ourselves in relation to the past, the present, and the future. In Renaissance writing, as in our own, the relationship between these two forms of historiographic rhetoric is uneasy, combative, and effacing, suggesting further that our shared modernity is constituted by the dialectic between the desire to produce history, and the desire to be produced by it. Shifting the identification debate towards the rhetorical forms of historiography is intended, in this essay, to shift attention from the competition between glib conflations of then and now, and anxious disavowals of similarity, towards a consideration of how the discourses of modernity function to establish difference within the present, both then and now.

I begin by discussing the two main rhetorical forms by means of which continuous identity between the early modern and the postmodern is construed, and the ways in which these tropes generally function in Renaissance writing. I then turn to my principal example, the writings of Anne Clifford, diarist, family biographer, and historian, whose ambivalent relationships to the past, present, and future sparked my consideration of the historical and critical issues addressed in this paper. At first glance, conditioned as we are to seek particular markers of modernity, Clifford seems a paradoxical and conflictual figure selection:

ultramodern in her choice of genre, of fashion, of reading, and of subjectivities, she is at the same time ultra-premodern in her reference to and
reverence for her family's and the aristocratic past, her re-instatement of
feudal land management systems and cultural practices on her estates,
and her desire, ultimately fulfilled, to become not a new woman but
an old queen, or, barring that, a wise patriarch. Yet if viewed with an
eye to her construction of herself and her narrative as capable of both
producing and *being produced* by history, however, Clifford can be seen to
represent the necessarily paradoxical nature of modernity. In particular,
Clifford exemplifies how radical our sense of individual discontinuity –
between, for example, a middle-class academic feminist such as myself
and a dowager queen of an aristocrat, who would call the steward to
have me evicted should I show up in her chamber, step on her rush
mats, and take her pen in my hand – can be within a rhetorical and
instrumental sense of modernity.

II

The first form of identification I should like to discuss, as employed by
Greenblatt, Dollimore, and feminist 'gynocritics' of the 1980s, situates
modernity in the subject or consciousness. The emblem of the relation
between the early modern and the postmodern in the works of these
critics is the conversation, an exchange of voices and the transcendence
of history that are made possible by the similarity between the subjectivities involved. The quotation from Steen above is an allusion to
Greenblatt's formulation of his critical desires and practice: 'I began
with the desire to speak with the dead ... If I never believed that the
dead could hear me, and if I knew the dead could not speak, I was
nonetheless certain that I could re-create a conversation with them ...
It was true that I could hear only my own voice, but my own voice
was the voice of the dead ...' (*Shakespearean Negotiations* 1). Similarly,
Elizabeth Harvey writes that 'historical reconstructions are always a
kind of ventriloquization, ... a matter of making the past seem to speak
in the voice that the present gives it' (6). The privileging of voice and
presence and the assumption of transhistorical conversation construct
what Jacques Derrida describes as a 'philosophy of presence' (2–26);
but because it does so within a nominally historiographic discourse,
our attention is further drawn to this conversation's relationship to the
representation of history. In all of these works, history, as the sum
of social, economic, discursive, and other practices, is said to produce

subjectivities, both then and now. During the conversation, however, history as such is set aside, only to be discovered to have been created anew by the conversation itself. This return to history reveals the nature of the shared modernity of the two subjects, for within the history constructed by the conversation a hierarchy exists between the remembering, encompassing, *knowing* subject, which is the critic, and the other, which is the early modern writer or individual. Within this metonymic relationship the postmodern critic, despite gestures towards his or her own fragmentary, dispersed identity, is represented as the whole, from which the part, the early modern identity, takes its signification. This whole is constituted by its ability to function outside of history, by its ability to take both sides in the conversation and master the tropes of subjectivity then and now, and to create history in the process of undertaking the conversation; in brief, it is characterized by its metahistorical and philosophical disposition.[4] Modernity is asserted in this discourse by the fact that the present is effectively all that exists, and it exists as the beginning of meaningful history. The making of *history* therefore marks a radical break with the *past*.

Much attention has been paid within new historical, cultural materialist, feminist, and queer criticisms to the conflictual nature of the imagined 'unitary' subject in Renaissance literature and culture. This figure is usually viewed psychoanalytically, or in a psycho-cultural fashion. Viewed as a trope, rather than as a condition of consciousness, the speaking subject, able to step aside from, or above, the matter of the past in order to create the very history of which it speaks, is more clearly a figure of self-conscious modernity, marking a locus of difference from the present. This 'convenient fiction,' to cite Gayatri Spivak's description of Derrida's commentary upon the proper name (Spivak liv), enables the construction of a metahistorical relationship with the audience. Through this relationship the subject – which is more often *he* than *she* – can, according to the first half of Pocock's definition of the seventeenth-century radical, 'reconstruct the past in order to authorise the future' (261). The *in situ* modernity of the speaking subject is often established in this way in Renaissance literature. One thinks of the ability of tragic protagonists in Renaissance drama to set themselves apart from the present action, constructing a metahistorical relationship with the audience through the soliloquy. One thinks also of the authority to create history and

---

4 On the opposition between 'history' and 'philosophy' established by the dialogue form, see Arthur C. Danto, passim.

story established by the speaker of the epic poem in particular, but also the lyric and other shorter genres. In the genres in which I am most interested in this paper, namely, autobiography, biography, and historiography, the ability of the speaking subject to construct himself or herself as an authority over a history that has previously existed only as the past is necessary to establish the authority of the narrative. Considered as a rhetorical technique, rather than as a psychoanalytic or psycho-cultural condition, the instrumentality of constructing a position for the speaking voice within the imaginary time of the differential present (to refer to Hawking's statement cited at the beginning of this essay), from which real time is made legible in the form of history, is clear.

The second trope of modernity I should like to address is that in which the identification with 'history' itself takes precedence over the identification with the individual subject. Whereas the favoured figure of the representation of history in the criticism of modernity discussed above is the conversation, invoking as that does the privileging of voice over writing, the preferred figure of representation of this second kind of historical criticism is the materiality, profusion, and indeterminacy of the written and printed word. These works are often conceived of in opposition to the privileging of the ahistorical subject by historical and feminist critics of the 1980s. Historical criticism takes its cues from Foucault, who writes that 'genealogy is gray, meticulous, and patiently documentary. It operates on a field of entangled and confused parchments, on documents that have been scratched over and recopied many times' (139), and from Derrida, for whom 'historicity itself is tied to the possibility of writing' (27). These discourses attempt to situate themselves in the historical, textual matter that precedes the establishment of the unitary self with its speaking voice, and other 'hegemonic' categories of identity. Wendy Wall's The Imprint of Gender and Mark Rose's Authors and Owners, for example, are concerned with the diverse positions of writerly authority that precede the invention of the 'author'; Jeff Masten's essay on Beaumont and Fletcher in Queering the Renaissance discusses homoeroticism and collaboration before the 'invention' of both the 'author' and 'homosexuality' as categories of identity; Valerie Traub's essay on lesbian desire in the same volume, which also appears in the Zimmerman volume, similarly discusses female-female desire preceding the 'lesbian' as a subject of social discourse; Jonathan Dollimore's work on the masculine subject of early modern tragedy, in Radical Tragedy and parts of Sexual Dissidence, also locates itself within a material and textual history preceding the invention of the modern, unitary subject. Gary Taylor's and Margreta de Grazia's works on the editing of Shakespeare similarly historicize the invention of the playwright as a 'genius,' and their arguments rely much upon the multiplicity of the dramatic text preceding the unification constructed by eighteenth-century editors. By privileging the multiplicity of history and textuality over the unity of the subject and the coherence of the transhistorical conversation, these critics reverse the process of the earlier critical practices outlined above, by using what Hawking refers to as 'real time' to describe 'imaginary time.' In these cases, imaginary time is both the time *after* the events discussed, in which the categories of author, homosexual, and so on were consolidated, and the unfulfilled possibility that these histories offer of a time in which these categories were refused. Rather than a metonymic relationship with the past, these critics construct a metaphoric relationship between the present and the past. The similarity between the two terms in the metaphor, terms that are materially different things, is the position they occupy (or desire to occupy) from which will emerge change – the position, that is, of modernity. In these writings modernity is established by the imaginary presents made possible by real histories. These imaginary presents, including the time in which the writer now exists, resemble metaphorically the 'real' presents, both then and now.

The establishment of a metaphoric relationship between the past and the present, the return to the documentation of the past, and the identification with that which precedes, rather than that which is, are also characteristic of Renaissance or early modern writing. In literary texts, one of the conventional markers of the Renaissance is the 'return,' strategically mediated, to classical sources and forms, a technique that disperses origins, disrupts continuity with the present, and seeks to locate a point within real time that might legitimately and differentially precede the imagined future. Thus the modernity of Spenser's and Milton's epics lies in part in the revision of the field of origins, of that which precedes and constitutes the speaking voice and its implied subject. The authority of the poems is thus partly gained through a metaphoric, rather than a metonymic, relationship with the classical sources. Similarly, the modernity and radical discontinuity of Reformation Christianity are figured as a return to texts that precede their hegemonic interpretations by church authorities, interpretations through which a metaphoric, rather than a metonymic, relationship between interpretation and Scripture is asserted. Autobiography, biography, and historical writing also reclaim the documentation of history in order to establish the emergence within the present of the differentiated subject of the narrative. Modernity is established through a paradox mediated by the figure of metaphor, for within the overriding historical framework, to be the same as they were in the past is to be different within the present. In this sense, this discourse correlates with the second half of Pocock's definition of the seventeenth-century radical, as one who 'historicises the present in order to deprive it of authority' (261).

These techniques exist together uneasily in both postmodern critical texts and early modern literary and non-literary texts. Together, they produce a complex, dialectical image of the relationships between the writing subjects, the narratives and the texts on the one hand, and the matter of the past and the idea of history on the other. What they do not produce is grounds for identification, in the sense of funda-mental similarity, for both figures of speech cast continuity within the framing tropes of discontinuity. The early modern is not, to cite and disagree with Marcus, 'postmodernism in embryo' (43); neither is our basis for identification genetic. We may, however, identify with the competing use of these tropes in our writings about history, and we may further identify with the fact that these tropes offer at least the illusion of instrumentality, of intervention in a history that is, and is not, our own.

III

Anne Clifford (1590–1676),[5] subject of and subject to this historical narrative, is most remembered, in literary and historical circles, for the documentation of her own life, probably the most extensive such record of the seventeenth century. Surviving are her memoir of the year 1603, a diary of the years 1616, 1617, and 1619, an autobiography written between 1652 and 1653, annual accounts of the years 1650 to 1675, and a diary of the final year of her life, 1676.[6] In addition to these autobiographical works, Clifford dictated brief histories of members

---

5 Biographical accounts are available in George C. Williamson, Martin Holmes, and the *Dictionary of National Biography*, as well as in eighteenth- and nineteenth-century collections of lives of noble worthies and exceptional women. See also chap. 5 of Barbara Kiefer Lewalski's *Writing Women in Jacobean England* both for biographical information and for a cogent reading of the relationships between Clifford's biography (particularly her struggles over her patrimony) and her autobiographies.
6 The 1603 memoir survives in two manuscript copies, each appended to the manuscripts of the 1616–19 diary; they are the Portland Papers XXIII ff 74–9, and

of her family dating back to William the Conqueror on one side and
Edward II on the other, for inclusion in *The Great Books of the Clifford
Family*. Although her autobiography begins with her conception, perhaps the single most important event in Clifford's long life was the
death of her father, which brought into effect his will, in which he
bequeathed to his brother Francis the titles and properties attached to
the Clifford, Vesci, and Veteripont baronies (extensive estates in the
north of England). Anne Clifford and her mother, Elizabeth Russell

---

Knole/Sackville Papers U269 F48/1 I leaves 1–17. The memoir is included in both
Sackville-West's and D.J.H. Clifford's editions of the diary and was first published
in 1795 in William Seward's *Anecdotes of Some Distinguished Persons*. Although it has
been considered (by Sackville-West and D.J.H. Clifford) to be part of the diary of
1616–19, it is clearly retrospective, a feature that, together with the differences in the
editorial history, suggests that the two manuscripts should be considered separately.

The diary of the years 1616, 1617, and 1619 survives in two manuscript copies. One
is written in the hand of Elizabeth Cavendish Harley Bentinck, Duchess of Portland
(and granddaughter of Robert Harley), Portland Papers XXIII ff 80–117 (Longleat
House, property of the marquess of Bath), committed sometime in the latter part
of the eighteenth century. The other is in the hand of Elizabeth Sackville, Countess
de la Warr, descendant of Clifford's brother-in-law Edward Sackville, dated 1826,
now in the collection from Knole House at the Centre for Kentish Studies, Maidstone
(U269 F48/1–3). The latter copy, as I argue in a forthcoming edition of the diary,
was made from and only from the Portland copy, and was used to prepare the two
editions of the diary prior to mine (Sackville-West 1923; D.J.H. Clifford 1990). In this
essay I am citing from my PhD thesis edition of the Portland version (in which the
dates, scribes, and relationships of the manuscripts are argued in detail); I also give
references to D.J.H. Clifford.

The Great Books of the Clifford Family, which contains the genealogies of Clifford's
family, the autobiography (1652–3) and the annual accounts (1650–76), and which was
dictated by Clifford (with corrections and additions made in her hand), is preserved
in three copies. These are in the Hothfield Papers at the Cumbria Records Office
in Kendal (WD/Hoth/Great Books). There were, according to a note at the end of
one copy by Thomas Tufton, sixth earl of Thanet, Anne Clifford's heir, 'four setts
of these Books, one at Skipton, another sett at Applebey Castle and another sett at
Hothfield' and a fourth at London (Clifford 1916, xxxiv). The autobiography and
parts of the genealogy were abridged and copied by interested parties and members
of her family. I do not know how many of these were made or how many survive,
but I have seen the Fisher copy dated 1737 (Harley 6177), the Portland copy of the
autobiography and parts of the text of the annual summaries (Portland Papers XXIII
ff 49–72), which was apparently made from the Fisher copy, and an 'Abridgement'
made in 1914 (CRO-Carlisle, DX/227/5) for descendants of Clifford. The Fisher
manuscript containing the 'Lives of the Clifford Family …' and the 'Life of Me …' (as
the autobiography is called) was published by the Roxburghe Club, ed. J.P. Gilson,
in 1916; this edition is the source of the citations from the autobiography in this
paper.

Clifford (until her death in 1616), spent much of the next dozen years trying to reclaim the Clifford patrimony on the basis that baronies were entailed upon the heir of the body, regardless of gender.[7] In 1617 the case was heard by the king, who decided against her, even though, as she writes, 'I beseeched His Majesty to pardon me for that I wou'd never part with Westmorland while I lived upon any Condition

---

All citations from the diary of 1676 are from *The Diaries of Lady Anne Clifford*, ed. D.J.H. Clifford.

7 Williamson writes that this claim was based on a 'unique deed' (1) by which the baronial lands were entailed upon the heir of the body, rather than the 'heir male'; Lewalski cites this deed (127) as the basis for Clifford's 'exceptional legal circumstances' (126). My understanding is that the deed was quite conventional, but that although female inheritance had occurred according to such deeds during the Middle Ages, the practice in the fifteenth, sixteenth, and most of the seventeenth centuries was to pass the titles and lands to the nearest male relative, or to hold the title extinct and pass the lands to the nearest male. In the sixteenth century, there were a couple of instances of female inheritance, or inheritance of a barony through the female line, but these were exceptional in that they depended upon monarchical whim; an example was the case of William Cecil, who was permitted to inherit the title of Baron Ros through his mother in 1591, in a show of favour by Queen Elizabeth. The law concerning this matter was not actually settled until 1674; Clifford was posthumously recognized as baroness since her father's death upon her grandson's petition to be permitted to take a seat in the House of Lords in 1691 (Cokayne, 'Limitations' 295 and 295n). (The House of Lords had recognized Clifford's right since 1628, but this had no effect other than to keep Henry Clifford from taking a place there.)

Part of what was at stake in the legal argument was the inheritability of two different kinds of barony: those established by writ of summons to the Parliament of 1299, and those held by right of tenure. The differences were important to Clifford because some of the baronial properties had passed by female inheritance prior to 1299, through Isabella de Veteripont. Tenure did not in itself constitute the possession of an inheritable right (Doubleday 689); however, as the oldest basis for the title of baron, tenure was held to contribute to that right, particularly in cases in which the tenure was at some later date qualified by writ. The perceived significance of tenure can be seen in the diary in the actions of both Clifford and her uncle Francis, concerning in particular the death of her mother, when the actual physical possession of the estates and the loyalty of the tenants are contested between them. Similarly, in 1607, Clifford writes: 'by reason of those great suits in law my mother and I were in a manner forced for our own good to go together from London down into Westmoreland' (*Lives* 38); on the same trip, she notes, 'my mother and I would have gone into the Castle of Skypton to have seen it, but were not permitted so to do, the doors thereof being shut against us by my uncle of Cumberland's officers in an uncivil and disdainfull manner' (*Lives* 39). Another principle at stake in peerage law

Whatsoever. sometimes he used fair means & perswasions, & sometimes fowle means but I was resolved so as nothing would move me' (*Diary of Anne Clifford*, ed. Acheson 66). Clifford's last hope was the right of reversion established by her father's will; she set herself to surviving the male heirs, a goal that, upon the death of her cousin Henry, she accomplished. In 1643 Anne Clifford inherited the estates and became (in addition to her existing titles of Dowager Countess of Dorset and Countesses Pembroke and Montgomery) Baroness Clifford, Vesci, and Veteripont, Hereditary High Sheriffess of Westmoreland, and Lady of the Honour of Skipton Castle. When the wars cooled, she went north to ride her boundaries, repair her castles, reorganize her estates, meddle in politics, boss about her grandchildren, go on progresses between castles with hundreds of retainers and all her bedroom furniture in tow, shave her head and smoke a pipe, and set down her histories.

Clifford's texts, her self-representation, as well as her activities – reading, fashions, and friendships – certainly bear some of the conventional markers of the modernity of the early modern subject: for example, her accounts of her legal struggles show, as Barbara Lewalski argues, that she 'contested Jacobean patriarchal ideology' (125), suggesting her prototypical identity with modern women. Her 'self-fashioning' also conforms to Greenblatt's paradigm as it is construed in relation to a 'threatening Other,' in this case nominally patriarchy (and especially her evil male relatives), and manifested 'in language' through her self-documentation and legal arguments (*Renaissance Self-Fashioning* 9). On more mundane matters – her arguments with her husband, her care for her child, her isolation in the country, her relationship with her mother, the fact that she kept diaries and personal memoirs – her diary of 1616–19 (henceforth referred to as the diary) reveals some affinities with contemporary women's lives. At the same time, other aspects and, more pointedly, texts other than the diary, reveal Clifford's resolute

---

was the 'doctrine of attraction,' by which it was held that an earldom, or some other such honour, magnetically attracted all other attached honours. Francis Clifford's lawyers argued that since the earldom unquestionably descended to him, so too did the associated baronies; this argument was the foundation of the king's decision. The matter, which is somewhat more complex than a single 'unique deed' would have it be, helps us to understand not only how protracted and complicated the legal proceedings were, but also some of the otherwise inexplicable activity recounted in the diary. Moreover, although Clifford never states her cause as pertaining to that of women in general, success in this matter would have set important precedents for noblewomen.

refusal of what we might call nascent feminism,[8] as is evidenced by her abiding attachment to her noble family's history and the sense of aristocratic entitlement that history represented, as well as by her construction of herself in later years as a feudal patriarch, coding rack-renting, legal harassment,[9] and the bestowal of alms and kisses as 'the contentments and innocent pleasures of a country life' (*Lives* 59). These aspects of her conduct, together with her texts and her self-representation, bestow on Clifford an inalienable *strangeness*, an ineradicable resistance to who *we* are, which disrupts the identification of the modernity of the early modern subject that her works sometimes encourage. Read in terms of the rhetorical figurations of her ambivalent, conflictual desire to have been preceded, at the same time as she desired to be made anew, Clifford's texts respond more fully and more coherently to the analysis of modernity as an oscillation between a metonymic and a metaphoric relation to history than they do to conventional modes of identification.

Clifford's metonymic relationship with the past is best represented in the two of her works that are most self-monumentalizing, both of which were commissioned soon after her inheritance of the baronial lands. In both texts, the 'Life of Me' and *The Great Picture of the Clifford Family*, Clifford is pre-eminently concerned with establishing herself

8 Clifford's attitude toward the 'modern' woman may be inferred from an extraordinary action she undertook when, in 1611, Anthony Stafford dedicated part 2 of his *Niobe* to her. The dedication is effusive in its praise, the locus of which is the identity of the new Eve as found in the body and being of Lady Anne Clifford: 'I am astonisht Madame I am astonisht; and could finde in my heart, to pray you, and such as you are (if there be anie such) to desist from doing well: for, I am afraide, that (ere longe) you will disable my sex, falsifie the Scriptures and make Woman the stronger vessel. But it is not I alone, whom you hauve troubled and amazed: you grow cruell, and disquiet the first of your owne Sex, Eve whose grieved Ghost methinks I see rising out of her lowe-built bedde, looking upoun you with an envious blush ... For whereas she was created in perfection, and made her selfe imperfect; you beeing created in imperfection, have almost made your selfe perfect ...' (Williamson 516). Although Clifford left no direct record of her feelings regarding the dedication, the fact that the gathering in which it appeared was torn from the binding of almost every copy suggests that she, or perhaps her husband, took great offence.

9 According to an unsubstantiated story about Clifford, a tenant who owed her a boon hen each year refused to pay, in protest over larger matters; she took him to court, spending hundreds of pounds, finally got her hen, and invited him to dinner, at which the bird in question was served. Both Sackville-West and Williamson cite the story, and its apocryphal nature; although the story is probably untrue, it none the less indicates Clifford's reputation for the rigorous, even ruthless, management of her estates.

as the legitimate heir to and head of the Clifford family, representing herself as the distillation of the essence of Clifforddom and the sum of its significant parts. 'I was very happy,' she writes at the beginning of the autobiography, 'in my first constitution both in mind and body, both for internal and external endowments, for never was there child more equally resembling both father and mother than myself. The color of mine eyes were black like my father, and the form and aspect of them was quick and lively like my mother's; the hair of my head was brown and very thick, and so long that it reached to the calf of my legs when I stood upright, with a peak of hair on my forehead, and a dimple in my chin, like my father, full cheeks and round face like my mother, and an exquisite shape of body resembling my father' (*Lives* 34–5).

Fig. 1 The Great Picture of the Clifford Family; attributed to Jan van Belcamp (c. 1647). Reproduced by permission of the Abbot Hall Art Gallery and Museum, Kendal, Cumbria.

'The Great Picture' (fig. 1) similarly represents Clifford as the sum of her parents' parts. The painting is a triptych, and the two panels flanking the centre depict Clifford first at the age at which she abstractly inherited the property (15), at least in her own mind, and, on the right, at the age of 56, when she physically inherited the property. The younger Lady Anne resembles her mother in the attitude of her head, her hairstyle, and her dress; the older resembles her father: her black hood looks like his hair, her sombre clothes echo his dark outfit, and her stance is almost identical to his. In the later portrait she wears her mother's pearls, but she does so in a fashion resembling her father's sword belt, rather than draped at the neck as Margaret Russell wears them. The past is therefore represented in metonymic parts that form the whole of the body of the head and heir of the Clifford family.

Clifford's self-representation in the painting also subordinates 'real time,' the time when she struggled for and was kept from the property, and when her legitimacy as the head of and heir to the family was questioned, to 'imaginary time,' the time when she was always the head and heir and when her legitimacy was never questioned. For example, Anne Clifford was the youngest child of the Cliffords; she is shown, however, in the left-hand portrait to be older than either of her brothers, suggesting her pre-eminence as heir to the patrimony. She is furthermore depicted, in the right-hand panel, as older than either of her parents, suggesting that she is not only the heir, but also the wise and elder progenitor of the Clifford family. The line of inheritance is figured directly in the painting as continuing from the father, through the body of the mother, to the bodies of the little boys; the line is disrupted, however, by the flanking portraits of the actual heir in both her dispossessed and possessed states. Between the two portraits of herself, time has obviously passed, as is illustrated by the disarray of the library in the later portrait. The intention, however, is to show that despite time, Anne Clifford now physically occupies the place that she abstractly occupied at the time of her father's death. The metonymic relationship of the parts of the past to the body of the present, and the subordination of real time to imaginary, non-linear time, signify her position as the creator of history whose authority derives from her ability both to embody the otherwise unformed or deformed past, and exceed the material present.[10] According to the terms developed earlier in this essay, Anne Clifford is distinctively modern because she

---

10 Clifford's success in creating a transhistorical image of herself is evident in the accounts of her since her death. As recently as 1990, in the edition of the 1616–19 diary by D.J.H. Clifford, the editor notes 'the impress of her character and her actions [which] can still be felt in the rural areas of Westmorland and Craven as if she had been alive just a few years ago' (x). Clifford closes his text with an anecdote attesting to her continuing presence in the localities in which she once reigned:

I cannot end without recounting a delightful story which so well illustrates how much the spirit and the memory of Lady Anne still lingers in the minds of Westmorland folk to this day.

constructed herself, within a historiographic discourse, as separate from the present in which she lived.

Clifford also constructed herself in terms of a metaphoric relationship to the past. This is apparent in the ways in which she selects certain figures – all of them exceptional women taken from her panoply of ancestors – with whom she identifies in a metaphoric, rather than metonymic, fashion. Her Russell aunts, for example, are memorialized in *The Great Books*, depicted in the painting, and written of many times in her other works, always inasmuch as they represent the possibilities that once existed (that is, at the court of Elizabeth) for the dignified, pious, learned conduct of power by women, possibilities lost in the frivolous courts of James and Anne. Clifford's more distant ancestresses, Idonea de Vipont and Isabella de Veteripont, also figure metaphorically in Clifford's accounts as representing the legitimacy of Clifford women inheriting property. Margaret Russell is depicted, in her biographical portrait in *The Great Books*, as a paragon of piety, intelligence, kindness, and perseverance, whose sufferings, like Clifford's, were at the hands of powerful, philandering, profligate men. Margaret Russell provides a model, therefore, both for what Clifford is, and for what she might have become. In a more complex manner, however, Clifford's metaphoric relationship with the histories that precede her own is reflected in her attitude toward textuality. Clifford recognized, even enjoyed, the multiplicity of the textual past, and the possible, imaginary presents that those texts portended. Even her most staunchly metonymic works are marked by the profusion of texts that are only nominally, and imperfectly, controlled. *The Great Books*, which concludes with the autobiography, contains dozens of biographies as well as direct copies of legal documents, deeds, gifts, letters from royalty, and the like. *The Great Picture* similarly represents something of an excess of documentation: several

---

Not long after the Second World War Lord Hothfield offered to install electricity for the first time in the almshouses in Appleby which Lady Anne had founded some three hundred years before. His proposal was politely declined, the reason being given that, 'Lady Anne would not have liked it' (270).

The ability of the commentator in 1990 to commune and converse with the long-dead subject is partly, obviously, a function of Clifford's aristocracy and her material wealth, through which she was able to insist that she be remembered. Equally obvious, however, is the extent to which this identification is made possible by her self-construction, her situation of herself at the beginning of a meaningful history, her positioning of herself as authority over, rather than subject to, the past and the present in which her works were written.

scrolls, on which the writing is legible, are depicted, as are dozens of books, their titles clearly legible and their editions identifiable by their size. Surrounding the central panel are thirty-five coats of arms, each accompanied by a biography of the holder; and each escutcheon portrait, of which there are eight, is explained with a textual biography. Clifford's investment in textuality is described by Bishop Edward Rainbow in his funeral sermon: 'She would frequently bring out of the rich Store-house of her Memory, things new and old, Sentences, or Sayings of remark, which she had read or learned out of Authors and with these her Walls, her Bed, her Hangings, and Furniture must be adorned; causing her Servants to write them in Papers, and her Maids to pin them up, that she, or they, in the time of their dressing, or as occasion served, might remember, and make discants with them. So that, though she had not many Books in her Chamber, yet it was dressed up with the flowers of a Library' (40). Most interesting in this respect, however, is Clifford's relationship with her own, rather than others', texts. The extent to which she reread, rather than rewrote, her past indicates that she maintained a metaphorical relationship with her past selves. Her textual remains, although fragmentary and sometimes ambiguous, also suggest that she intended to pass on her multiple, metaphorical selves, even as she constructed her transcendental, immortal form.

In her lifetime, Clifford wrote three kinds of autobiographical document. The first is the day-to-day book, from which she seems to have later written up the second kind, namely, annual summaries; the third is the autobiography, of which there is only one. There is some evidence that the later versions of the autobiography supplanted the earlier ones in an orderly fashion, erasing conflicts as they grew in span of years. For example, in the earlier diary, Clifford's relationship with Richard Sackville, who ambivalently opposed her suits, is depicted as volatile, argumentative, affectionate, and almost passionate; similarly, letters surviving from her second marriage to the choleric Philip Herbert suggest that their relationship, although not as affectionate as her first marriage, was equally tempestuous. In the autobiography, Clifford separates herself from both husbands and her strife-ridden relationships in a striking demonstration of how the metonymic approach to the past constructs an isolated speaking subject: 'the marble pillars of Knowle in Kent and Wilton in Wiltshire were to me often times but the gay arbour of anguish. Insomuch as a wise man that knew the insides of my fortune would often say that I lived in both these my lords' great familys as the river of Roan or Rodamus runs through the lake of Geneva, without mingling any part of its streams with that lake; for I gave myself wholly to retiredness, as much as I could, in both those great families, and made good books and virtuous thoughts my companions ...' (*Lives* 40).[11] At the same time, one must look to the survival of the diary as revealing Clifford's desire to preserve multiple versions of herself. In this respect, the diary is indeed anomalous, as it survives neither in her hand nor in a secretarial hand; nor is it included in *The Great Books*, nor is a copy of it to be found in the main collections of her papers. The diary survives only in two posthumous copies (see above, n6). Clifford's biographer, George C. Williamson, suggests that the original was destroyed because it was too embarrassing (366–7); Bishop Edward Rainbow, in his funeral sermon, cryptically refers to the 'censures others may pass on this exactness of *Diary* as too minute and trivial a *Diligence*,' and he later states: 'I confess, I have been informed, that after some reviews, these [the diaries] were laid aside' (51). As these accounts make clear, the diar[ies] were not destroyed, or set aside, by Clifford herself, but by her descendants. Although it is apparent that she did not want the diaries to survive in her formal documentation of herself, namely, *The Great Books*, it is also clear that she did intend that they survive, at least until she was through with them. Whatever function she may have imagined these documents would have for her descendants, they were of daily importance to Clifford herself. Throughout the diary of her final year, Clifford appears to have read over the earlier documents, 'remembering' things that happened in the past: 'I remembered how this day was 59 years I went with my first Lord to the Court at Whitehall, where in the inner withdrawing chamber King James desired & urged mee to submit to the Award which hee would make concerning my Lands of Inheritance, but I absolutly denyed to do so, wherein I was guided by a great Providence of Good for the good of mee & mine. And that day also have my first & then only childe a dangerous fit of her long Ague in Knowl house in Kent, where shee then lay' (240). Similarly, she recalls the hotel in which she stayed sixty years previously on her way to visit her mother, the christening of her nephew, the death of her second husband's first wife, all with dates, places, and full names and titles in place. Clifford's late rereading of her past recalls instances of rereading that she recorded in the diary: 'My Soul was much troubled,' she writes upon the receipt of the King's Award, '^&

11 Lewalski identifies the 'gay arbour' as an allusion to *The Countess of Pembroke's Arcadia* (372).

afflicted^ to see how things go, but my trust is still in God & compare things past with things present & reade over the Chronicles' (*Diary of Anne Clifford*, ed. Acheson 72). Her diaries are fragmentary, multiple, and intertextual, supplementing, but not superseding, the other selves she left for the enjoyment of her posterity. Her identification, through written records, with her past, 'metaphoric' selves ('compare things past …'), fulfils the other condition of 'early' modernity of which I have been writing, namely, the situation of introspection at that point that precedes the construction of the unitary self, subordinating the imaginary time in which the transcendental subject is constructed to 'real' time, in which the many possibilities of the historical self have been manifest. In the same instant as she self-consciously constructs her unitary, authoritative, speaking self, Clifford retains and rereads the records of her multiplicity, the textual evidence of herself within history. She regards the past not metonymically, but metaphorically, giving herself authority by the precedent of others.

IV

Anne Clifford's sense of herself as both subject to and subject of the matter of history, her oscillation between her conception of herself as at once unitary and fragmentary, and her ambivalent reliance on both the figures of metonymy and metaphor identify modernity as a rhetoric that inscribes a differential relationship with the present. Key to Clifford's modernity, and key to ours, is the sense of alienation from the present, figured as a problematical set of relationships with history. For Clifford, the present was variously the time when her claims and rights went unrecognized, her enemies conspired against her, her profligate and neglectful father and husbands injured her cause and reputation, and the morals of the aristocracy were tainted by injustices towards her and the wilful disregard of her version of history. Her historical discourses, in all of their forms, were ways in which she intervened in the present, refiguring herself in relation to her surroundings. Crucial, therefore, to our understanding of the discourses and rhetorical forms of modernity, in the case of Anne Clifford and of Renaissance and postmodern historiographic and literary writing, is the instrumentality of that discourse and those forms of rhetoric, that is, the ways in which we position ourselves differentially within the present through our uses of the past in order to refigure the future.

Despite their opposition on other issues of substance, the metonymic and metaphoric forms of literary historiography, if considered as instrumental rhetorical forms, reveal their common ground. The metonymic 'identity' politics of the 1970s and 1980s served to move the agendas of feminism and cultural materialism to the centre of early modern criticism, as is evidenced by their dominance in accounts given of the Renaissance (enthusiastically) by Marcus, and of seventeenth-century literary criticism (grudgingly) by William Kerrigan in a survey volume recently published by the Modern Language Association of America. The metaphoric identity politics of the 1990s, by which, in the words of Margaret Hunt, we 'attempt to claim a usable history in the face of an all too easily abusable past' (359), is further serving to entrench the discourses of newer feminist, queer, and materialist forms of criticism, by returning the site of inspection and introspection to the documentation and 'evidence' of history. Jonathan Dollimore wrote in 1989 that he was using the term 'early modern England' because it was 'a description of the period with less assumptions than "Renaissance"' (*Radical Tragedy* xxxi). As this essay has shown, the contrary is now true, both inasmuch as 'early modern' conventionally suggests the 'erroneous' conflation of which Dollimore also writes, and inasmuch as it suggests the rhetorical relationships with the past, the present, and history. According to the argument of this essay, the use of the term 'early modern' signifies, ironically, our attempts to construct ourselves differently from our post-modern present, either through claiming the authority of the speaking subject, and creating history anew, or by situating ourselves as subjects of a previously unknown history. Both early and post-modernity, although they may indeed be both producing of and produced by particular states of subjectivity or particular cultural formations, may best be viewed as 'convenient fictions' by which we grant ourselves, however much we are denied it elsewhere, and however much we know it to be an illusion, the authority, even the power, to enact difference in the present.

WORKS CITED

Acheson, Katherine, ed. *See* Clifford, Anne.

Beilin, Elaine V. *Redeeming Eve: Women Writers of the English Renaissance.* Princeton: Princeton UP, 1987.

Brant, Clare, and Diane Purkiss. 'Introduction: Minding the Story.' *Women, Texts and Histories 1575–1760.* Ed Claire Brant and Diane Purkiss. London and New York: Routledge, 1992. 1–12.

Butler, Judith. *Gender Trouble: Feminism and the Subversion of Identity.* New York and London: Routledge, 1990.

Butler, Marilyn. 'Against Tradition: The Case for a Particularized Historical Method.' *Historical Studies and Literary Criticism*. Ed. Jerome J. McGann. Madison: U of Wisconsin P, 1985. 25–47.

Chalmers, Hero. '"The person I am, or what they made me to be": The Construction of the Feminine Subject in the Autobiographies of Mary Carleton.' *Women, Texts and Histories 1575–1760*. Ed Clare Brant and Diane Purkiss. 1992. 164–94.

Clifford, Anne. *The Diaries of Lady Anne Clifford*. Ed. D.J.H. Clifford. Phoenix Mill, UK and Wolfeboro Falls, NH: Alan Sutton, 1990.

– *The Diary of Anne Clifford, 1616–1619: A Critical Edition*. Ed. Katherine Acheson. New York: Garland, 1995.

– *The Diary of the Lady Anne Clifford*. Ed. Vita Sackville-West. London: William Heinemann, 1923.

– *Lives of Lady Anne Clifford, Countess of Dorset, Pembroke and Montgomery (1590–1676) and of Her Parents, Summarized by Herself*. Ed. J.P. Gilson. London: Roxburghe Club, 1916.

Clifford, D.J.H. *See* Clifford, Anne.

Cokayne, G.E. *The Complete Peerage of England, Scotland, Ireland, Great Britain and the United Kingdom*. Ed. Vicary Gibbs. 2nd ed. 14 vols. London: St Catherines, 1910–1959.

– 'Limitations to "Heirs Male."' *The Complete Peerage*. Vol. 7. Appendix E. 1913. 718–33.

Danto, Arthur C. Foreword to *The Author, Art and the Market* by Martha Woodmansee. New York: Columbia UP, 1994. ix–xv.

Derrida, Jacques. *Of Grammatology*. Trans. Gayatri Chakravorty Spivak. Baltimore: Johns Hopkins UP, 1976.

Dollimore, Jonathan. *Radical Tragedy: Religion, Ideology and Power in the Drama of Shakespeare and His Contemporaries*. 2nd ed. London: Harvester Wheatsheaf, 1989.

– *Sexual Dissidence: Augustine to Wilde, Freud to Foucault*. London and New York: Oxford UP, 1991.

Doubleday, H.A. 'Earldoms and Baronies in History and in Law, and the Doctrine of Abeyance.' *The Complete Peerage*. Vol. 4. 1916. 651–760.

Epstein, Julia, and Kristina Straub. Introduction. *Body Guards: The Cultural Politics of Gender Ambiguity*. Ed. Julia Epstein and Kristina Straub. New York and London: Routledge, 1991. 1–28.

Ferguson, Kathy E. 'Interpretation and Genealogy in Feminism.' *Signs: Journal of Women in Culture and Society*. 16.2 (1991). 322–39.

Foucault, Michel. 'Nietszche, Genealogy, History.' Trans. Bouchard Simon and Sherry Simon. *Language, Counter-Memory, Practice: Selected Essays and Interviews*. Ed. Donald F. Bouchard. Ithaca: Cornell UP, 1977. 139–64.

Gilbert, Sandra M., and Susan Gubar. 'Introduction: Gender, Creativity and the Woman Poet.' *Shakespeare's Sisters: Feminist Essays on Women Poets.* Ed. Sandra M. Gilbert and Susan Gubar. Bloomington: Indiana UP, 1979. xv–xxvi.

– Preface. *The Norton Anthology of Literature by Women: The Tradition in English.* Ed. Sandra M. Gilbert and Susan Gubar. New York and London: Norton, 1985. xxvii–xxxii.

Gilson, J.P. *See* Clifford, Anne.

Goldberg, Jonathan. Introduction. *Queering the Renaissance.* Ed. Jonathan Goldberg. Durham, NC and London: Duke UP, 1994. 1–14.

Gordon, Linda. 'What's New in Women's History.' *Feminist Studies/Critical Studies.* Ed. Teresa de Lauretis. Bloomington: Indiana UP, 1986. 20–30.

Grazia, Margreta de. *Shakespeare Verbatim.* Oxford: Clarendon P, 1991.

Greenblatt, Stephen. *Renaissance Self-Fashioning: From More to Shakespeare.* Chicago and London: U of Chicago P, 1980.

– *Shakespearean Negotiations: The Circulation of Social Energy in Renaissance England.* Berkeley and Los Angeles: U of California P, 1988.

Greenblatt, Stephen, and Giles Gunn, eds. *Redrawing the Boundaries: The Transformation of English and American Literary Studies.* New York: MLA, 1992.

Halley, Janet E. '*Bowers v. Hardwick* in the Renaissance.' *Queering the Renaissance.* Ed. Jonathan Goldberg. 15–39.

Harvey, Elizabeth D. *Ventriloquized Voices: Feminist Theory and English Renaissance Texts.* London and New York: Routledge, 1992.

Hawking, Stephen W. *A Brief History of Time from the Big Bang to Black Holes.* Toronto and New York: Bantam, 1988.

Holmes, Martin. *Proud Northern Lady: Lady Anne Clifford, 1590–1676.* London and Chichester: Phillimore, 1975.

Hunt, Margaret. Afterword. *Queering the Renaissance.* Ed. Jonathan Goldberg. 359–77.

Jakobson, Roman. *Fundamentals of Language.* Trans. Morris Halle. 2nd ed. The Hague and Paris: Mouton, 1971.

Kerrigan, William. 'Seventeenth-Century Studies.' *Redrawing the Boundaries.* Ed. Stephen Greenblatt and Giles Gunn. 64–78.

Lewalski, Barbara Kiefer. *Writing Women in Jacobean England.* Cambridge, MA and London: Harvard UP, 1993.

Liu, Alan. 'The Power of Formalism: The New Historicism.' *ELH* 56.1 (1989): 721–71.

Marcus, Leah S. 'Renaissance/Early Modern Studies.' *Redrawing the Boundaries.* Ed. Stephen Greenblatt and Giles Gunn. 41–63.

Mason, Mary G. 'The Other Voice: Autobiographies of Women Writers.'
  Autobiography: Essays Theoretical and Critical. Ed. James Onley. Princeton:
  Princeton UP, 1980. 207–35.
Masten, Jeff. 'My Two Dads: Collaboration and the Reproduction of Beaumont
  and Fletcher.' *Queering the Renaissance.* Ed. Jonathan Goldberg. 280–309.
McGann, Jerome J. *A Critique of Modern Textual Criticism.* 2nd ed. Charlottesville
  and London: UP of Virginia, 1992.
– *The Textual Condition.* Princeton: Princeton UP, 1991.
Meschonnic, Henri. *Modernité, Modernité.* Paris: Gallimard, 1988.
Neely, Carol Thomas. 'Constructing the Subject: Feminist Practice and the
  New Renaissance Discourses.' *English Literary Renaissance* 18.1 (1988): 5–18.
Patterson, Lee. 'On the Margin: Postmodernism, Ironic History, and Medieval
  Studies.' *Speculum* 65.1 (1990): 87–108.
Pocock, J.G.A. 'Time, Institutions and Action: An Essay on Traditions and Their
  Understanding.' *Politics, Language and Time: Essays on Political Thought and
  History.* New York: Atheneum, 1973. 233–72.
Porter, Carolyn. 'History and Literature: "After the New Historicism."' *New
  Literary History* 21.2 (1990): 253–72.
Rainbow, Edward. *A Sermon Preached at the Funeral of the Right Honorable Anne
  Countess of Pembroke Dorset and Montgomery.* London, 1677.
Riley, Denise. *'Am I That Name?':* Feminism and the Category of 'Women' in
  History. Basingstoke: Macmillan; Minneapolis: U of Minnesota P, 1988.
Rose, Mark. *Authors and Owners: The Invention of Copyright.* Cambridge, MA
  and London: Harvard UP, 1993.
Sackville-West, Vita. *See* Clifford, Anne.
Spivak, Gayatri Shakravorty. Preface to *Of Grammatology,* by Jacques Derrida.
  Trans. Gayatri Shakravorty Spivak. Baltimore and London: Johns Hopkins
  UP, 1976. ix–lxxxvii.
Stanton, Domna C. 'Autogynography: Is the Subject Different?' *The Female
  Autograph.* Ed. Domna C. Stanton. Chicago and London: U of Chicago P,
  1984. 3–20.
Steen, Sara Jayne. 'Behind the Arras: Editing Renaissance Women's Letters.'
  Voices of Silence: Editing the Letters of Renaissance Women. Papers Presented at
  the Renaissance English Text Society. MLA Annual Convention. 1990.
Stimpson, Catharine R. 'Woolf's Room, Our Project.' *The Future of Literary
  Theory.* Ed. Ralph Cohen. Madison: U of Wisconsin P, 1989. 129–43.
Taylor, Gary. *Reinventing Shakespeare: A Cultural History from the Restoration to
  the Present.* New York, Oxford: Oxford UP, 1989.
Taylor, Gary, and Michael Warren, eds. *The Division of the Kingdoms:
  Shakespeare's Two Versions of 'King Lear.'* Oxford: Clarendon P, 1983.

Traub, Valerie. 'The (In)Significance of "Lesbian" Desire in Early Modern England.' *Queering the Renaissance*. Ed. Jonathan Goldberg. 62–83.

Travitsky, Betty S. 'Introduction: Placing Women in the English Renaissance.' *The Renaissance Englishwoman in Print: Counterbalancing the Canon*. Ed. Anne M. Haselkorn and Betty S. Travitsky. Amherst, MA: U of Massachusetts P, 1990. 3–41.

– *The Paradise of Women: Writings by Englishwomen of the Renaissance*. Westport, CO and London: Greenwood, 1981.

Wall, Wendy. *The Imprint of Gender: Authorship and Publication in the English Renaissance*. Ithaca: Cornell UP, 1993.

Williams, Linda R. 'Happy Families? Feminist Reproduction and Matrilineal Thought.' *New Feminist Discourses: Critical Essays on Theories and Texts*. Ed. Isobel Armstrong. London and New York: Routledge, 1992. 48–64.

Williamson, George C. *Lady Anne Clifford, Countess of Dorset, Pembroke and Montgomery, 1590–1676, Her Life, Letters and Work*. Kendal: Titus Wilson and Son, 1923.

Woolf, Virginia. *A Room of One's Own*. 1929. Toronto: McClelland and Stewart, 1932.

Zimmerman, Susan. 'Disruptive Desire: Artifice and Indeterminacy in Jacobean Comedy.' *Erotic Politics: Desire on the Renaissance Stage*. Ed. Susan Zimmerman. New York and London: Routledge, 1992. 39–63.

– 'Introduction: Erotic Politics: The Dynamics of Desire on the English Renaissance Stage.' *Erotic Politics: Desire on the Renaissance Stage*. Ed. Susan Zimmerman. 1–11.

3

Dark Ladies: Women, Social History, and English Renaissance Literature

LINDA WOODBRIDGE

'She hath no name,' Sir Thomas Wyatt writes of the woman he is ostensibly immortalizing in verse: 'it doth suffice she doth me wrong.' Renaissance literature abounds in nameless sonnet mistresses and the male sonneteers who immortalized themselves by writing of the pain those mistresses caused. Modern readers have often wanted to name those women – not only the anonymous sonnet mistresses but the women who went about their lives in London, maybe read sonnets themselves, maybe wrote sonnets themselves, and then were lost to memory. What history and literary history have forgotten, we have wanted to remember. How much can we recover of the real lives of women in that era, what can we say about how literature represented women, and what connections can we make between the two? Here I shall consider only women in the literature of love and marriage – not much of a narrowing, since love and marriage are central Renaissance themes, and since the ideology of the day tried to restrict women's action to just this 'private' and domestic sphere – to speak of women in Renaissance literature is almost necessarily to speak of love and marriage.

In *life*, marriage was changing – Protestants declared it a worthier state than celibacy, inverting the medieval hierarchy of these two states, and they considered marriage a contract, where Catholics had viewed it as a sacrament. Among Catholics *and* Protestants, the ideal of companionate marriage was growing, partly owing to the influence of humanist ideology. The dissolution of convents and the increasing exclusion of

Small portions of this essay have previously appeared in reviews published in *Shakespeare Quarterly*, *Renaissance Quarterly*, and *Modern Philology*, and are reprinted by permission of those journals.

craftswomen by trade guilds were abolishing women's alternatives to marriage – for the woman who wished to eat, marriage was becoming compulsory. In *literature,* writers such as Spenser and Shakespeare took the crucial if illogical step of linking courtly love, with its tradition of female dominance and male grovelling, to marriage, with its ideology of male dominance and female subjection. Turning courtly love into courtship, a step towards marriage, significantly changed the medieval notion of marriage as a matter of dynastic preservation and economic survival; courtly love had been a matter of delightful adultery never expected to eventuate in marriage. Both changes in life and changes in literature valorized love and marriage; both embedded love and marriage in an ideological discourse designed to produce a stable society. The temptation to read the literature in light of social history has proved irresistible.

The new historicism, still the reigning critical approach to Renaissance literature, focuses on the monarchy and the court; and women lose by this monarchomania. What is gained for women by a focus on Elizabeth is lost in the neglect of ordinary women. Since few Renaissance women were active in public life, the study of women loses even more than the study of men by a narrow focus on national politics. While literary study in recent decades has witnessed historicisms old and new, equally monarchic, historiography has travelled in the opposite direction. From the Annales school to Lawrence Stone's social history, we can see that political, constitutional, military, and diplomatic history has yielded to the history of ordinary folk. Having hoped that literary study would move in the same direction, I *should* welcome recent applications, often by feminist scholars, of social history to the study of women in the Renaissance – here is an attempt to study ordinary women. And yet I'm bothered by the fact that applying social history to literature often just doesn't work very well.

A useful case study is Ann Jennalie Cook's *Making a Match: Courtship in Shakespeare and His Society.* This exhaustively researched, interesting book sets out to link social history with Shakespeare, with seemingly unintended results. Cook often finds significant discontinuity between the plays and Elizabethan life: young men in the audience might dream of a Juliet, Marina, Perdita, or Miranda, 'but they generally married women of twenty or more, not girls of fourteen or sixteen. They might spin fantasies of loving a shepherdess ... or a damsel on an enchanted island ... Yet the majority actually married wives of suitable age and suitable background from suitable families' (34). In life, Cook says,

Rosalind and Orlando in *As You Like It* would have been 'a patently impossible match' (59); if *Twelfth Night* were life, Orsino would have wed Olivia, since 'the twins do not have even lesser titles' (61); Sir Toby Belch could never have married Maria. The whole idea of founding marriages on falling in love belongs less to life than to literature, Cook argues. Duly noting each discontinuity between life and literature, Cook is not bothered by the way they are accumulating: the plays seem to depart from normal Elizabethan social practice much more often than they adhere to it. Cook reads this as Shakespeare's 'radical challenge to the institutions of Elizabethan-Jacobean culture. The centrality of marriage to the self, the family, the community, the church, the state, the very cosmos meant that it was guarded by rules, rituals, customs, and beliefs designed to ensure its stability. Onstage, however, stability disappears. Any aspect of courtship may be questioned' (262). Rather than mystifying Shakespeare as uniquely capable of rising above the ideology of his age – a bit of bardolatry facilitated by Cook's focus on Shakespeare in isolation from his contemporary writers – one might ask whether discontinuity between plays and life does not undermine the project of interpreting plays via social history. Is it possible that literature follows its own rules rather than the rules of normal social life, that the blustering *senex iratus* of Elizabethan comedy has more in common with the blustering *senex* of Roman New Comedy than with the Elizabethan patriarch? Too often we wield social history as a blunt instrument that rasps off all the fine edges of literariness.

Elizabethan audience members must often, I think, have suspended ordinary attitudes and accepted a play's contract of belief: revenge tragedy asks a Christian audience to suppress the text 'vengeance is mine, I will repay, saith the Lord'; an amoral superman such as Tamburlaine could be enjoyed and applauded only by shelving one's workaday Christian aversion to violence, boasting, and mindless territorial conquest. In these cases, how helpful *is* it to dig out actual attitudes towards vengeance or bloodshed? Are actual attitudes and real practices the question here? This issue is nowhere more acute than with marriage, a ubiquitous motif in drama and in life. Love and marriage provide a perfect test case for the validity of applying social history to literature; and the pervasive discontinuity between social history and Shakespeare as documented by Cook raises serious questions about that validity.

Cook's findings are valuable because they help to problematize the historicizing of drama. Cook herself, however, just keeps trying to show that social history can illuminate plays. Sometimes this works, as with her approach to Bertram or Petruchio; at other times one feels real strain, as when Cook suggests that Capulet in *Romeo and Juliet* and Egeus in *A Midsummer Night's Dream* would have been seen as being within their rights in seeking to dictate 'the marriage of a minor daughter' (100). *Would* audience sympathy have been with these heavy fathers and against the daughters? It seems doubtful. Capulet and Egeus are not Elizabethan patriarchs but examples of a stock literary figure, the *senex iratus* or angry old man, who opposes his child's marriage in a time-honoured literary convention going back to Roman comedy; such figures are set up to be outwitted by the young, and little suggests that in the long history of the *senex* the audience was ever invited to sympathize with him. Cook's study succeeds in its goal of giving 'equal treatment [to] social history and Shakespearean drama' (15). It is the *connection* between them that troubles me.

One problem dogging literary scholars who use social history on the marriage question has been the baneful influence of Lawrence Stone's *The Family, Sex, and Marriage in England 1500 to 1800*. Stone's most controversial conclusion, that the early modern family displayed 'low affect' since parents did not allow themselves much emotional investment in children due to high infant mortality, was strenuously questioned by historians the moment the book appeared in 1977. Historian Keith Thomas found evidence to the contrary, interestingly, in Ben Jonson's poems on the death of his children. And feminist scholars helped to refute Stone's dismal view. In the essay collection *The Renaissance Englishwoman in Print* (1990), for example, Betty Travitsky sees a plain refutation of the 'low affect' theory in Elizabeth Egerton's anguished 'efforts to come to grips with the pain of her daughter Katherine's death' (249). But despite the fact that both *The Family, Sex, and Marriage* and Stone's other influential book *The Crisis of the Aristocracy* came under heavy attack from prominent historians such as Alan Macfarlane, as reaching dubious conclusions from unreliable evidence, many Renaissance literary scholars have continued to use Stone as if he were gospel. At the 1990 conference of the Shakespeare Association of America in Philadelphia, a forum on literary uses of the work of Lawrence Stone and Michel Foucault featured three historians, who heavily reiterated the slim credibility of Stone and Foucault in history departments, evincing considerable surprise at the veneration in which literary scholars hold them. One speaker, social historian David Cressy, detailed Stone's scholarly failings and demonstrated how widely and often uncritically his work is used by Renaissance scholars, quoting a number of recent books on English Renaissance literature that cite Stone as if he were tablets of stone. Now, this might have been a little tactless, since most of the offending scholars were sitting in the room at the time, but I was still surprised at the reaction to the forum: not so much indignation at Cressy's having pilloried literary scholars as rage that he had attacked Stone, mingled with irritation at the Shakespeare Association for having invited historians to lecture us so sanctimoniously, when they had little notion of our discipline's special needs.

I was sorry we literary folk were deaf to historians' opinions of the work of their fellows – work that we were after all using, whether our needs were special or not. We had to some extent left ourselves open to their criticism, by forgetting how different history and literature can be. But would the problem disappear if we pitched out Stone and Foucault and adopted Keith Thomas and David Cressy as our pet historians? The problem is partly that we have rested our foundations on some rather sandy historians, but it is a good deal more complicated than that.

In appealing to History, are we trying to make English scientific, maybe even respectably 'masculine'? A sad project from a feminist point of view. It is also epistemologically problematic: by trying to anchor literature in the solid sea floor of History, we have cast an anchor into shifting sand. History is no less epistemologically bedevilled than literary study. Our craving for something certain in which to ground literary study leads us to privilege historical over literary texts as repositories of truth. Although new historicism differs from old historicism in recognizing that we ourselves inevitably rewrite history from our own ideological standpoint, in practice the slipperiness of 'history' is too often overlooked. Stephen Greenblatt, treating Harsnett's *Declaration of Egregious Popish Impostures* as a historical document in which to ground *King Lear*, gives Harsnett's text, according to Edward Pechter, 'the objective status of a stable point of reference'; Pechter notes: *King Lear* 'is said to be produced by its ideological and historical situation; it is unambiguously dependent, while the culture is unambiguously determining' (293). Historian Hayden White attributes such subservience to the pressure on humanistic studies to 'aspire to the status of sciences' ('Historical Pluralism' 484). 'To enable research in any field of humanistic studies,' argues White, 'investigators must presuppose that at least one other field of study or discipline is ... effectively free of the kind of epistemological and methodological disputes that agitate their own area of inquiry. [For some literary critics] history appears to serve this function' (484). But theorists such as David Carroll, Leo Braudy, and White himself have argued that historical documents closely resemble literary texts, falling into similar genres, employing similar rhetorical strategies, and often being classifiable as narrative. (Is the history profession's current distaste for 'old-fashioned narrative history' partly a subconscious attempt to deny the fictiveness of history-making?) Few now believe naïvely that historians discover patterns in human events: historians clearly *impose* patterns on human events, in imaginative acts that Hayden White likens to the novelist's. But to abandon the notion of objective truth in historical investigation is to invite abuses, such as the rewriting of history to suit the purposes of any repressive ideologue; we must go on trying to falsify the past as little as possible. I shall never forget J.H. Hexter's moving tribute to his fellow historian Garrett Mattingly for believing so fervently that setting the record straight on the Spanish commander of the Armada really *mattered*. Being as fair and objective as we can to people of the past *does* matter; and yet prisoners of our own culture as we are, it is notoriously difficult. I'm not sure that we literary scholars remind ourselves often enough just how difficult it is, or take enough care to remember when we use historical documents that history is itself a construction, not a raw chunk of objective reality. I am not attacking social history as a discipline, but problematizing our borrowings from it. Social historians have similar conversations about the validity of using literary evidence in their discipline.

To illustrate problems of method facing a feminist-historicist-literary critic studying love and marriage, take Desdemona's elopement in *Othello*. Would Shakespeare's audience have seen it as a horrific abrogation of patriarchal authority that positively *invites* smothering in one's bed? Or as a dashingly romantic expression of *jouissance*, bearing the audience away on wings of romance and adventure? Shakespeare's audience was a historical entity, and this is a historical question. A social historian would recognize that descrying the beliefs about elopement held by Shakespeare's contemporaries will take a lot of digging – into letters, diaries, court records, legal statutes, sermons, ecclesiastical documents, and the like, correcting for differences of attitude across social classes, geographical regions, age groups, genders, religious denominations. Since Shakespeare's audience was socially, geographically, religiously, generationally, and sexually heterogeneous, part of the social historian's conclusion might well be that an audience cannot be regarded as an entity that holds 'attitudes': members of the audience may well have disagreed on the most fundamental matters. The problem with studies of context, as posed by deconstructionists, is that, as Jonathan Culler puts it, 'meaning is context-bound, but context is boundless' (123).

But suppose a social historian working on the Elopement Attitudes Problem believed that the study of context could at least bring us closer to a text's meaning, although it could not determine it absolutely, and in this faith she handed over her results to a literary historian with whom she was collaborating on the *Othello* question. First, the literary historian should have learned enough from the historian to find out if the data are reliable, representative, complete. Our literary historian would also need to consider genre differences – when lovers elope in the festive air of a comedy, even draconian patriarchs in the audience may prove sentimentally tolerant; but what happens when this act is translated into a tragedy like *Othello*?

Next, the literary historian should ask whether the data of social history are relevant to drama at all. Plays are *not* life, and it is possible that an audience may suspend its ordinary beliefs when accepting the contract of belief that a play provides – again, a Christian audience, accepting the biblical injunction 'vengeance is mine, I will repay, saith the Lord,' might still applaud the artistic vindictiveness of a revenge-tragedy hero, since those are the terms of the play. It might do so in defiance also of Tudor ideology, which also condemned private vengeance in order to maintain the state's monopoly of violence. The current widely held belief that ideology is virtually inescapable, that the individual subject is as incapable of standing outside of ideology as of choosing not to breathe the air of planet Earth, does not always square with literary experience: if an audience was not capable of putting its ideology on hold for the duration of a play, the very genre of revenge tragedy would be unintelligible. The tendency to accept a text's contract of belief may be especially strong in drama, where because an audience is sharing an oral experience rather than reading in isolation, a group psychology may encourage acceptance of the play's terms.

Finally, our literary historian might ask whether the diaries, letters, sermons, and other 'historical documents' used as windows onto the social attitudes of real people should not themselves be regarded and analysed as literary texts. Among the many problems of maintaining a literary 'canon' as if it were a stable of fine horses is that we may habitually analyse the thoroughbred literary documents safe in their stalls according to recognized conventions, rhetorical devices, and so on, while assuming that the cart-horse texts outside the stable do not follow such rules. Isolating literary texts as different *in kind* from 'historical documents' encourages the old vice of regarding historical documents as chunks of unprocessed reality, somehow closer to Truth than are literary texts. If 'literary' documents, like plays, operate in a different mental world from that of everyday experience, so may diaries, letters, and sermons.

We cannot regard social history as a freshly washed window onto early modern reality. Historical texts are as subject to interpretation as literary texts, and if we want to use social history to interpret literature, we must resist any inclination to construe History as standing firm on the shore, throwing out the lifeline to Literature, 'across the dark wave.' Literature follows its own rules and invites attitudes towards its characters that may not faintly resemble attitudes that real people would have held towards one another. And neither literature nor history is science: we will never make literary study into an 'objective' science by hanging it onto history. Even scientists nowadays talk about their theories as the 'stories' that best make sense of the data; is this a time to be selling our birthright as *specialists* in stories for a mess of social-science pottage?

Among many good books on women and gender in early modern England, at least one study of love and marriage takes the kind of rigorous look at social history that I have been advocating. Heather Dubrow's *A Happier Eden: The Politics of Marriage in the Stuart Epithalamium* takes a hard look at the feasibility of using marriage sermons and marriage treatises to illuminate that genre of marriage poetry, the epithalamium. Noting the 'striking degree of inconsistency from treatise to treatise and within the same treatise' (12) Dubrow asks tough questions about whether sermons and marriage treatises are indexes of social attitudes: sermons were always written by clergymen, and marriage treatises most often were. Might not any clergyman 'have biased and partial views on marriage'? Are writers of marriage manuals 'representative even of their own profession? It is likely that a certain type of clergyman would be attracted' to writing such books. 'To what extent were readers actually influenced by [their] pronouncements?' (10–12). Insisting that there was little agreement on any aspect of marriage, Dubrow sure-footedly negotiates the slippery passages between social history and literature. She neither forgets the surrounding context of social attitudes nor lets us forget that literature forges its own world: a patriarch benignly applauding an elopement in a comedy would not necessarily feel benevolent about his own daughter's elopement. Treating marriage manuals themselves as literary documents rather than peepholes into social attitudes, Dubrow writes that 'the very act of writing a manual or delivering a sermon on marriage ... implies that wedlock is an

institution that can indeed be regulated, controlled, and ordered ...
And the rhetoric of the marriage manuals in particular is grounded in
ordering ...' (26–7). In such writings, a rhetoric of debts and duty serves,
Dubrow claims, to 'socialize and civilize sexual desire. It becomes not
an irresistible passion but an obligation; the bride and groom will make
love, such rhetoric implies, because they should rather than because they
want to' (88); she comments drily, 'it is hard to think of a more potent
anaphrodisiac than the concept of duty' (26). Neither epithalamia nor
marriage sermons, Dubrow argues, are windows onto any Elizabethan
World Picture; they are ideologically committed attempts to instil Renaissance attitudes, and to do so both use rhetoric, art, the techniques
of literature.

I turn now from marriage to the Renaissance continuation of a medieval tradition, courtly love, a tradition flourishing in sonnets. An early
approach to women in Renaissance love poetry was to identify them
with living women. Who was Shakespeare's dark lady? Was Sidney's
Stella really Penelope Rich? This is in some ways a post-Romantic par-
lour game, reflecting the Romantic conception of poetry as a personal
effusion; but to some extent it was fostered by Renaissance love poets
themselves. Sidney points us towards a living woman by punning on
the name Rich; in one poem, Wyatt seems to glance at a forbidden
relationship with the queen, and in another he alludes to his period
of house arrest. Several first-person speakers talk about their craft as
poets, and are thereby constructed not as generic lovers but specifically
poets-as-lovers, thus inviting identification of the speaker with the poet.
Nevertheless, naïve quests for the identity of the dark lady have, at
least in academic criticism of the past several decades, been distinctly
out of style, partly because of the critical and theoretical de-emphasis
on the author as an autonomous individual. When the Death of the
Author is announced, the dark lady goes down with him. Interest in
such topical concerns, however, is reviving, owing I think to a basic internal contradiction in new historicist and cultural materialist thinking:
on the one hand historicists declare the autonomous individual subject
a chimera or at least the invention of a later age than Shakespeare's;
on the other hand their desire to historicize literary study leads many
of them, such as, for example, Leah Marcus and Louis Montrose, into
minutely topical criticism, which involves, again, the identification of
historical individuals, usually those at court (because new historicists
are deeply concerned with power). Since Renaissance love poetry is
often courtly, we arrive back at identifying the sonnet mistress with a

historical woman, the difference being that the lover's interest in her is now seen as a displacement of his desire for power at court. Re-enter Penelope Rich.

Topicality surfaces in another useful case study, Ann Rosalind Jones's *The Currency of Eros: Women's Love Lyric in Europe, 1540–1620*. This impressive cross-cultural study treats English, French, and Italian love poets: Isabella Whitney, Mary Wroth, Louise Labé, Catherine des Roches, Pernette du Guillet, Tullia d'Aragona, Gaspara Stampa, and Veronica Franco. One of the best features of Jones's excellent study is her use of the Marxist concept of *negotiation*, the 'mixed process of acceptance and resistance' by which 'subordinated groups respond to the assumptions encoded into dominant cultural forms …' (2), an approach that goes well beyond those which have dwelled only on women's oppressed silence: 'Definitions of proper feminine conduct,' writes Jones, 'were inserted into a gamut of oral and printed forms whose diversity suggests how persistently and in how many media these messages proliferated …' (12). Jones's determination to 'resist interpretative frameworks that doom women of the past – or the present – to a relentlessly disempowered relation to political and cultural practices' (9) is refreshing. But what again gives me pause is Jones's foray into history, into the lives of real early modern women – in this case the poets. Jones does not explore the fact that female love poets often invert an inversion: male-authored courtly love poetry constructs the male as the female's inferior, subject to her tyranny, cruelty, and scorn – an inversion of received gender hierarchy in the real world. When women poets enter this discourse, they often reinvert it: rather than adopting the sonnet mistress's voice, as one might expect female writers to do, they most often speak as the spurned lover, a role that in male-authored sonnets is gendered male. The male is now remote and aloof: Gaspara Stampa, for example, laments her social inferiority to the man who cruelly scorns her. This double reversal brings a highly conventional discourse much closer to 'normal' gender hierarchies and real women's experience of male tyranny and cruelty in early modern life. This accidental by-product of women poets' adaptations of male conventions may also tempt us to read the poems biographically at the expense of recognizing their conventionality – at the expense of remembering that they are subject to the by-laws of *literature*'s counties and municipalities. Stampa's references to 'a pitiless gaze untouched by my suffering,' and 'a laugh at my death as I lie perishing' (Sonnet 174; quoted in Jones 137) closely resemble Spenser's description of the mistress in *Amoretti*: '… she kills with cruell pryde, / and feeds at pleasure on the wretched pray: / Yet euen whylst her bloody hands them slay, / her eyes … vpon them smyle' (Sonnet 47); but by discussing Stampa's lines in the context of her thwarted love for Collaltino di Collalto, Jones positions them as personal experience rather than manipulation of poetic convention. In a reader less sophisticated than Jones, such positioning might spawn biographical approaches of the who-was-the-dark-lady sort, and at times Jones's work slides in that direction: she tells us at one point, 'the biographical question of who Labé's lover was is a vexed one' (160).

Although these women merit treatment as poets in their own right, separating them from the male tradition involves losses as well as gains. Once female poets are severed from familiar literary conventions, the sort of statement recognized as conventional in a male poet is interpreted as a cry from the heart in a female poet: male poets rationally manipulate literary convention, and female poets respond emotionally to the heart's promptings. Men inhabit the realm of artifice, women the realm of nature, a version of the identification, which anthropologist Sherry Ortner has posited, of men with culture, women with nature. Men in this formulation inhabit literature-land; women inhabit history-land. Interpreting the poems in this way abets the tendency to exclude women writers from the literary canon because their work is viewed in entirely different terms. A few years ago in my book *Women and the English Renaissance* I complained that *women* authors taking part in the formal debate over the nature of womankind have usually been seen as incapable of aesthetic detachment: their writings are uncontrolled emotional outbursts, while men writing in the same genre are considered rational, calculating, in full artistic control. As I wrote then, 'to assume that female writers were sincerely indignant, male writers playing gracefully with a convention, is merely sexist' (65). I still believe this, and still find too many contemporary critics, at times even a first-rate critic such as Ann Jones, willing to position women love poets as artless creatures of the heart, male love poets as skilful virtuosi of literary convention.

What is only a problem in embryo in Jones's work becomes a serious difficulty in Barbara Lewalski's ambitious survey *Writing Women in Jacobean England*. Although Lewalski's title is not misleading if closely considered – it reads *Writing Women* and not *Women's Writing* – readers interested in these women *as writers* may regret the disproportionate amount of space allotted to their biographies, especially in the first half of the book. Only 2 of 20 pages on Princess Elizabeth are devoted to her writing; just over 10 pages of 25 on Arbella Stuart, 8 pages of 28 on the countess of Bedford, and some 15 of 25 pages on Anne Clifford deal with writing. The proportion improves in later chapters, largely because Rachel Speght, Elizabeth Cary, Aemilia Lanyer, and Mary Wroth were published authors who actively defined writerly roles: the earlier figures did not publish, and, in the case of Queen Anne, really did not write.[1] I question whether some are 'writing women' at all. Perhaps 'Writing Women' is a construction along the lines of 'writing the body,' referring to Lewalski's own act of writing.

Queen Anne, although not a writer, 'often proposed the governing concept for a masque' (28), and so Lewalski considers her its 'author.' The strategy allows Lewalski to appropriate for Anne certain masques by Jonson and Daniel, whose own contributions she ignores almost entirely, ascribing everything 'oppositional' in the masques to Anne: 'in Jonson's first masque, as in Daniel's, the Queen's authorial and directorial presence proves subversive' (33). In the absence of evidence of Anne's precise role in the composition, this is a dubious move. When these masques defend women, Lewalski smells deliberate subversion, by 'the Queen's "authorial" presence' (34), of James's misogyny and patriarchal ideology; but in Jonson's and Daniel's mouths, a defence of women might be only conventional praise of the fair sex, and therefore hardly subversive.

Princess Elizabeth is 'also an author of sorts' (45), which means that she tried to script her life via roles gleaned from chivalric romance, and wrote letters. Although she 'wrote hundreds of letters – vivacious, witty, shrewd, informed, incisive – to King Charles, to John Donne … to Thomas Roe …, and to Buckingham, Montrose, Laud, and Charles Lewis' (65), Lewalski finds room to quote only brief segments from a half dozen letters, and subjects these to no literary analysis except to call them 'forthright, urgent, incisive' (59). Lewalski does undertake some literary analysis of Arbella Stuart's letters, but still chiefly mines them in order to shed light on the biography. Lewalski's neglect of the literary is especially apparent in comparison with Sara Jayne Steen's analysis of Arbella Stuart's letters; in contrast to Lewalski's chronological ordering of letters as part of a biographical narrative, Steen organizes and discusses them by type and style, distinguishing between stream-of-consciousness letters and those heavily revised and polished with artful rhetoric.

---

1 The countess of Bedford, subject of chapter 4, is a writer by virtue of only one surviving poem – but for sheer technical skill it is probably the best poem that Lewalski quotes.

The Renaissance regarded letters as a literary genre, and scholars have been analysing their style for a long time. Morris W. Croll's classic essay, 'The Baroque Style in Prose,' provides a model for analysing letters written in Senecan or Ciceronian styles.[2] Theory is also available in, for example, Claudio Guillén's 'Notes toward the Study of the Renaissance Letter,' which appeared in a volume edited by Lewalski but is not cited in *Writing Women*.[3] If Lewalski had wanted to treat the letters *as writing*, a critical vocabulary and conceptual frameworks are not lacking. Similarly, autobiography – a genre Anne Clifford essayed – can be analysed in *literary* terms. Instead, Lewalski uses autobiographies as a pretext for writing biographies. This strategy may be valuable, although we already have numerous biographies of Princess Elizabeth, Arbella Stuart, and Anne Clifford. But do these women whose lives are given more space than their writings belong in the same book with women whose writings are analysed? And why should the former be given pride of place in the first half of the book while the women who actually published are relegated to second place? The reason might have to do with the fact that the first five writers were among the kingdom's highest-ranking women, while Rachel Speght was only a minister's daughter and Aemilia Lanyer the wife of a court musician. Two of the final four, however, have elegant pedigrees as well, and so it seems more likely that Lewalski is placing first those actively involved in national politics. The true centre of Lewalski's interest appears to lie in politics – she seems happier writing history than literary criticism. And not only is social history here being used as an interpretive tool for literature, but it is a social history narrowed to favour the few women who had some (at least peripheral) influence on national politics, to the exclusion of ordinary women, a recentring of the decentring move that social history had promised us.

Lewalski does not justify or reflect upon her approach, and one might well ask why straightforward biographical criticism, long out of fashion in criticism of male writers, should be deemed the best approach to female writers. The choice could be justified – some of these women do choose biography-linked genres such as letters and autobiography,

2 See *Studies in English Philology: A Miscellany in Honor of Frederick Klaeber*, ed. Kemp Malone and Martin B. Rund (Minneapolis: U of Minnesota P 1929) 427–56.

3 See *Renaissance Genres: Essays on Theory, History, and Interpretation*, ed. Barbara Kiefer Lewalski, Harvard English Studies 14 (Cambridge, MA and London: Harvard UP, 1986) 70–101.

and perhaps, given the cultural conditions under which they wrote, women *were* more likely than male writers to link their writings to their lives. But Lewalski has not made the case, one way or another. Even within biographical criticism, Lewalski could have asked more pertinent questions of her material. For example, what should we make of the persistent link between a sexually transgressive life and a writing life – visible in all but one of Lewalski's writers[4] and in most of the writers discussed by Ann Jones? This pattern would seem to ratify the Renaissance stereotype linking female publishing to sexual looseness, a ratification that many feminist scholars ignore, perhaps as an embarrassment, although Maureen Quilligan has argued that sexual transgression was discursively empowering (272). Only two aspects of the lives and writing really interest Lewalski: self-fashioning and oppositionality or subversion. To the latter she returns with discouraging regularity – discouraging because it relegates these women to an unremittingly negative stance. Like Milton's Satan, who renders himself dependent on God by vowing to do nothing but oppose God's will, oppositional women lose the initiative, lose the capacity for creative, constructive human endeavour. A Queen Anne systematically undermining and embarrassing her husband is not ultimately a more edifying spectacle than a King James denigrating women.

Given that feminist critics are sometimes positioned as radicals within the academy, it seems ironic that after Barthes has proclaimed the death of the author and Foucault has demanded 'What does it matter who is speaking?', critics of early modern women's writing are nearly the sole remaining practitioners of a rather naïve form of biographical criticism.

What might a more purely *literary*, a less dark-ladyish approach to women's love poetry look like? To begin with, it might ask why *didn't* the sonnet mistress become a subject position for female poets? Although Shakespeare had three main characters, the typical male-authored sonnet cycle had a cast of two: disdainful mistress and suffering lover. Writing within this tradition, the female poet had a choice of these two positions. Although the mistress was female and the suffering lover male, the majority of women love poets of the period chose the position of the suffering lover. Why?

---

4 The writer is Rachel Speght. Queen Anne was not sexually transgressive but I cannot bring myself to call her a writer.

For one thing, the stance of the disdainful mistress is unattractive: how many poets relish the voice of super-bitch? What would the sonnet mistress say, were she actually to speak rather than smile contemptuously, laughing in mockery of her lover's pain, or frowning in displeasure that he has offended her by not grovelling enthusiastically enough? Perhaps she would say something like 'Hello down there, pathetic grovelling sniveller! Penning sonnets again, are we?' It's fine for a humble sonnet-maker to praise a proud beauty as long as she does not speak, but were a *female* poet to speak in her voice, it would suggest an unseemly revelling in power, and women poets were under considerable pressure to exhibit modesty; here is a clear collision between sonnet-land,[5] where women had freedom and power, and history-land, where women were to be chaste, silent, and obedient. But even assuming that a woman could rise artistically above the material reality of her life – I have been arguing, after all, that literature is to some extent a separate world – the subject position of sonnet mistress was not one to adopt if one sought to escape strictures on female speech; this position, in male-authored poetry, did not allow speech. Stella in Sidney's *Astrophil and Stella* is one of the few sonnet mistresses occasionally allowed to say something, and even then it isn't much. In one song she asks who is complaining under her window and tells him to 'begone' and 'come no more'; in another she repeats the same line nine times, once at the end of each sexual proposition by Astrophil; her lines mostly consist of repeating the same word four times, and the word reiterated thirty-six times is 'no.' Which brings us to the sonnet mistress's frigidity: she often says no, and imagery often associates her with winter. This desexualized being is not a promising subject position from which a female poet could address the topic of female sexual desire. Silence and frigidity were connected, just as female loquacity was linked with sexual profligacy: putting a woman on a pedestal in Petrarchan poetry was a way of freeze-drying her and of shutting her up. Adopting the traditionally male subject position at the bottom of the pedestal gave women the 'male' privilege of a virtually infinite amount of complaining, languishing, and other profligate uses of language.

Some people still believe that women want to be put on pedestals; my daughter's high-school social studies teacher said that the shrillness of feminists irritated him so much that he wasn't going to put women on

5 'Sonnet-land' is a coinage of graduate student Robert Barratt.

a pedestal anymore; no more chivalrous door-opening for him. Those who still believe in the pleasures of the pedestal should look at the historical period when women were first put there – during the courtly tradition of the late Middle Ages and the Renaissance – and note that if the chosen voice of Renaissance women poets is anything to go by, women definitely did *not* identify with the lady on the pedestal, or wish to adopt her proud, scornful persona.

Female poets may have experienced the Petrarchan sonnet mistress as a particularly negative construction of male fantasy: the scornful lady, ostensibly a tribute to female power, seems to project male resentment of the sexual attraction women exercise over men, resentment of the meagre power women actually possessed – the power to say no. The refusal to write in her voice may have been a political decision by the woman writer alert to sexual politics not to mollify male sexual anxiety by abetting such a literary construction of women.

Trying to construct a category of 'literary' that does not interpenetrate in some way with 'history' is very problematic; no sooner had literary criticism rejected centuries of readings that treated Renaissance literary characters as if they were real people than new historicists proposed that real people are constructed as if they were literary characters. Both approaches blur the line between literature and life. Probably the line must necessarily be blurred, but I am concerned that it not be obliterated. It is difficult to avoid social history, and it is dangerous too, since cutting literature off from life can be an act of social and political irresponsibility; yet, as I've tried to show, the relationship between literature and social history is notoriously hard to pin down. And if we position ourselves in a line of theorists from Russian formalists through deconstructionists in insisting on literariness, we run up against the fact that literature is no more a stable point of reference than history. I have cited conventions of genre as a corrective to more purely 'social historical' approaches, yet Renaissance literature displays an astounding instability of genre: texts in which two or more genres intersect and modify each other are the rule. And genres themselves are not ideologically innocent, as writers such as Montrose on pastoral or Marotti on sonnets have shown.

I have tried to problematize the reading of early modern texts, but too much of this sort of thing can produce paralysis: stretched on a hermeneutical torture rack with new historicists pulling on our arms and deconstructionists on our feet, we may become unable to read or interpret at all. Some theorists of hermeneutics posit two poles: first, clearly determinate meaning (the author put in the meaning and we extract it); and second, complete indeterminacy (since we can never determine with certainty what a text 'means,' it therefore means nothing). Such theorists seem to construct the very kind of binary opposition that Derridean deconstruction always found suspicious. Can there be no middle ground – readings that, given what we know about social history and literary history, are more probable than others? The problem of meaning in texts is analogous to the problem at the heart of syllogisms: syllogisms cannot *prove* anything, because they all exemplify circular reasoning. In the syllogism 'all men are mortal; Socrates is a man; therefore Socrates is mortal,' we must know that Socrates is mortal before we can know whether the major premise is true. The major premise on which deduction rests is derived from induction, from observing a large number of human lives that have proved mortal; but Socrates could still be the one exception that invalidates the premise, and therefore we cannot rest the case for his mortality on the premise 'all men are mortal.' Our reasoning rests ultimately on probability – since so many humans have proved mortal, Socrates probably will too. The middle ground of probability deconstructs the binary opposition between absolute certainty and total indeterminacy. Sidestepping the horrifying prospect that to regard meaning in terms of probability might ultimately embroil us in the disciplines of statistical probability, I simply suggest that accepting the middle ground as the best epistemological standpoint that our fallen nature can find involves a pragmatism like that of William James. We accept the enabling fiction that we can read something and know what it means, in preference to the disabling truth that when we read something we can never be sure what it means. We do this in order to go on reading. This double-mindedness is not unlike our capacity to weep at the death of a Desdemona we know to be a literary construct and an actress. But in accepting such enabling fictions, we are not just pretending to understand what is finally incomprehensible; through historicizing – making use of both social history and literary history – we are seeking a foothold on a middle ground of probable meaning. That, I think, is entirely appropriate, fruitful activity for literary scholars. In this paper I have tried simply to remind readers how slippery that middle ground can be.

Feminist scholars have understandably turned to social history to illuminate the material conditions under which early modern women lived. One of their most important contributions has been in showing why so few women published literary works – of 26,098 items extant in print from the English Renaissance to 1642, only about 70 are known to be by women. Social history has shown that few women were educated, that even the educated were encouraged to do translations rather than original work and to take up religious rather than secular subject matter; they were encouraged to imitate the styles of others rather than developing an original style; and they were discouraged from publication by stereotypes linking women's utterance with sexual looseness. Such studies *have* been useful, and I don't want to discourage Renaissance feminist literary scholars from forays into social history. But I urge caution: contextual study seeking to ground literature in history, although currently the most fashionable critical pursuit, is of all approaches to literature perhaps the trickiest, most elusive, most treacherous. In seeking to shine searchlights or researchlights into the dark recesses of that undiscovered country, the past, we must take care not merely to deepen the shadows, or to leave those dark ladies, the women characters and women writers of the English Renaissance, in ever deepening darkness.

WORKS CITED

Beaumont, Francis, and John Fletcher. *The Woman-Hater*. STC 1692.
Braudy, Leo. *Narrative Form in History and Fiction: Hume, Fielding and Gibbon.* Princeton: Princeton UP, 1970.
Carroll, David. 'History as Writing.' *Clio: An Interdisciplinary Journal of Literature, History and the Philosophy of History* 7.3 (1978): 443–60.
Cook, Ann Jennalie. *Making a Match: Courtship in Shakespeare and His Society.* Princeton: Princeton UP, 1991.
Culler, Jonathan. *On Deconstruction: Theory and Criticism after Structuralism.* Ithaca: Cornell UP, 1982.
Dubrow, Heather. *A Happier Eden: The Politics of Marriage in the Stuart Epithalamium*. Ithaca and London: Cornell UP, 1990.
Greenblatt, Stephen. 'Shakespeare and the Exorcists.' *Shakespeare and the Question of Theory*. Ed. Patricia Parker and Geoffrey Hartman. New York and London: Methuen, 1985. 163–87.
Hall, Joseph. *Virgidemiarum*. STC 12716, 1597. Book I, Satire VII.
Hexter, J.H. *Doing History*. Bloomington: Indiana UP, 1971.
Jones, Ann Rosalind. *The Currency of Eros: Women's Love Lyric in Europe, 1540–1620*. Bloomington and Indianapolis: Indiana UP, 1990.

70   Linda Woodbridge

Lewalski, Barbara Kiefer. *Writing Women in Jacobean England*. Cambridge, MA and London: Harvard UP, 1993.

Macfarlane, Alan. [Review of Lawrence Stone, *The Family, Sex, and Marriage in England 1500–1800*.] *History and Theory* 18.1 (1979): 103–26.

Marotti, Arthur F. '"Love is Not Love": Elizabethan Sonnet Sequences and the Social Order.' *ELH* 49.2 (1982): 396–428.

Montrose, Louis Adrian. '"Eliza, Queene of shepheardes," and the Pastoral of Power.' *English Literary Renaissance* 10.2 (1980): 153–82.

– 'Of Gentlemen and Shepherds: The Politics of Elizabethan Pastoral Form.' *ELH* 50.3 (1983): 415–59.

– "The perfecte paterne of a Poete': The Poetics of Courtship in *The Shepheardes Calender*.' *Texas Studies in Literature and Language* 21.1 (1979): 34–67.

Ortner, Sherry B. 'Is Female to Male as Nature Is to Culture?' *Woman, Culture, and Society*. Ed. Michelle Zimbalist Rosaldo and Louise Lamphere. Stanford: Stanford UP, 1974. 67–87.

Pechter, Edward. 'The New Historicism and Its Discontents: Politicizing Renaissance Drama.' *PMLA* 102.3 (1987): 292–303.

Quilligan, Maureen. 'Lady Mary Wroth: Female Authority and the Family Romance.' *Unfolded Tales: Essays on Renaissance Romance*. Ed. George M. Logan and Gordon Teskey. Ithaca: Cornell UP, 1989. 257–80.

Sidney, Sir Philip. *The Poems of Sir Philip Sidney*. Ed. William A. Ringler, Jr. Oxford: Clarendon, 1962.

Spenser, Edmund. *Spenser: Poetical Works*. Ed. J.C. Smith and E. De Selincourt. 1912. London: Oxford UP, 1970.

Steen, Jayne. 'Fashioning an Acceptable Self: Arbella Stuart.' *ELR* 18 (1988): 78–95.

Stone, Lawrence. *The Crisis of the Aristocracy 1558–1641*. Oxford: Clarendon, 1965.

– *The Family, Sex, and Marriage in England 1500 to 1800*. London: Weidenfeld and Nicolson; New York: Harper and Row, 1977.

Thomas, Keith. 'The Changing Family.' *Times Literary Supplement*. 21 Oct. 1977, no. 3, 943, 1226+.

Travitsky, Betty S. '"His wife's prayers and meditations": MS Egerton 607.' *The Renaissance Englishwoman in Print: Counterbalancing the Canon*. Ed. Anne M. Haselkorn and Betty S. Travitsky. Amherst: U of Massachusetts P, 1990. 241–60.

White, Hayden. 'The Fictions of Factual Representation.' *The Literature of Fact: Selected Papers from the English Institute*. Ed. Angus Fletcher. New York: Columbia UP, 1976. 21–44.

– 'Historical Pluralism.' *Critical Inquiry* 12.3 (1986): 480–93.

Woodbridge, Linda. *Women and the English Renaissance: Literature and the Nature of Womankind, 1540–1620*. Urbana and Chicago: U of Illinois P; Brighton: Harvester, 1984.

Wyatt, Sir Thomas. *Collected Poems of Sir Thomas Wyatt*. Ed. Kenneth Muir and Patricia Thomson. Liverpool: Liverpool UP, 1969.

PART TWO
WHAT TO DO WITH SHAKESPEARE?

4

Against a Synecdochic Shakespeare

ELIZABETH HANSON

Scholars of English Renaissance drama have in recent years come to identify their object of study as an instance of 'culture' rather than 'literature.' The shift in nomenclature insists on the drama's participation in discursive fields that include medicine, law, politics, commerce, and religion. Moreover, the work performed is considered in light of the construction of sex and gender, the discipline of the subject, or the invention of the nation rather than the achievement of aesthetic unity, characterization, or the revelation of eternal truths. Despite this significant change in professional assumptions about what it means to study Renaissance drama, current critical practice has not seriously challenged the overwhelming centrality of Shakespeare to the endeavour. To make this point one need only recite the titles of those invaluable essay anthologies that have marked the rise to hegemony of the 'politico-cultural' version of Renaissance drama: *Shakespeare and the Question of Theory, Alternative Shakespeares, Political Shakespeare, Shakespeare Reproduced, The Matter of Difference: Materialist Feminist Criticism of Shakespeare.* Only David Scott Kastan and Peter Stallybrass's *Staging the Renaissance* and Richard Dutton and Richard Wilson's *New Historicism and Renaissance Drama* range beyond the Shakespeare canon, although in the latter more than half the essays are also concerned with Shakespeare. Crucial studies by single authors such as Stephen Greenblatt, Steven Mullaney, Leah Marcus, Leonard Tennenhouse, Karen Newman,

This essay is deeply indebted to discussions with Jean Howard and Kate McLuskie on the relation between the dramatic literature and the culture of early modern England. I am also grateful to the members of Queen's University's English Work-in-Progress group and to Edward Pechter for insightful commentary on earlier drafts.

and Valerie Traub are also focused either exclusively or predominantly on Shakespeare, although some cultural materialists, such as Catherine Belsey, Jonathan Dollimore, Jean E. Howard, and Kathleen McLuskie, have cast their nets more widely.

The persistent focus on Shakespeare is in part the result of institutional practices that survive from the days when the drama was 'literature' rather than 'culture.' Whatever else scholars of Renaissance drama do, most of us every year teach a course called simply 'Shakespeare,' which means that we are conversant with that playwright's canon and have frequent occasion to work out arguments about his plays and their relation to early modern culture. The centrality of Shakespeare to the undergraduate curriculum also means that we consume vast quantities of Shakespeare criticism, ensuring a readership for *Shakespeare Quarterly* and encouraging publishers to favour books on Shakespeare.

Of course, the institutional prestige that makes work on Shakespeare professionally convenient renders such work politically significant. In the British cultural materialist work of the mid-1980s, for instance, the Shakespeare-centrism appears to be a strategic attempt to appropriate the 'Shakespeare' who is already a signifier in contemporary cultural politics, to make him stand not for 'literature' but for 'history,' not for a mythologized England but for class, gender, and racial struggles that fissured the construct of the nation. And yet what is striking about this work, as well as that of the American new historicists and the successors of both schools, is the reticence that surrounds the question, logically anterior to any claim about the meaning of 'Shakespeare,' of how this playwright and canon were situated in the cultural field of early modern England – a question that embraces his relation to other playwrights and poets of the period. Stephen Greenblatt's wistful confession at the beginning of *Shakespearean Negotiations* that 'conventional in my tastes, I found the most satisfying intensity [of representation] in Shakespeare' (1) is the only instance I have found of a critic who even acknowledges having chosen Shakespeare as the subject from a field of writers and canons. The weak explanation that Greenblatt offers for his choice, namely, his own personal taste, suggests that he has difficulty making the choice meaningful for his theory that plays are 'textual traces ... of contingent social practices' (5). Greenblatt's choice, it would seem, is the residue of his investment in a category ('the total artist') that his sociocultural vision of the drama has forced him to abandon; but it is apparently harmless to that vision because Greenblatt no longer attempts to ground the choice theoretically (2).

In subsequent criticism, in which the idea that Renaissance plays are textual traces of contingent social practices is axiomatic rather than arrived at, the decision to work on Shakespeare receives no attention at all.

My purpose is to demonstrate that the ongoing, reflexive Shakespeare-centrism is unjustifiable in a criticism that purports to explicate the culture of early modern England rather than just its highest aesthetic achievements.[1] This is so, not because the focus on Shakespeare represents an invidious survival of literary value-judgments (although that may be the case) but because if we consider plays to be 'textual traces ... of contingent social practices' then surely playwrights and the companies for which they work must be considered crucial social practitioners whose differences are constitutive of culture. The question of what difference the playwright makes, I argue, is not merely unasked but actually repressed as a result of a politically motivated, theoretically incoherent deployment of the concepts of agency and subjecthood in the politico-cultural criticism of Renaissance drama. I conclude this essay with a comparative analysis of a play by Shakespeare and a collaborative work by three of his contemporaries in order to indicate the kinds of issues that become available to a specifically politico-cultural criticism when we situate Shakespeare in relation to his contemporaries, rather than letting him simply stand for them.

I

Gary Taylor explores the difference it would make to the theory and practice of editing Renaissance drama if Middleton's canon rather than Shakespeare's set the norm. Taylor concludes that the most influential poststructuralist notions of intertextuality pre-empt any precise mapping of 'textual space,' that is, a plotting of the degree to which texts do (or do not) approximate one another by replicating, borrowing from, influencing, or following the same generic rules as, or sharing

---

1 I should clarify that Shakespeare-centrism does not seem to me problematic if a critic construes her task to be the explication of a literary text for the sake either of the profound meanings presumed to reside therein, or the illuminations achieved by thinking with the text. Then the emphasis on the Shakespeare canon requires no justification beyond an ongoing demonstration that it yields the most interesting literary criticism. My arguments here pertain only to criticism that undertakes to explicate cultural dynamics rather than simply literary ones.

a common ideology with one another. In the Derridean universe of discourse, according to Taylor, every text or utterance 'is equidistant from every other' (126); 'the absence of a center or origin extend[s] the play of signification infinitely' (126), while in the Foucaultian one there are 'only two degrees of proximity': the discontinuity that separates epistemes and the direct overlay of 'disciplines or genres of discourse within an episteme' (129). Perhaps reductive as a reading of Derrida and Foucault, Taylor's account none the less usefully suggests why the same critics who appropriated first Derridean notions of textuality and then Foucaultian concepts of discourse in order to dissolve the mind-forged boundaries between text and context, social experience and literary representation, would have also developed synecdochic habits of thought, so that virtually any instance of discourse could be adduced to represent the new object of study: early modern culture. To be sure, the Marxist critic Walter Cohen also observed this phenomenon several years ago; in a critique of the political criticism of Shakespeare that had developed in the 1980s, Cohen objected to the 'assumption of arbitrary connectedness' in which 'a single text or group of texts stands in for all texts and thus exhausts the discursive field' ('Political Criticism' 38). Since that time most critics would hasten to acknowledge that a few medical treatises do not a sex/gender system make, that discourses are heterogeneous. Yet what is striking about both the critique and the acknowledgments it has elicited is that while they readily locate heterogeneity across discursive fields (defined by categories such as the body, gender, class, or sexuality) and even within individual texts, they do not do so across the dramatic texts of the period. Indeed, in the course of his review essay Cohen notes without elaboration that his own exclusive focus on Shakespeare criticism is 'difficult to justify on theoretical grounds,' but he concludes in the same paragraph that it is also inconsequential (20).[2]

The double standard in the recognition of discursive heterogeneity arises, I think, because behind the concepts of textual space that Taylor criticizes lie deeply political issues of agency. After all, accounts of

2 I should like to emphasize that Cohen's remark pertains to his exclusive focus on Shakespeare *criticism*. But the assertion that criticism of Shakespeare can represent the criticism of Renaissance drama generally only recapitulates the problem I am describing on another plane. The assertion denies the possibility that the 'culture,' when seen through the filter of another dramatic canon, might look different enough to push critical discourse in different directions from that taken by the current Shakespeare-centred enterprise.

the relationships between *texts* derive in almost every instance from theories about the *activity* involved in textual production and therefore the relationships between producers. The 'old-fashioned' editor defines the relationship between a bad quarto and a good through theories about imperfect actors patching up memorial reconstructions and the owners of acting company taking promptbooks to the press. The student of sources or influences reveals that Shakespeare read North's Plutarch and Golding's Ovid. The feminist argues that Elizabeth Cary read Josephus's *Antiquities* as a woman and made Mariam rather than Herod the central character in her *Tragedy of Mariam*. A new historicist critic of the 1980s reads *A Midsummer Night's Dream* and Simon Forman's diary as expressions of a common sexual fantasy about dominating the queen, because he presumes that the playwright and the astrological physician participated in the same cultural unconscious.[3]

If Derridean and Foucaultian notions of textual space seem to lack degrees of separation or proximity it is because the privileged agents of textual production in these models are the perpetual-motion machines of language or discourse themselves rather than differentiated subjects such as writers or actors. And as imagined agents of textual production, language and discourse are singular, in relationship only with themselves, although in their simultaneous conception as the *site* of textual effects they are characterized by considerable internal heterogeneity and dynamism. 'Culture,' as it emerges in the criticism of English Renaissance drama during the 1980s and early 1990s, is an evolved form of 'discourse,' an amalgam, we might say, of discourse and material life. 'Language,' in contrast, seems to have dropped out of critical consideration over the same period.[4] But if 'culture' is a more inclusive category than discourse, its structural function within critical argument remains the same, that is, of primary agent of textual production.

---

3 I am referring, of course, to Louis Montrose's widely influential essay 'A Midsummer Night's Dream and the Shaping Fantasies of Elizabethan Culture,' in Ferguson, Quilligan, and Vickers, eds., *Rewriting the Renaissance*. My first two examples are, as is said of music, 'traditional.' The argument about Elizabeth Cary has been made by numerous commentators on *The Tragedy of Mariam*; it is a point I routinely make when I teach the play.

4 The speedy dwindling of the deconstructive engagement with language over the 1980s can be seen in a comparison of the essays in *Shakespeare and the Question of Theory*, ed. Patricia Parker and Geoffrey Hartman (1985) and those in *The Matter of Difference*, ed. Valerie Wayne (1991) or even in *Shakespeare Reproduced*, ed. Jean E. Howard and Marion F. O'Connor (1987).

I should hasten to clarify that I think these theoretical developments are a good thing. Perhaps the most fruitful effect of the emergence of language / discourse / culture as textual prime mover[s] has been the de-ontologizing of the entities that formerly had been privileged agents of textual production, most notably, the author. This process has made visible previously obscured or unthinkable factors in textual production, ranging from social forces such as patriarchal anxieties or the commercialization of culture to the activities of other kinds of textual producers such as publishers and editors. More important, such a shift in perception has the potential to reveal the constructed nature of all agents of textual production, that who or what is construed as origin of text, or as medium of its dissemination, is the result of ongoing interplay among writers, technologies of reproduction, publishers, regulating authorities, readers, and scholars.

But the effects on critical practice of the author's dissolution and displacement by 'culture' are complicated by the political significance that the event has come to bear. For the author had been above all a privileged subject, unified, implicitly male, influenced by history yet also freed from it by the power of the literary imagination. 'Literature,' with its explicit formalism, its Sidneian power 'to grow in effect another nature,' is the objective realization of this subject's freedom. Thus to step over the toppled author into the realm of 'culture' is to be 'political,' which among academics in the humanities usually means 'progressive,' both because to be 'progressive' revokes the privileges of an advantaged subject and because it takes the critic out of the formal world that reifies that subject's putative transcendence and into a zone where all the anxieties and violence that hierarchical relationships entail are visibly in play. However, as astute onlookers have noted, the 'culture' conjured up by some critics of Renaissance drama (particularly the new historicist pioneers) reproduced or even intensified aspects of the power relations lurking within the concepts of author and literature. While politico-cultural analysis stripped Renaissance literature of its ethical prestige, exposing its implication in imperialism and the disciplinary agenda of the early modern state, it also construed culture as an ultimately unitary if internally dynamic entity, not a site of struggle but the agent of its own relentless reproduction. In other words, what critics of the new historicism recognized was that the power of the author / literature complex had been abstracted from a specific class of subjects and discourse and projected onto 'culture' as the putative source of all consciousness.

Feminist critics were the first to challenge the politics of the new historicists, noting that many new historicist analyses marginalized female characters or erased women from the culture altogether. (The most infamous example is Greenblatt's argument that women in Renaissance medical discourses are merely undeveloped men, so that 'Shakespearean women are in this sense merely the representation of Shakespearean men ...' [92].) The feminist critique was, at least potentially, both political and methodological, embracing not only the new historicists' blindness to women but also the conception of culture that permits it. In Cohen's review essay cited above, for example, a rehearsal of the myriad ways in which new historicists demonstrated their obliviousness or even hostility to women is the vehicle through which the argument about 'arbitrary connectedness' is conducted; attending to women exemplifies a more general recognition of the reality of social conflict and the heterogeneity of discourse. These concerns are articulated together, I think, because the notion of a politically meaningful discursive heterogeneity requires attention to how different subjects received and reproduced discourse. As long as the culture itself is the agent of this work, questions pertaining to how childbirth, nursing, running a household, not being taught to read or being taught to read but not to write, enjoying the society of other women, having sex with husbands or lovers, being beaten by husbands, engaging in prostitution, or supervising the religious education of children might have affected what women did with discourse, are not questions that have urged themselves, especially to male critics. As Cohen remarks, to the new historicist 'influenced by Foucault's relative indifference to gender ... women cease to be historical actors or subjects. They can be victims or objects, but it is not, however complexly, their experience that matters' ('Political Criticism' 38).

What interests me about this and other similar observations is that while we can tease out of them the implication that critics need to recalibrate the relationship between subject and culture, their real energy derives from their defence of women against objectification or victimization by men. In other words, the critical effacement of the subject becomes troubling only when it reiterates the historical denial of subjecthood to a specific class of persons. Thus a fundamentally theoretical move, the restoration of the subject to discursive agency, is both enabled and cloaked by its political meaning in a particular instance. Agency and its relation to the subject have become a critical obsession in the nineties, just as subjection had been in the eighties. The concept of agency is now central to all political criticism, which increasingly means criticism that advocates for groups that have been othered, abjected, or effaced by canonical literature or its traditional criticism. As long as the particular subject in question aligns with one of these categories, rehabilitating the subject's agency serves something of the same political needs that shaped the North American reception of poststructuralism, its dismantling of the sovereign male subject, and the re-attribution of his usurped agency. But surely the same recognition that activates questions about women's experience should also activate questions like the following: How does possessing a university education, lacking a university education, being obsessed with classical literature, being a gentleman, or a citizen, or a hireling of Philip Henslowe, or a share-holder in the King's Men, who perform at the Globe, or a shareholder in the Children of the Queen's Revels, who perform at the Blackfriars, having an aristocratic patron, a good ear for verse, or a reputation for certain kinds of plotting, affect what playwrights do with discourse? If different experiences of the sex/gender system produce discursive heterogeneity, then should not different experiences of what Richard Helgerson has called 'the literary system' (*Self-Crowned Laureates* 20) do the same?

These questions remain unasked, I would suggest, because while the concept of a literary system becomes thinkable in part through analogy with the sex/gender system, it also problematizes habits of thought that have characterized much of the critical work on gender and other cultural issues pertaining to Renaissance drama.[5] Imagining a literary system entails the recognition that participation in the system as a writer

---

5 The kind of social and economic situatedness of individual writers' practices that Helgerson's *Self-Crowned Laureates* explores has received far more attention in recent scholarship on non-dramatic literature than it has in work on the drama. The notable exception is the extensive body of scholarship on Ben Jonson's authorial self-construction. (I am thinking of recent studies by Joseph Loewenstein, Timothy Murray, Peter Stallybrass and Allon White, Don Wayne, Richard Burt, and Helgerson himself.) Even here, however, Jonson's efforts tend to be set against a generalized 'loathed stage' that effaces authorial labour. The possibility that the differences among the positions of Shakespeare, Marston, Heywood, and Middleton, for instance, might be significant is lost in the attention to the single distinction that Jonson sought to establish between himself as classical author and the degraded role of professional playwright. These patterns in recent criticism suggest a possible complicity between current critical practice and the economic structures of early modern commercial theatres, a sidelining of the playwright's labour, which permits play texts to be treated as evidence of generalized social fantasy at the same time that sonnet

is linked to possession of technical skills – in metrical composition, scene construction, or plotting – a knowledge, in short, of how forms work.[6] A corollary of this recognition is literature's deployment of linguistic resources, a deployment that is not wholly and immediately ideological, in so far as the logic of forms and tropes inhibits as well as enables socially interested expression. But if such an insistence on the relative autonomy of literary discourse seems to risk the return of 'literature' and the fantasy of the transcendent subject that it serves, the idea of a literary *system* also insists upon the subjection of literary practitioners to historically specific social, economic, and discursive arrangements: patronage, for example, or the print market, or censorship. In addition, the literary system necessarily overlaps with other regimes of subjection such as the sex/gender and class/status systems, yoking the writer's imagination to concerns such as patriarchal anxiety (or perhaps feminine subversion), aspiration to preferment, or aristocratic self-display. Thus the idea of a literary system threatens to disorganize the opposition – between 'culture' and 'literature' or between 'political' and 'formalist' criticisms – that in recent years have fuelled the professional discussion of Renaissance drama. Moreover, it imposes a certain intellectual re-striction on the critic, a requirement that she renounce the spaciousness not only of 'literature' but also of 'history' for a narrower discursive domain in which the formal and the social intersect with each other in highly specific ways. And in so far as this intersection is mediated by writers' labour, she must confront a subject defined neither by the grandeur of poetic imagination nor by the pathos of interpellation and resistance, but by the banalities of professional practice and local ideo-logical investments.

'Shakespeare,' I would suggest, remains at the centre of cultural criticism of Renaissance drama because his long-established centrality masks the interference that literary practice introduces in the transmis-

---

sequences or narrative poetry are being read as expressions of the writer's specific economic, social, or institutional situation.

6 The literary system as I conceive it is constituted by the total deployment of cultural and material resources within a society. Thus all members of that society participate in that system, even if only by virtue of their marginalization. An illiterate person, for instance, may serve as audience for a ballad seller or a play, thus ensuring the ongoing production of these materials, at the same time that her comparative deprivation enforces the class/gender significance of literacy. For the purposes of argument, however, I am focusing on those whose participation is principally through writing.

sion of early modern social consciousness. Working on Shakespeare is the 'default mode,' as it were, for critics of Renaissance drama; the choice involved has always already been made, its implications long since naturalized. The choice, therefore, seems transparent in a way that the choice to work on Middleton, Dekker, or Webster does not. The remainder of this essay denaturalizes the Shakespearean choice by situating Shakespeare's writing practice and its institutional context in relation to those of some of his contemporaries. My topic is the different ways in which Shakespeare and a group of playwrights writing for the Children of the Queen's Revels used the resources and associations of the romance mode in order to represent the social relations organized by emergent merchant capitalism, a choice influenced by recent critical interest in the connection between the theatre and the accelerating commercialization of English society during the early modern period.[7]

Before turning to the texts themselves, however, a moment of methodological self-reflection is in order. My object here is to read plays as traces of complex interactions between literary resources and the social fantasies of particular groups. The figure of the playwright, whose agency I have sought to restore to critical attention, is a heuristic device for specifying and organizing the contents of any given interaction. There is no more possibility of, or point to, establishing the intention (or in the case of one of the plays I consider here, the precise contribution) of any given playwright than there is of discovering the thoughts of actual women who went to the theatre. All we can do is attempt to reconstruct from the play text some of the imaginative experiences it allows for, disciplining these efforts with whatever evidence remains (and it is always insufficient) of the circumstances under which a play was written and produced. What follows, then, is neither a biographical nor bibliographic exercise but a demonstration of a reading strategy that resists synecdochic thinking and enables a more nuanced model of cultural production than the one underlying current Shakespeare-centred critical practice.

II

The Merchant of Venice is widely acknowledged among political critics of Renaissance drama to be a crucial imaginative event of England's

---

7 See, for instance, Agnew, Bruster, and Cohen (*Drama of a Nation*).

proto-capitalist phase, an attempt to manage, or perhaps expose, ideological discontinuities within the relationships of aristocratic land-based wealth, merchant capital, evolving mechanisms of finance, and older systems of thought such as Christianity and patriarchy. I need hardly say that this recognition is not vouchsafed to Jonson, Chapman, and Marston's *Eastward Ho!*, which was performed by the Children of the Queen's Revels at Blackfriars in 1605, a year in which *The Merchant of Venice* was performed at least once, at court (Brown, Introduction, *MV*, xxxii). Yet *Eastward Ho!* thematizes many of the same issues that concern Shakespeare's play: merchants and their relation to moneylenders and to the (supposedly) landed gentry, venture capital and its relation to other forms of wealth, thrift, and prodigality. The play also contains similar plot elements: a virtuous merchant who shuns usury, a 'lady richly left,' a suitor in dire financial need, a usurer, and seagoing investments that founder. These similarities, however, are perhaps easily missed because in tone and atmosphere the two plays are considerably different, as are the resolutions. But this is precisely the point: responding to the same economic developments as *The Merchant of Venice* and making use of similar cultural materials, *Eastward Ho!* reveals the contingency of the conjunction of aesthetic and ideological effects in Shakespeare's play. And, of course, *The Merchant of Venice* forces a similar recognition about *Eastward Ho!*

The *Merchant of Venice*, it might be argued, exemplifies Fredric Jameson's definition of romance as a literary mode characterized by ethical oppositions, magical forces, and 'salvational historicity,' a mode that 'is to be found in a transitional moment in which two distinct modes of production, or moments of socio-economic development, coexist [and] their antagonism is not yet articulated in terms of the struggle of social classes, so that its resolution can be projected in the form of a nostalgic (or less often, a Utopian) harmony' (148). In its presentation of two worlds of urban commerce and of mysterious aristocratic wealth, the play figures the two distinct but overlapping socio-economic moments, subjecting the conflicts of the former to the magical resolving influences of the latter. But if the two-world structure seems explicitly to reveal the economic doubleness of the play's historical moment, there are also mystifications in the play's representations of economic relationships. Most notably, the sharp distinction between Shylock, the usurer, and Antonio, the merchant who lends money without charge, is belied by the fact that the taking of interest at ten per cent was legal in England and that merchants tended also to be moneylenders (Ferber 445; Cohen,

'*The Merchant of Venice*' 368–9). Michael Ferber argues convincingly that in Antonio Shakespeare has written a merchant as though he were an aristocrat: both his refusal to take interest, which Shylock so deeply resents, and his reckless generosity to Bassanio associate Antonio with the aristocratic virtue of liberality, and, in so far as Portia also embodies this virtue, with Belmont as well as the Rialto (436–7). The aristocratic elements of the play are, however, framed in terms of mercantile interests and desires. Belmont, with its lady richly left, three caskets, questing suitors, and moonlight, is the site of romance ethos, and Portia the bearer of its 'salvational historicity.' But the romance world of Belmont at once celebrates the mercantile virtue of risk-taking by means of the leaden casket that rewards the one who will 'give and hazard all he hath' (2.7.16), at the same time that it construes this choice as a preference for spiritual over material wealth. More generally, we might argue that the romance ethos saturates the play because the journeying and the susceptibility to accident and to miraculous recovery that characterize maritime mercantile activity invite construction in romance terms. The point is underlined by Portia's final revelation that 'by … strange accident' (5.1.278) she possesses a sealed letter that will reveal that 'three' of Antonio's 'argosies / Are richly come to harbour suddenly' (276–7).[8]

One of the play's effects, then, is the figuration of an ideological alliance between the merchant class and the aristocracy, an alliance in which mercantile desire and practice are constructed in terms of aristocratic virtue, and supported by aristocratic wealth, which, as Lars Engle points out, is enhanced in the transaction only in so far as Portia's interventions in the play's exchanges make all goods flow 'toward Belmont' (97). Thus we might argue that the play affirms aristocratic dominance at the same time that its energies, desires, and fantasies, which animate not only Antonio's and Bassanio's choices but also Portia's improvisations, are those of merchants.

This account of the play must be complicated, however, by an acknowledgment of its famous 'problems,' which trouble the ethical oppositions around which romance is organized as well as the sense of wonder that it produces. Most notable is the propensity for the distinction between spiritual and material wealth to collapse or invert itself, as when the audience sees all too clearly that Bassanio's 'love' for Portia is linked to her money; or when, in Shylock's lament for

---

8 On the connections between romance and mercantile interests, see Quint 248–67.

Leah's ring, which the absconding Jessica has sold for a monkey, the opposition between liberality and greed suddenly becomes one between prodigality and love. These problems arise in part because the play cannot fully contain the ideological discontinuities that it means to resolve. However much the play's valorization of liberality produces comparative freedom for the female characters, through whom the transition of wealth is effected, the anxiety that Jessica's flight (and female freedom and power generally) arouses in patriarchal minds permits a proto-bourgeois investment in thrift to surface. Or it may be that Shakespeare has at certain points made overt what Jameson claims is the latent content of the romance mode, namely, the coexistence of two distinct socio-economic orders. The result is that the play is morally overbalanced by the details of its own representation. However fantastic the terms Shylock exacts, the Rialto may be too realistically rendered and its logic too persuasive for urban audiences and players not to register the bad faith in the magic of Belmont. This is not to say, however, that Shakespeare treats ironically the romance elements that produce the ideological effects described above. Instead, I would argue that we experience the problems in *Merchant* precisely as *problems,* rather than as explicit conflicts, because the meanings conveyed by the forms Shakespeare employs are so strong that they prevail despite the numerous local disturbances that the play generates at the mimetic level. In other words, I am positing a dramaturgical correlative for the play's work of articulating mercantile aspirations through aristocratic values, a conservative use of forms that does not entirely control the play's mimetic effects but that generates its dominant meanings. Such a dramaturgy lends itself well to discussion in terms of politicized binaries (Greenblatt's subversion and containment model; Robert Weimann's *locus* and *platea* effects), but it does not exhaust what theatricality meant in the early modern period.

If *Merchant* plays forms straight, *Eastward Ho!* relentlessly parodies them. A send-up of the prodigal dramas that were popular among citizens, *Eastward Ho!* tells the tale of Touchstone, a goldsmith, and his two apprentices, the prodigal Francis Quicksilver, who nearly comes to a bad end, and the thrifty and obedient Golding, who achieves a ridiculously speedy prosperity, becoming a liveryman of the Goldsmiths' Company on the first day of his freedom. More generally, however, the play presents a world in which a character's consciousness is reducible to literary forms – the maxim, the bombast speeches of the public theatre, chivalric romance, the gallows repentance ballad –

forms whose meanings carry as formal effects rather than as truths. This is not to say, however, that the play does not do ideological work; indeed *Eastward Ho!*, just as much as *Merchant*, constructs a mystified version of the relations of nascent capitalism. But *Eastward Ho!* serves different interests, and in doing so trades in a very different kind of theatricality.

As a goldsmith, Touchstone is a member of one of the wealthiest London guilds; as such, he is engaged in a trade in which the activities of the merchant and the financier overlapped, although it would be another thirty years before the goldsmiths would assume the role of deposit bankers. Touchstone insistently constructs himself as a thrifty and humble shopkeeper, however, and the relationship between this traditional role and the opportunities afforded by an expanding economy fuels the quarrel between him and Quicksilver, the prodigal apprentice. In the opening scene, Quicksilver, having reminded his master that he is the younger son of a gentleman, suggests the economic utility of his unwillingness to stay confined to the shop:

... by God's lid, 'tis for your worship and for your commodity that I keep company. I am entertained among gallants, true! They call me cousin Frank, right! I lend them moneys, good! They spend it, well! But when they are spent, must not they strive to get more? Must not their land fly? And to whom? Shall not your worship ha' the refusal? Well, I am a good member of the City, if I were well considered. How would merchants thrive, if gentlemen would not be unthrifts? How could gentlemen be unthrifts, if their humours were not fed? How should their humours be fed but by white-meat and cunning secondings? Well, the City might consider us. I am going to an ordinary now: the gallants fall to play; I carry light gold with me; the gallants call, 'Cousin Frank, some gold for silver!'; I change, gain by it; the gallants lose the gold, and then call, 'Cousin Frank, lend me some silver!' (1.1.25–40)

Touchstone replies by denying his participation in the economy described by Quicksilver:

Did I gain my wealth by ordinaries? No! By exchanging of gold? No! By keeping of gallants' company? No! I hired me a little shop, sought low, took small gain, kept no debt-book, garnished my shop for want of plate, with good wholesome thrifty sentences, as, 'Touchstone, keep thy shop, and thy shop will keep thee.' 'Light gains makes heavy purses.' 'Tis good to be merry and wise' ... (44–9)

The significance of this exchange lies not simply in the contradiction that it voices between the middle-class valorization of thrift and the dependence of commercial life on prodigality, but in the fact that, unlike Touchstone, Quicksilver seems to be describing actual economic activity: the sale of land, which intensified in the first two decades of the seventeenth century, and the goldsmith's role in (and profit from) the exchange of gold and silver necessitated by the bi-metallic system of currency.[9] In contrast, Touchstone's claim that he has furnished his shop with 'good wholesome thrifty sentences' (47–8) instead of plate makes clear that his maxims are unusable as economic advice, that unlike Quicksilver's accounting they contain no information on how one might profitably conduct oneself as a goldsmith or even enter the London marketplace. However much Quicksilver himself may be sent up for his enthusiasm for the public stage, he knows his way around and functions as a bearer of economic truth in the play, of a meaning that, unlike Touchstone's wisdom, is not merely the effect of an ossified form.

Quicksilver's subsequent career offers a map of the commercial interconnections that Touchstone's maxims occlude. Thrown out of his master's house, he takes shelter with the usurer Security, who keeps the profits of Quicksilver's activities for himself and his punk, Sindefy. Security and Quicksilver concoct a plan to fleece Sir Petronel Flash, a newly made knight who is to marry Touchstone's prodigal daughter Gertrude, who possesses a small country estate that she inherited from her grandmother. Sir Petronel has invested all of the money he could raise on a ship bound for Virginia, and Security agrees that he will lend money to Sir Petronel, taking as security the property that Gertrude will have signed over. All goes well until the would-be voyagers and Quicksilver get drunk at the farewell party, and, taking to the boats despite foul weather, are wrecked on the Isle of Dogs, where they are all arrested. Repenting in the Counter, Quicksilver concocts a neck-verse, warning his fellow apprentices:

> *Seek not to go beyond your tether,*
> *But cut your thongs unto your leather;*
> *So shall you thrive by little and little,*
> *'Scape Tyburn, Counters, and the Spital!*   (5.5.111–14)

---

9 I am indebted to Janelle Jenstad for the connection between Quicksilver's account of his activities and the practices of goldsmiths during the period.

The verse causes Touchstone to recognize true contrition and to take Quicksilver back. Quicksilver's only punishment is to marry Sindefy, for whom Security is commanded to provide a dowry that, Golding announces, 'shall be all the restitution he shall make of that huge mass he hath so unlawfully gotten' (166–8). As a result, Quicksilver returns to Touchstone's house, bringing with him at least some and, depending on how we interpret 'all,' possibly the entire profits of the operation.[10] Like Portia, Quicksilver is the master, through his improvisatorial skill, of the play's exchange relations. But instead of securing the triumph of one morally coded site at the expense of another, he serves both as mechanism and sign of their systemic connection, of the inevitable collusion between the house of Security and the house of Touchstone. The play thus represents an alliance between financiers, merchants, and gentry, an alliance effected through a savvy younger son of the latter. While the alliance reveals the inadequacy and hypocrisy of the citizens' ideology of thrift, an inadequacy stemming from the necessary entanglement of trade in finance and of finance in prodigality, it also confirms the merchant's power to profit from the system.

10 It is not clear whether Golding's command to Security to 'give her a dower, which shall be all the restitution he shall make of that huge mass he hath so unlawfully gotten' (5.5.166–8), is meant to divest Security of his profits altogether, transferring them to Quicksilver and Sindefy, who are now harboured by Touchstone, or mercifully to permit Quicksilver to keep most of his money (and thus his practice) even as he is knit into the festive conclusion. In other words, do we read 'all the restitution' to mean 'the entire restitution,' or 'the only restitution'? The exaggerated spirit of forgiveness that characterizes the scene would suggest the latter, but Security's reply – 'I say anything, sir, what you'll ha' me say. Would I were no cuckold!' (171-2) – suggests that he is submitting to a real punishment, albeit a lesser one than the misery of being a cuckold. It is also worth noting that the editor, C.G. Petter, interprets the alchemical references in the scene as suggesting that Security 'is here cast out of society' like sulphur precipitated from an alchemical solution (line 176n). If Security is indeed ordered to give up all of his wealth, then we can read the conclusion as marking a (hypocritical) moment of consolidation in which the house of Touchstone is reconstructed as a financial institution rather than as a shop, and Quicksilver as the canny if comic agent and beneficiary of this profitable outcome. If, on the other hand, Security is forced to give up only a portion of his wealth, then the ending would appear to restore the *status quo ante*, which confirms the ongoing connection, via Quicksilver's antics, of Touchstone's and Security's establishments. In either case, however, the moral opposition between usurer and merchant is undermined, and what it takes to play the system is revealed by Quicksilver's improvisational capacities.

If *Eastward Ho!* seems to herald a capitalist ascendancy in the alliance of Quicksilver's capacities with Touchstone's establishment, however, it strikingly disavows both the mercantile ethos of risk-taking and the romance mode that expresses it in *Merchant*. When Quicksilver takes up with Security he explicitly eschews the risks of mercantile life, refusing to 'trust my estate in a wooden trough' (2.2.59), a sentiment with which Security heartily concurs, ridiculing the merchant who 'at every shaking of a leaf ... falls into an agony to think what danger his ship is in ... Where we, that trade nothing but money, are free from all this' (105–15). Underpinning their discussion is the distinction that anti-usury discourse promulgates, between the illegitimate gains of the usurer and the just profits of the merchant that reward him for the risks he has run. As numerous critics have noted, the distinction also underlies the moral opposition between Antonio and Shylock. But if the distinction informs the meaning that Security bears, it does not hold across the play's structure, for his opponent, Touchstone, who 'sought low and took small gain,' is no less averse to risk. The play's great risk-taker instead is Security's dupe, Sir Petronel Flash, knight adventurer bound for Virginia, who never gets past the Isle of Dogs, an outcome confirming the wisdom of Quicksilver's and Security's choice.

Sir Petronel is matched in his thwarted desires to get out of town by Touchstone's daughter Gertrude, who has married Sir Petronel thinking that her knight has a castle where she will preside as lady. Sent off into the country in her coach while her husband makes her estate over to Security, Gertrude discovers that the castle is a fiction, and returns to London wondering 'would the Knight o' the Sun, or Palmerin of England, have used their ladies so ...? or Sir Lancelot? or Sir Tristram?' (5.1.28–30). Confronting her destitution, Gertrude laments that 'there are no fairies nowadays ... To do miracles, and bring ladies money' (74–7); ever resilient, however, she hopes that 'a fairy may come, and bring a pearl or a diamond' (80), or that 'there may be a pot of gold hid o' the backside ...' (81–2). As in *Merchant*, romance in *Eastward Ho!* is associated with women, with miraculous economic events, and a place outside of the city. But romance possesses no transformative power, having withered to the commonplace chivalric costuming of a City girl's greedy fantasies. The reduction is not only ethical but epistemological. Like Touchstone's maxims, Gertrude's romance clichés are presented as delusions; they embody a way of thinking that is useless in the play's economic world, and they provoke laughter from those who are in the know.

Eastward Ho! vouchsafes its audience a sense of epistemological mastery, exposing the collusion of apparently opposed elements of the economic system, and the illusions of literary form that underlie the beliefs of that system's participants. What is interesting about the ridicule that Sir Petronel's and Gertrude's schemes elicit is that while the ridicule trades on the audience's and Quicksilver's supposed mastery of exchange relations, it produces a historically false picture of the economic world, limiting the circuit of activity to London, exploding as fantasy present and future bases of wealth: the colonies, and alliances between mercantile and landed wealth. The sense of mastery that the play affords its audience is primarily an aesthetic rather than an epistemological phenomenon, the ironic anti-mimetic vision that was the Children's companies' stock-in-trade. Parodying the formal resources of the theatre and social life, the Children of the Queen's Revels offered their audiences the experience of not being taken in, as Gertrude is, by the expectations generated by literary forms. My point is not that the play's effects must be understood in formal rather than economic terms but that what makes *Eastward Ho!* significant is its insistent presentation of an ironic literary vision, as though it were epistemological mastery of proto-capitalist exchange relations, a presentation that reveals the ideological work performed by the Blackfriars' brand of theatricality.

A truism of theatre history is that the Blackfriars catered principally to a male élite: court gallants, students of the Inns of Court, and probably some merchants. While the designation 'élite' suggests exclusivity and homogeneity, Andrew Gurr has argued that this élite in fact represented a site of constant conversion and reconversion across the boundary between gentry and citizen, a point underscored by the fact that in a wealthy company such as the Goldsmiths, one third of the apprentices were, like Quicksilver, sons of gentlemen (Gurr 52). The men associated with the Blackfriars represented a new and heterogeneous social group whose energies and resources would be crucial in the expanding economy, and whose identity was defined not only by membership in institutions such as the guild system or the Inns of Court, but also by participation in a looser, homosocial network in which the theatre functioned as binding agent. It is worth noting that in a few years Marston – playwright, gentleman, and member of the Middle Temple – would sell his shares in the Children of the Queen's

Revels to the goldsmith Robert Keysar, to whom Francis Beaumont, another gentleman and playwright, would sympathetically dedicate *The Knight of the Burning Pestle*. In the career of the younger brother Quicksilver and in the demise of the schemes of Sir Petronel and Lady Gertrude, *Eastward Ho!* works to interpellate the members of this group as subjects within a capitalizing economy, offering them a fantasy of participation in which literary mastery leads to profit while taking risks leads nowhere. The play grants its privileged audience an experience that the rapidly changing economy necessarily denies all of its participants: epistemological control and freedom from uncertainty.

It is more difficult to define the work that *The Merchant of Venice* stages. The court performance of 1605 is the only recorded performance in the pre-Civil War period, although the title-page of the 1600 quarto states that the play had 'beene diverse times acted by the Lord Chamberlaine his servants,' presumably at the Theatre and/or the Globes. The play is therefore associated with at least two playing sites, and one of them, the public theatre, probably possessed a more heterogeneous audience than did the Blackfriars. Moreover, the play's displacements, its Venetian setting, its construction of merchants and aristocrats on each others' terms, and its powerful romance elements obscure local interests and interpellations. These displacements, however, are directly connected to the circumstances of the plays' production, evidence perhaps of a dramaturgical strategy developed by Shakespeare's company in order to maximize its audience base. At the very least we need to notice that the mimetic distancing that Shakespeare's conservative use of forms produces is well suited to the situation that Gurr claims prevailed in the pre-1599 period, before the commercial-theatre market began to diversify (59–79). Yet it is precisely this representational practice of blurring the interests of specific social groups, and of disrupting any clear reference to them, that encourages modern critics to take Shakespeare's play as evidence of the culture as a whole. Reconstructing the dramatic field in which Shakespeare's company was working permits us to recognize that its practice is universalizing, but not universal.

WORKS CITED

Agnew, Jean-Christophe. *Worlds Apart: The Market and the Theater in Anglo-American Thought, 1550–1750*. Cambridge: Cambridge UP, 1986.

Beaumont, Francis. *The Knight of the Burning Pestle*. Ed. Michael Hattaway. London: Benn, 1969.

Bruster, Douglas. *Drama and the Market in the Age of Shakespeare*. Cambridge: Cambridge UP, 1992.

Cohen, Walter. *Drama of a Nation: Public Theater in Renaissance England and Spain*. Ithaca and London: Cornell UP, 1985.

– '*The Merchant of Venice* and the Possibilities of Historical Criticism.' *ELH* 49.4 (1982): 765–89.

– 'Political Criticism of Shakespeare.' *Shakespeare Reproduced: The Text in History and Ideology*. Ed. Jean E. Howard and Marion F. O'Connor. 18–46.

Dollimore, Jonathan, and Alan Sinfield, eds. *Political Shakespeare: New Essays in Cultural Materialism*. Manchester: Manchester UP; Ithaca: Cornell UP, 1985.

Drakakis, John, ed. *Alternative Shakespeares*. London: Methuen, 1985.

Dutton, Richard, and Richard Wilson, eds. *New Historicism and Renaissance Drama*. London and New York: Longman, 1992.

Engle, Lars. *Shakespearean Pragmatism: Market of His Time*. Chicago and London: U of Chicago P, 1993.

Ferber, Michael, 'The Ideology of *The Merchant of Venice*.' *English Literary Renaissance* 20.3 (1990): 431–64.

Ferguson, Margaret W., et al., eds. *Rewriting the Renaissance: The Discourses of Sexual Difference in Early Modern Europe*. Chicago and London: U of Chicago P, 1986.

Greenblatt, Stephen. *Shakespearean Negotiations: The Circulation of Social Energy in Renaissance England*. Berkeley and Los Angeles: U of California P, 1988.

Gurr, Andrew. *Playgoing in Shakespeare's London*. Cambridge: Cambridge UP, 1987.

Helgerson, Richard. *Forms of Nationhood: The Elizabethan Writing of England*. Chicago and London: U of Chicago P, 1992.

– *Self-Crowned Laureates: Spenser, Jonson, Milton, and the Literary System*. Berkeley: U of California P, 1983.

Howard, Jean E. *The Stage and Social Struggle in Early Modern England*. London and New York: Routledge, 1994.

Howard, Jean E., and Marion F. O'Connor, eds. *Shakespeare Reproduced: The Text in History and Ideology*. New York and London: Methuen, 1987.

Jameson, Fredric. *The Political Unconscious: Narrative as a Socially Symbolic Act*. Ithaca: Cornell UP, 1981.

Jonson, Ben, George Chapman, and John Marston. *Eastward Ho!* Ed. C.G. Petter. London: Benn, 1973.

Kastan, David Scott, and Peter Stallybrass, eds. *Staging the Renaissance: Reinterpretations of Elizabethan and Jacobean Drama*. New York and London: Routledge, 1991.

5

Cultural Capital's Gold Standard: Shakespeare and the Critical Apostrophe in Renaissance Studies

KAREN NEWMAN

that curious and mad public that cries continually for the new and original while admiring only the tried and true

(Gauguin on painting)

Recent critiques of new historicism and cultural poetics complain that for all their attention to non-canonical texts – historical, scientific, popular, written from the 'margins' – Shakespeare and Milton remain the signal points of reference of most of these investigations. Typically, it is argued, such essays marshal and analyse a host of texts once considered 'non-literary' – diaries, cookbooks, anatomies, travelogues, court cases, pamphlets, wills, texts written by women – but the pay-off is analysis of a canonical author, more often than not, Shakespeare. In what follows, I want to examine that critique and its assumptions, first, by considering carefully what constitutes 'cultural capital' in the late twentieth-century United States academy, and then turning to a particular case that I shall use to exemplify the complex of issues at stake in these debates, *Timon of Athens*, a play that because it is 'Shakespeare' is now always already canonical, and yet of all Shakespeare's plays, perhaps the most canonically problematic. That double status, *Timon*'s dubious canonicity within Shakespeare studies coupled with the continuing canonical power of Shakespeare more generally within the schools and the culture at large, suggests the way in which the canon works through a logic of the supplement and not by way of, so to speak, a gold standard.

By the gold standard, I mean to invoke debates about coined and paper money that shaped political discourse in nineteenth-century Amer-

Marcus, Leah. *Puzzling Shakespeare: Local Reading and Its Discontents*. Berkeley: U of California P, 1988.

Montrose, Louis A. '*A Midsummer Night's Dream* and the Shaping Fantasies of Elizabethan Culture: Gender, Power, Form.' *Rewriting the Renaissance: The Discourses of Sexual Difference in Early Modern Europe*. Ed. Margaret W. Ferguson et al. 65–87.

Mullaney, Steven. *The Place of the Stage: License, Play, and Power in Renaissance England*. Chicago: U of Chicago P, 1988.

Newman, Karen. *Fashioning Femininity and English Renaissance Drama*. Chicago and London: U of Chicago P, 1991.

Parker, Patricia, and Geoffrey Hartman, eds. *Shakespeare and the Question of Theory*. New York and London: Methuen, 1985.

Quint, David. *Epic and Empire: Politics and Generic Form from Virgil to Milton*. Princeton: Princeton UP, 1993.

Shakespeare, William. *The Merchant of Venice*. Ed. John Russell Brown. 7th ed. 1955. London: Methuen, 1959.

Taylor, Gary. 'The Renaissance and the End of Editing.' *Palimpsest: Editorial Theory in the Humanities*. Ed. George Bornstein and Ralph G. Williams. Ann Arbor: U of Michigan P, 1993. 121–49.

Tennenhouse, Leonard. *Power on Display: The Politics of Shakespeare's Genres*. New York and London: Methuen, 1986.

Traub, Valerie. *Desire and Anxiety: Circulations of Sexuality in Shakespearean Drama*. New York and London: Routledge, 1992.

Wayne, Valerie, ed. *The Matter of Difference: Materialist Feminist Criticism of Shakespeare*. Ithaca: Cornell UP, 1991.

Weimann, Robert. 'Bifold Authority in Shakespeare's Theatre.' *Shakespeare Quarterly* 39.4 (1988): 401–17.

ica, debates that recent commentators have recognized as concerned with 'symbolization in general, and hence not only with money but also with aesthetics. Symbolization in this context concerns the relationship between the substantial thing and its sign' (Shell 6).[1] At stake in the gold-standard controversy and the logic of general equivalence that it presupposes is the referent – proponents of the gold standard, and to a lesser but shared degree, the silver money men, believed in the intrinsic value of precious metals, particularly gold, which 'stood behind' paper money. Paper money, unlike gold, has no intrinsic value, only that which is bestowed by statutory alchemy, by act of Congress and the willingness of the society in which it is a medium of exchange to accept that denomination. As the history of political economy demonstrates, that value is never stable, but changes over time, in different historical circumstances. Within debates about the canon, cultural conservatives argue on behalf of the intrinsic value of works of literature, for a sort of gold standard of cultural capital. Paper money men are like those cultural critics who challenge arguments on behalf of literature's intrinsic value and recognize instead the way in which a given text's or author's value as symbolic currency changes over time. When the new historicist or cultural materialist situates Shakespeare, or less frequently, Milton in relation to a host of texts not usually considered canonical, he or she recognizes not only the lesson that to be read or viewed, one must repeat, produce what is recognizable but never identical, the simulacrum that is not the copy, but also the way in which canonicity is always a question of rereading, that it is produced, not ontological, natural, innate.[2] The changing canonical fortunes of various authors and texts, including Shakespeare, via recent protocols of reading, criticism, and consumption, show canonicity to be always retrospective, anachronistic, constructed through the various ways in which a text is endowed with value and made consumable at a particular cultural moment. In the final section of this essay I want to inflate *Timon*'s canonical value by reading it as a chapter in the history of early

---

1 On the gold standard, see also Michaels and especially Goux.
2 In so far as the production of any early author continues to constitute cultural capital, Shakespeare is that author; the plays epitomize the canon as the continuing proliferation of new editions and texts demonstrate, even as the standard plays of Jonson, Marlowe, and others go out of print. The availability of Middleton in Gary Taylor's mammoth new edition will inevitably shift pedagogic interest even further away from Marlowe and Jonson, though it is unlikely even to jostle the Shakespeare industry.

modern sexuality, to apostrophize, that is, reanimate *Timon* in today's academy.

Before turning to *Timon*, however, I shall consider briefly the concept 'cultural capital,' which derives from the important work of French sociologist/anthropologist Pierre Bourdieu. Bourdieu's work forms a part of the French movement that has been loosely termed post-marxist because of its willingness to question classical Marxist accounts of capitalism, class, subjectivity, and domination. Bourdieu criticizes solely economic accounts of class formation and insists on the importance of what he terms symbolic capital. However, as the debates about the gold standard and recent work on symbolic economies demonstrate, economics has always been implicated in the processes of symbolization, and symbolization in the economic. Although commentators – new historicist and feminist alike – on the 'canon debates' and new paradigms in Renaissance studies have appropriated the concept of 'cultural capital' since the publication of Bourdieu's earliest discussions, John Guillory's *Cultural Capital: The Problem of Literary Canon Formation* has given it its recent currency in literary studies.

Guillory opens his argument by stating boldly his claim that 'the concept of cultural capital can provide the basis for a new historical account of both the process of canon formation and the immediate social conditions giving rise to the debate about the canon' (viii). Guillory challenges notions of canon formation organized on the model of *representation*, arguing that social conditions – class, not identity – determine the distribution of cultural resources. The canon, as Guillory observes, has always been subject to revision over time, even if those pressures that lead to canon revision are now represented as social and extrinsic rather than intrinsic and value-based. For example, Guillory, Gerald Graff, and others have shown how in the eighteenth and nineteenth centuries the move in the schools away from Greek and Latin culture to the vernacular, and from poetry to the novel, represented the formation of new forms of cultural capital. Guillory's chapter on Gray's 'Elegy' and Wordsworth is a dazzling demonstration of the shift from the classical to the vernacular canon in response to the shifting hegemonic status of an emergent bourgeoisie. Subsequently Guillory analyses Eliot, New Criticism, and de Man as toiling in the production of the 'literary,' a category that he claims is produced in order to ensure distinction and cultural hegemony.

Guillory assumes, then, that 'literature' continues to represent cultural capital. I want to argue instead that mass cultural forms are fast superseding 'literature' as cultural capital: even in the narrower confines of the academy, work on television, contemporary movies, popular musical forms such as rap, cultural icons – Elvis, Madonna, O.J. Simpson – refracted through the categorical grids of race, gender, sexuality, nationality, and (too infrequently) class, garner the highest enrolments and would seem to produce the highest economic rewards and prestige.[3] Just as the shift away from classical culture towards the vernacular has been historicized, so we need to historicize the shift in the late twentieth century towards mass cultural forms that are being constituted *in the schools* as symbolic capital. To return to Guillory's argument, economic analysis and historical specificity drop out as he turns to the recent history of literature and theory and rehearses what may be described as a nostalgic narrative of 'high' cultural texts – literature – producing class distinctions. Historical and economic enquiry of the kind Guillory so painstakingly performs in the chapter on Gray needs to be undertaken in analysing the status of literature as a contemporary form of cultural capital: publishing practices (what is in print and available for 'consumption'), reading lists, syllabuses and course enrolments, period choices in graduate training, faculty compensation both across disciplines and in relation to the producers of other forms of symbolic capital, from coaches to entertainers, as well as a host of other factors, challenge literature's assumed status as cultural capital. New forms of cultural capital with their own complex protocols of reception and interpretation are being produced through the institutionalization in the university of mass culture. Their enormous exchange value contrasts sharply with that of early modern canonical and non-canonical texts and their inordinate demands on today's reader, such as knowledge of Latin and classical culture, of early forms of English and other romance languages, of literary genres, of social and political history, of rhetoric and figuration. Let me be clear. My tone should not be heard as elegiac so much as hard-boiled: I am suggesting that we recognize the momentous shift in cultural practices and objects in which we are taking part, as significant as was, for example, the advent of print culture in the early modern period.

3 See, for example, Peder J. Zane's report in the *New York Times*, 6 Aug. 1995 on the upcoming First Annual International Conference on Elvis Presley, at the University of Mississippi, at which well-known Elvis impersonators, 'The Mexican Elvis,' and other 'media personalities' were to take part. According to university sources interviewed by the *Times*, academic conferences are boring and in need of juicing up (2).

And what of Shakespeare? Shakespeare has long been considered by some the gold standard in English studies, cultural capital of unquestioned value that stands behind other symbolic forms. In the schools, 'the canon' is increasingly being reduced to a synecdoche – Shakespeare – a Shakespeare represented by a small and predictable series of plays deemed properly Shakespearean. If the cultural capital that was 'literature' and that Guillory assumes in his analysis of de Man still confers distinction, has been superseded by mass cultural forms, and Shakespeare remains the signal reference point of 'the canonical,' then to complain as some have of bad faith on the part of the new historicists is to misunderstand how cultural capital works under late twentieth-century U.S. capitalism. The constriction of what is in print, of student and collegial interest in and knowledge of the larger tradition, much less of non-canonical authors of the early modern period, presses for the continued turn to Shakespeare, the *auctor rex* of a literary Jurassic Park. The new historicist, cultural materialist, or feminist turn to Shakespeare allows the contemporary critic working in the early modern period to be read, given the many forces that militate against the continued status of older canonical writers, much less non-canonical writers of earlier periods.

In his discussion of the importance of access to literacy, to the means of literary production and consumption through the regulation of reading and writing – in short, the educational system – in producing and revising what counts as canonical, Guillory poses a series of questions: 'Who reads? What do they read? How do they read? In what social and institutional circumstances? Who writes? In what social and institutional contexts? For whom?' (18). Oh *Timon of Athens*! Who will read you? How will you be read? In what follows, I want to read and write about *Timon of Athens* in the institutional context of the academy and professional Shakespeare studies. In doing so, I will bear in mind the shifts in what constitutes cultural capital at the *fin de siècle* in order to produce *Timon of Athens* as such within the circumscribed limits of the university and the discursive topography of literary study in the 1990s.

Perverting the Canonical: An Apostrophe

Out of perverseness, I turn to perhaps the most dubiously canonical of Shakespeare's plays, to look at a text by a male, non-minority, canonical writer of the early modern period, a text that professional Shakespeareans barely afford the status of a Shakespearean play, to read it by *not* repeating what has become the canonical commentary about it, that it may have been collaborative, and therefore not 'authentically, fully Shakespearean,' that it has 'unusual imperfections,' is 'unpleasant,' 'incoherent,' 'unfinished.'[4] *Timon's* problematic canonical status is already gestured at in its peripatetic textual history. Although first printed in the 1623 Folio, between *Romeo and Juliet* and *Julius Caesar*, it apparently owes its inclusion to the copyright misfortunes of *Troilus and Cressida*. In other words, the canonical status of *Timon* seems already to have been troublesome in the seventeenth century. Editors surmise that the spot was planned for *Troilus* because copies of the Folio survive with the end of *Romeo* on one side of the leaf, and the beginning of *Troilus* on the other. In addition, at the other end, there is a gap in the pagination between *Timon* and *Julius Caesar*, a gap that conforms to the difference in length between the printed texts of *Timon* and *Troilus*. Frank Kermode ends his discussion of *Timon's* textual fortunes by observing that 'whether *Timon* would have been left out altogether if that emergency had not arisen it is impossible to say for certain' (1441).

Although *Timon* has been largely ignored by critics until recently, the play began to be reread and produced in the 1980s, presumably, it is sometimes said, 'because of its emphasis on an affluent and decadent society' (Charney, '"Timon of Athens" on Stage and Screen' 249). Since Bradley, *Timon* has been characterized as unfinished, 'weak, ill-constructed and confused' (Bradley 200), linked to *King Lear* either as a failed first sketch, or alternatively as an after-vibration, with a protagonist ridiculous rather than tragic.[5] Recently such judgments have shifted as critical norms have changed. Readers have pointed to *Timon's* topical relation to Jacobean gift-giving at court, and its links to new forms of monetary exchange and credit specific to late sixteenth- and

4 Although Charney claimed in his 1973 bibliographic essay on *Timon* that 'older studies of divided or non-Shakespearian authorship are now more or less obsolete,' ('*Coriolanus* and *Timon*' 225) *Timon of Athens* will be included in Gary Taylor's projected edition of Middleton's works. Also on authorship see Smith, 'The Authorship of *Timon of Athens*.' Titles of recent essays include 'An Embryonic *Lear*,' 'Notes toward a more Finished *Timon*,' and 'Word Links between *Timon of Athens* and *King Lear*.' The *locus classicus* for the play as unfinished is Ellis-Fermor's essay, 270–83; see also Mellamphy 170.

5 In his review of *Timon* criticism and bibliography, Charney notes that Coleridge established the comparison with *Lear*, which 'pairing is one of the commonplaces of *Timon* criticism, although there is no external evidence at all, or even a specific allusion, by which to date the play' ('*Coriolanus* and *Timon*' 226).

early seventeenth-century London. Readers have articulated that historical context in terms of psychological and psychoanalytic structures – primary narcissism, fantasies of maternal power and castration.[6] To appropriate the title of an unpublished essay on *Timon of Athens* by Barbara Correll, the poles of recent criticism might be alliteratively described as capitalism and castration.[7] But I want to read *Timon* not in terms that would recuperate it to contemporary normative historicist or psychoanalytic protocols in Renaissance studies, but instead by way of different economies of figure and address.

Readers of *Timon of Athens* have often remarked that the play begins with a *paragone*, the dialogue between the poet and the painter (see Hunt 47–63). Unlike a classic *paragone*, however, Shakespeare's poet and painter do not in fact argue over the relative merits of their respective arts, or even compete for Timon's patronage; instead they describe, discuss, and admire the work each has executed. Even a cursory look, for example, at the opening scene of Molière's *Le Bourgeois Gentilhomme*, in which the various masters of philosophy, music, dance, and fencing quarrel and brawl over whose art is best, shows how differently Shakespeare conceives of this scene and its function. More important than any implied debate among the arts is the initial invocation of poetry in the poet's first speech, with its odd figure initiating a rhetoric of apostrophe that comes to dominate the play, particularly in its 'difficult' second half. In response to the painter's commonplace observation about how the world wears, the poet responds: '… See, / Magic of bounty, all these spirits thy power / Hath conjur'd to attend!' (1.1.5–7). The poet's imperative 'see' initially seems to be addressed to the painter, with 'magic of bounty' the object. See the magic of bounty, the poet seems to say to the painter. But in the second half of the line, the second person 'thy' shifts our understanding of the lines. 'Magic of

6 See especially the important essay by Kahn; see also Chorost. *Timon* has been wildly successful onstage in Michael Langham's stunning production at Stratford, Ontario in 1991.

7 For a recent essay still concerned with Jacobean patronage and gift-giving, but in terms of what she calls its sodomitical economy, see Greene, whose essay came to my attention after I had written my own; although our approaches to *Timon* differ, we share an interest in the play's adumbration of sodomy. Whereas Greene's attention is focused on 'the impossibility of writing a play about the limits of male friendship in the Renaissance without recourse to the vocabulary of sodomy' (165), I am concerned with the ways in which commentators have turned away from *Timon*'s sodomitical economy.

bounty' is a periphrastic epithet for Timon, an apostrophe summoning him to see the 'spirits' that his generosity has conjured up, the swarm of dealers, artisans, and flatterers that surrounds his door awaiting his return. Barbara Johnson defines apostrophe as 'the direct address of an absent, dead, or inanimate being by a first person speaker ... Apostrophe is thus both direct and indirect: based etymologically on the notion of turning aside, of digressing from straight speech, it manipulates the I/Thou structure of *direct* address in an indirect, fictionalized way. The absent, dead, or inanimate entity addressed is thereby made present, animate, and anthropomorphic. Apostrophe is a form of ventriloquism through which the speaker throws voice, life, and human form into the addressee, turning its silence into mute responsiveness' (29–30). Timon is not named at the outset of the play, but is introduced in a periphrastic apostrophe suggesting the seemingly infinite, even supernatural quality of his generosity figured as 'bounty.' The word *bounty* or its forms is repeated fourteen more times in descriptions of Timon; the word derives from the Old French *bontet*, meaning goodness in persons, virtue, or high estate. Interestingly, the second meaning is warlike prowess, which would seem to adumbrate the later obscure allusion, at 4.3.95–6, to Timon's 'great deeds, when neighbour states, / But for thy sword and fortune, trod upon them' [i.e., the Athenians]. The third meaning of *bounty* is related to things – good quality or property. Finally, *bounty* means an act of kindness or good turn, a kindness that can also be shown through giving and liberality; *bounty*, in this final sense, which is certainly the primary sense here and in the play generally, is usually attributed to God or to the great or wealthy who have power to give liberally and lavishly. In the opening apostrophe, the poet not only introduces Timon; he also tells Timon what otherwise he could not outside the linguistic figure of apostrophe, namely, that the 'spirits' he conjures up are merely there for rewards.

Many readers have commented on Timon as a gift-giver, and on the topical suggestiveness of his generosity when considered in relation to early modern gift culture. Although in Act 1 we see Timon release Ventidius from prison by paying off his creditors, and dower his manservant Lucilius, we know about Timon's material generosity more by what is said of him, and by the enumeration of his favours when he sends his servants for returns in Act 3, than by seeing that generosity enacted. In fact, what Timon gives most generously, even in the first half of the play when he has property to give, is words; he never handles money, rarely handles a gift. We never see him engaged in the work of exchange, although the play would perhaps allow him to take up the proffered jewel in Act 1.1. Instead, Timon's gift-giving is linguistic, performative; saying is doing. He gives by means of words: 'I'll pay the debt,' (1.1.106); 'I will send his ransom' (108); 'I'll counterpoise' (148); 'you shall find I like it. Wait attendance / Till you hear further from me' (164–5); 'I gave it freely ever' (1.2.10). Flavius's aside in Act 1.2 calls attention to a disjunction between the material and the linguistic:

> He [Timon] commands us to provide, and give great gifts,
> And all out of an empty coffer;
> Nor will he know his purse, or yield me this,
> To show him what a beggar his heart is,
> Being of no power to make his wishes good.
> His promises fly so beyond his state
> That what he speaks is all in debt; he owes for ev'ry word ...   (1.2.190–6)

When Timon offers his bay courser to a friend because that friend has praised it, he gives it saying, 'You may take my word' (1.2.212). But perhaps the most emphatic example of the displacement of things by words is Flavius's comment – 'O my good lord, the world is but a word: / Were it all yours, to give it in a breath, / How quickly were it gone!' (2.2.156–8).

Viewed from this perspective, the two 'halves' of the play are not as opposed as the criticism has usually represented them; in the play's second half, we must remember, Timon continues giving. He continues his 'magic of bounty,' which conjures up spirits through the 'performative' linguistic figure of apostrophe. Timon spews words, lavishing them as liberally as he has lavished gifts earlier, calling upon the gods, the heavens, the earth, apostrophizing the city walls, Athenian matrons, slaves, fools, bankrupts, servants, masters, even cold sciatica with his impassioned, misanthropic poetic gifts. To apostrophize is to 'will' a state of affairs; for Barbara Johnson and Jonathan Culler the apostrophe figures the performativity of language not so much in the technical Austinian sense, although such an argument could certainly be made, but in the sense of language as constitutive.[8] Timon employs the apostrophe because he is a visionary poet engaged in a dialogue with the universe:

8 On apostrophe as performative, see esp. Johnson.

> ... O thou wall
> That girdles in those wolves, dive in the earth
> And fence not Athens! Matrons, turn incontinent!
> Obedience fail in children! Slaves and fools,
> Pluck the grave wrinkled senate from the bench
> ...
> ... Bankrupts, hold fast;
> Rather than render back, out with your knives,
> And cut your trusters' throats! Bound servants, steal!
> ...
> ... Maid, to thy master's bed;
> ...
> ... Piety and fear,
> Religion to the gods, peace, justice, truth,
> Domestic awe, night-rest and neighbourhood,
> Instruction, manners, mysteries and trades,
> Degrees, observances, customs and laws,
> Decline to your confounding contraries;
> And yet confusion live! (4.1.1–21)

Timon's impossible imperatives pre-empt the place of the *you* in the I/Thou structure of direct address and thereby enact what the lines demand – the annihilation of the *you*, the Athenians whom Timon so abhors.[9] The apostrophes in this notorious diatribe animate the inanimate by constituting death and destruction through language: incontinence, disobedience, treason, fornication, pillage, murder, parricide, plague, confusion.

In *Symbolic Economies: After Marx and Freud* Jean-Joseph Goux analyses 'the intersections and conceptual parallels' (1) among and between semiotics, structural psychoanalysis, and political economy, particularly what he terms 'the notion of the *general equivalent*' (3). For Goux, after Marx, gold is that general equivalent, the measuring object, the 'metaphor for the transcendental guarantee of meaning' (103), the referential 'gold standard.' Goux analyses three functions of gold: as a form of the imaginary or the ideal, as a *measure of values*; as a symbolic

---

9 If, as Culler argues, apostrophe substitutes the 'temporality of discourse' for 'referential temporality,' the lyric *now* for narrative, or in this case, dramatic, extension (149, 154), then apostrophe also helps to make sense of other of the play's so-called unusual imperfections, particularly its episodic structure.

form in its function as a circulating medium or instrument; and as a real form of payment, no longer an image, but 'as real money, as cold, hard cash' (48). In *Timon*, gold works in all three capacities; it is an ideal measure, a form of the imaginary, a function highlighted by the notorious confusion of numbers – the five, fifty, and five hundred talents (Spencer, 'Shakespeare Learns' 75–8). That reckoning disorder merely serves to emphasize the idealized status of gold, its role as excess, 'pure superfluity, excess par excellence' (Goux 28). Gold also functions in the second sense as a symbolic form or instrument – as jewels and the bay courser – in the form of the gift that stands in for gold. Finally, in the opening scene it circulates as cold, hard cash to make Lucilius equivalent to the daughter of the old Athenian, and to pay Ventidius's debts and thereby release him from prison; later in the play, it enables Alcibiades to pay his soldiers and wage war against Athens. The homology that Goux explores between the economic and the linguistic is foregrounded in Act 4.3 when Timon, in a famously anti-pastoral moment, digs for roots and instead finds gold, gold that is summoned from the earth in the form of the apostrophe:

> ... Earth, yield me roots.
> Who seeks for better of thee, sauce his palate
> With thy most operant poison. What is here?
> Gold? Yellow, glittering, precious gold?
> No, gods, I am no idle votarist.
> Roots, you clear heavens! Thus much of this will make
> Black, white; foul, fair; wrong, right;
> Base, noble; old, young; coward, valiant.
> Ha, you gods! Why this? What this, you gods? Why, this
> Will lug your priests and servants from your sides,
> Pluck stout men's pillows from below their heads.
> This yellow slave
> Will knit and break religions, bless th'accurs'd,
> Make the hoar leprosy ador'd, place thieves,
> And give them title, knee and approbation
> With senators on the bench. This is it
> That makes the wappen'd widow wed again:
> She whom the spital-house and ulcerous sores
> Would cast the gorge at, this embalms and spices
> To th'April day again. Come, damn'd earth,
> Thou common whore of mankind, that puts odds

Among the rout of nations, I will make thee
Do thy right nature.   (4.3.23–45)

Conventionally these lines, like Volpone's at the opening of Jonson's
play, are glossed in terms of the reversible world; gold turns the world
upside down, reverses the values of family, state, nature.

I want instead to focus on the figure of address itself, apostrophe's
power to animate – the earth, the gods, roots, finally gold itself:

> *Timon.* ... O thou sweet king-killer, and dear divorce
> 'Twixt natural son and sire, thou bright defiler
> Of Hymen's purest bed, thou valiant Mars,
> Thou ever young, fresh, loved and delicate wooer,
> Whose blush doth thaw the consecrated snow
> That lies on Dian's lap! thou visible god,
> That sold'rest close impossibilities,
> And mak'st them kiss; that speak'st with every tongue,
> To every purpose! O thou touch of hearts,
> Think thy slave Man rebels, and by thy virtue
> Set them into confounding odds, that beasts
> May have the world in empire!   (4.3.384–95)

Unlike most tropes, as Jonathan Culler points out, apostrophe tropes not
on the meaning of a word, but on the circuit or situation of communication itself – apostrophe is a trope of reciprocity and giving – it animates,
gives life, bestows qualities, agency; but it may also 'complicate or
disrupt the circuit of communication, raising questions about who is
the addressee' (135). As such, apostrophe is a pre-eminently suitable
trope for *Timon*; it is the 'gold' of the play in its powers of performance
and address. Apostrophe may also be the pre-eminent critical trope
of academic discourse. Stephen Greenblatt famously opens his book
on Shakespeare with the gnomic utterance 'I began with the desire to
speak with the dead' (Greenblatt 1); in other words, with the desire, we
might say, for apostrophe: 'My own voice was the voice of the dead, for
the dead had contrived to leave textual traces of themselves, and those
traces make themselves heard in the voices of the living' (1). Criticism
is always in some sense an act of apostrophe.

Early in his discussion of the canon debates, John Guillory points
out that consumption is determined by the knowledge required to read
historical works; but cultural capital within the university, however

dependent on *knowledge* produced in the schools, is also disabled by the limits of that knowledge, by the canons of reading and gate-keeping protocols that keep the dead from speaking, that inhibit the critical apostrophe. Oh Plutarch! Speak what cannot be spoken. Speak the love that dares not speak its name! Shakespeareans have been almost unanimous in their judgment that Plutarch's *Lives* is not important to *Timon*.[10] Although Kenneth Muir admits the playwright used Plutarch 'somewhat perfunctorily for the scenes in which Alcibiades appears,' and mentions Shakespeare's use of the life of Antonius in the portrayal of Timon, he emphasizes 'the anonymous *Timon'* (218). T.J.B. Spencer, in *Shakespeare's Plutarch*, does not include the Life of Alcibiades; in *Plutarch Revisited* David Green tells us that Shakespeare's use of Plutarch in *Timon* is 'slight,' and that the play is not only 'unfinished,' but 'inferior Shakespeare' (1). Geoffrey Bullough discounts Plutarch in his review of *Timon's* sources, stating that Shakespeare uses the Life of Alcibiades although 'but slightly,' and emphasizes instead Lucian and the anonymous academic *Timon* (249). Why the continuing critical censure of *Timon*? Why the determination to read the play through Lucian and the Dyce ms *Timon* and not through Plutarch? Can we animate Plutarch, make him speak, and in an act of critical apostrophe, animate a different *Timon of Athens*?

Plutarch is suggestive for our understanding of many aspects of the play. In both the Life of Marcus Antonius (Plutarch 4: 290–360) and the Life of Alcibiades (1: 346–89), Timon the misanthrope warmly commends Alcibiades' power and wishes the Athenians 'undone.' The Life of Alcibiades contributes the name of the whore Timandra. It recounts Alcibiades' intervention to save a friend in an incident suggestive of the strange scene (3.5) in which Alcibiades petitions on behalf of 'a friend of mine' whose 'hot blood' / 'Hath stepp'd into the law ...' (3.5.11–13), a man 'of comely virtues' (15). But more important than these isolated parallels is the characterization of Alcibiades and his homoerotic attachments. In North's translation of the Life of Marcus Antonius we learn that Timon was mocked by the Athenians, who called him 'a vyper, and malicious man unto mankind, to shunne all other mens companies, but the companie of young Alcibiades, a bolde

---

10 An exception is H.J. Oliver, who states that 'North's *Plutarch*' was 'Shakespeare's main source for the story of Timon' (xxxii). But Oliver claims of the Life of Alcibiades that Shakespeare merely 'glanced through it at this or a later stage of his career' (xxxiii) and ignores the Life's insistence on Alcibiades' homoerotic attachments.

and insolent youth, whom he woulde greatly feast, and make much of, and kissed him very gladly' (Plutarch 4: 348). The Life of Alcibiades begins with a description of his physical beauty, his lisping speech; it recounts his relationships with male suitors, particularly Socrates, and remarks on his propensity to dress in long, sweeping robes. The Life tells of Alcibiades' dream at the time of his death, in which he was made up and dressed in women's clothes. These aspects are emphasized as fully as is Alcibiades' ambitious involvement in Athenian politics and the Peloponnesian War. Alcibiades is presented as subject to flattery, blandishment, extravagance, and as often saved by Socrates, with whom it is twice repeated that he often shared his tent. North's Plutarch emphasizes Alcibiades' beauty and his 'familliar friendshippe with Socrates': they played together, wrestled, and lodged together in the war (350). North includes Thucydides' reputed characterization of Alcibiades as 'incontinent of bodie, and dissolute of life' (352). The Life ends with the protagonist's death following a transvestite dream. Is the refusal on the part of critics to animate Plutarch's Life a turning away from its homoeroticism, from its account of same-sex relations and desire that potentially changes our reading of *Timon*? Is *Timon* deemed an embryonic or, alternatively, a failed *King Lear* because it lacks a heterosexual familial attachment? Does Bullough's portrayal of Alcibiades as a womanizer and a prodigal, and his emphasis on Lucian and the Dyce ms *Timon*, in which the protagonist falls in love with and marries a woman, Callimela, rather than on Plutarch, represent a turning away from the play's avowed homoeroticism? Does Plutarch's Life suggest a different reading of male friendship in the play, a different understanding of the emotional power of Timon's disappointment at his friends' betrayal, a different understanding of what it means to be without 'gold'?

It has been often remarked that *Timon* is unusual, even among Shakespeare's Roman plays, in the intensity of its focus on homosocial relations and its exclusion of women. There are virtually no female characters, only the fleeting, almost speechless entrance of the masquing Amazons at the banquet in Act 1.2, who arrive only to be banished immediately by Timon, and the exchange in Act 4 with Timandra and Phrynia, whom Timon terms, after Plutarch, Alcibiades' whores. In that second exchange, Timandra asks Alcibiades about Timon: 'Is this th'Athenian minion whom the world / Voic'd so regardfully?' (4.3.82–3). *Minion* meant not only a specially favoured or beloved one, the idol of a people or community, but, of course, also a sexual favourite,

a wanton, a darling, a conflation of meanings that suggests a different
attention to the presentation of male friendship in the play, an attention
that takes into account Alan Bray's important challenge to the assumed
distinction between male friendship and sodomy in the early modern
period. Readers have often noted that Timon's investment in his male
friends and his sharp misanthropy in the second half are prompted not
so much by his loss of status or property as by his loss of friends, a
loss symbolized by his vanished gold. Jody Greene has recently read
Timon and its presentation of male friendship and clientage via sodomy
as it has begun to be analysed in reference to early modern England
by Alan Bray and Jonathan Goldberg. Greene's reading of the play's
language of orality and spending is powerful, if occasionally anachronistic, but critics of *Timon* have generally evaded the play's insistent
homoeroticism.

   That Alcibiades was understood in the early modern period to symbolize homoerotic relations is not in doubt.[11] In the January eclogue
of Spenser's *Shepheardes Calender*, E.K.'s gloss on Colin Clout's relation with Hobbinol describes Hobbinol as Colin Clout's 'most familiar
freend,' (Spenser 422) and alludes to the 'sauour of disorderly loue,
which the learned call paederastice,' exemplified by Socrates and Alcibiades, and protests that the philosopher loved Alcibiades' soul: 'And
so is paederastice much to be praeferred before gynerastice ...' (423).
E.K. goes on to demur that he does not defend 'execrable and horrible
sinnes of forbidden and vnlawful fleshlinesse,' but the association of
Alcibiades with homoerotic love is clear (423). In Marlowe's *Edward II*
the association is even more emphatic. There Mortimer Senior admon-
ishes his nephew to allow Edward his favourite since

   The mightiest kings have had their minions,
   Great Alexander loved Hephaestion,
   The conquering Hercules for Hylas wept,
   And for Patroclus stern Achilles drooped;
   And not kings only, but the wisest men:

11 T.J.B. Spencer's essay '"Greeks" and "Merrygreeks"' is particularly interesting in its
   avoidance of drawing the conclusion required by its own evidence. Spencer details
   the Greeks' general reputation for depravity by looking in turn at drunkenness,
   deceit, dishonesty, and the libidinous habits of Greek women, with only a brief
   reference to the '"Greek vice"' via a quotation from *Troilus* (231).

The Roman Tully loved Octavius,
Grave Socrates, wild Alcibiades ...   (1.4.390–6)

Socrates and Alcibiades are the final dyad in a series of classical parallels
representing same-sex love. Kings must have their minions whatever
they cost.

In *Timon* gold is the necessary instrument of 'friends.' Even the loyal
Flavius, whose speeches throughout the play foreground the indistinguishable languages of desire, friendship, and service, promises to
'serve his mind, with my best will; / Whilst I have gold ...' (4.2.50–1).
Gold is at once the imaginary form of love and loyalty and the signifier
of the death of love and friendship. In his discussion of what he terms a
general *'logic of the symbolization process'* (24), Jean-Joseph Goux analyses
not only the intersection of semiotic and monetary economies, but the
way in which 'all processes of exchange and valuation encountered in
economic practice set up mechanisms in relation to what I am inclined to
term a *symbology*, which is in no way restricted to the economic domain.
This symbology entails a system, a mode of symbolizing, which also
applies to signifying processes in which are implicated the constitution
of the subject, the use of language, the status of objects of desire – the
various overlapping systems of the imaginary, the signifying, the real'
(113). Goux's final sentence points clearly to Lacanian psychoanalysis
and specifically to Lacan's '"*equivalence function of the phallus*"' (Goux
23; quoting Lacan, *Écrits*). Timon's gold stands in for the phallus, but
not only the phallus as absence, castration, or fear of feminine or maternal power. Timon's '"*phallic standard*"' (Goux 23; quoting *Écrits*)
adumbrates a different *sexual* narrative in which the absence of women
is simply that, the absence of women. *Timon*'s world of male/male love
and passionate friendship speaks through Plutarch and the 'wild' figure
of Alcibiades, whose relation with Timon and his phallic, golden gifts
adumbrates another view of Jacobean gift-giving.

WORKS CITED

Bradley, A.C. *Shakespearean Tragedy*. 2nd ed. 1905. London: Macmillan; New
    York: St Martin's, 1966.
Bray, Alan. 'Homosexuality and the Signs of Male Friendship in Elizabethan
    England.' *Queering the Renaissance*. Ed. Jonathan Goldberg. Durham, NC
    and London: Duke UP, 1994. 40–61.

Bullough, Geoffrey. *Narrative and Dramatic Sources of Shakespeare*. Vol. 6. London: Routledge, 1964.

Charney, Maurice, ed. *'Bad' Shakespeare: Revaluations of the Shakespeare Canon*. Rutherford, NJ: Farleigh Dickinson UP; London and Toronto: Associated Univ. Presses, 1988.

– *'Coriolanus* and *Timon of Athens.' Shakespeare: Select Bibliographical Guides*. Ed. Stanley Wells. London: Oxford UP, 1973. 216–38.

– '"Timon of Athens" on Stage and Screen.' *The Tragedy of Titus Andronicus. The Life of Timon of Athens*. Ed. Sylvan Barnet. 1963. New York: New American Library; Markham, ON: Penguin, 1989. 245–53.

Chorost, Michael. 'Biological Finance in Shakespeare's *Timon of Athens.' English Literary Renaissance* 21.3 (1991): 349–70.

Correll, Barbara. 'Easy Come, Easy Go: Capitalism and Castration in *Timon of Athens* and *Old Fortunatus.'* Unpublished essay.

Culler, Jonathan. *The Pursuit of Signs*. Ithaca: Cornell UP, 1981. 135–55.

Ellis-Fermor, Una. '*Timon of Athens*: An Unfinished Play.' *Review of English Studies* 18 (1942): 270–83.

Goldberg, Jonathan. *Sodometries: Renaissance Texts, Modern Sexualities*. Stanford: Stanford UP, 1992.

Goux, Jean-Joseph. *Symbolic Economies: After Marx and Freud*. Trans. Jennifer Curtiss Gage. Ithaca and New York: Cornell UP, 1990.

Green, David C. *Plutarch Revisited: A Study of Shakespeare's Last Roman Tragedies and Their Source*. Salzburg: Universität Salzburg, 1979.

Greenblatt, Stephen. *Shakespearean Negotiations: The Circulation of Social Energy in Renaissance England*. Berkeley and Los Angeles: U of California P, 1988.

Greene, Jody. '"You Must Eat Men": The Sodomitic Economy of Renaissance Patronage.' *GLQ: A Journal of Lesbian and Gay Studies* 1.2 (1994): 163–97.

Guillory, John. *Cultural Capital: The Problem of Literary Canon Formation*. Chicago and London: U of Chicago P, 1993.

Holstun, James. 'Ranting at the New Historicism.' *English Literary Renaissance* 19.2 (1989): 189–225.

Hunt, John Dixon. 'Shakespeare and the Paragone: A Reading of *Timon of Athens.' Images of Shakespeare*. Ed. Werner Habicht, D.J. Palmer, Roger Pringle, and Philip J. Brockbank. Newark: U of Delaware P, 1988. 47–63.

Johnson, Barbara. 'Apostrophe, Animation, and Abortion.' *diacritics* 16.1 (1986): 29–47.

Kahn, Coppélia. '"Magic of Bounty": *Timon of Athens*, Jacobean Patronage, and Maternal Power.' *Shakespeare Quarterly* 38.1 (1987): 34–57.

Kermode, Frank. Introduction. *Timon of Athens. The Riverside Shakespeare*. Ed. G. Blakemore Evans. Boston: Houghton Mifflin, 1974. 1441–4.

Lacan, Jacques. *Écrits*. Paris: Seuil, 1966.

Marlowe, Christopher. *Edward the Second*. Ed. W. Moelwyn Merchant. The New Mermaids. London and Tonbridge: Benn, 1967.

Mellamphy, Ninian. 'Wormwood in the Wood outside Athens: *Timon* and the Problem for the Audience.' *'Bad' Shakespeare*. Ed. Maurice Charney. 166–75.

Michaels, Walter Benn. *The Gold Standard and the Logic of Naturalism*. Berkeley: U of California P, 1987.

Muir, Kenneth. *The Sources of Shakespeare's Plays*. New Haven: Yale UP, 1978.

Oliver, H.J. Introduction. *Timon of Athens*. The Arden Shakespeare. Ed. H.J. Oliver. 1929. London: Methuen, 1959. xiii–lii.

Plutarch. *The Lives of the Noble Grecians & Romans Compared Together by that Grave Learned Philosopher and Historiographer Plutarke of Chaeronea*. Trans. into French by James Amyot and from French into English by Thomas North. 1579; 1603. 5 vols. London: Nonesuch, 1929.

Shakespeare, William. *Timon of Athens*. Ed. H.J. Oliver. The Arden Shakespeare. 1929. London: Methuen, 1959.

Shell, Marc. *Money, Language, and Thought*. Berkeley: U of California P, 1982.

Smith, M.W.A. 'The Authorship of *Timon of Athens*.' *Transactions of the Society for Textual Scholarship* 5 (1991): 195–240.

Spencer, Terence [T.J.B.]. ' "Greeks" and "Merrygreeks": A Background to *Timon of Athens* and *Troilus and Cressida*.' *Essays on Shakespeare and Elizabethan Drama in Honor of Hardin Craig*. Ed. Richard Hosley. Columbia: U of Missouri P, 1962. 223–33.

– 'Shakespeare Learns the Value of Money: The Dramatist at Work on *Timon of Athens*.' *Shakespeare Survey* 6 (1953): 75–8.

– ed. *Shakespeare's Plutarch: The Lives of Julius Caesar, Brutus, Marcus Antonius, and Coriolanus in the Translation of Sir Thomas North*. Harmondsworth, Middlesex: Penguin, 1964.

Spenser, Edmund. *Spenser: Poetical Works*. Ed. J.C. Smith and E. De Selincourt. 1912. London: Oxford UP, 1970.

Zane, Peder J. 'When Scholars Dig Not Only Tassels but Sequins.' *New York Times*. 6 Aug. 1995, late ed., sec. 4: 2+.

PART THREE
RETHINKING SUBJECTIVITY: THE TURN TO
LACAN

6

Historicism and Renaissance Culture

TRACEY SEDINGER

Despite the rhetorical gestures towards Freud and Lacan, most criticism of early modern texts continues to perpetuate the orthodox estimation of psychoanalytic discourse conveyed in Stephen Greenblatt's 'Psychoanalysis and Renaissance Culture.' In his essay, Greenblatt dismisses what he characterizes as 'the totalizing of a universal mythology' in favour of 'repressed histories,' which retain their autonomy from the so-called master narratives (138). In addition, he rejects the application of psychoanalytic theory to early modern texts because psychoanalysis presumes that subjectivity is a proprietary self with a deep interiority. But, as Greenblatt argues, this model is belated and anachronistic in relation to Renaissance discourses on identity, which defined the self by reference to the individual's place within a complex network of social and political relations. In this model, authenticity, determinism by origins, and individuation are the incongruous impositions of a psychoanalysis that is reduced to a depth psychology. To the totalizing lures of a psychoanalytic discourse that bases interpretation on the stable foundation of an essential if alienated self, Greenblatt opposes '*histories* – multiple, complex, refractory stories': 'But if we reject both the totalizing of a universal mythology and the radical particularizing of relativism, what are we left with? We are left with a network of lived and narrated stories, practices, strategies, representations, fantasies, negotiations, and exchanges that, along with the surviving aural, tactile, and visual traces, fashion our experience of the past, of others, and of ourselves' (138). Greenblatt is here concerned with the *limits* of interpretation, with the ways in which early modern texts always elude, in the last instance, and hence reveal the limits of a psychoanalytic approach to interpretation. But rather than limit history by subordinating it to the critic's epistemological endeavour, Greenblatt assumes that history itself is a limit, that is, a limit to the psychoanalytic interpretation that history both invites and frustrates. Psychoanalysis, Greenblatt argues, opposes the complexity of a history that threatens to overwhelm interpretation via its appeals to a stable point of reference, namely, the authentic, albeit alienated, self. Licensing a totalizing interpretation, psychoanalysis demonstrates both epistemological and political bad faith.

Although recent theory and criticism, especially feminist and queer, have turned to psychoanalysis for their articulation of the relation between large-scale ideological state apparatuses and individual bodies and pleasures, the substance of Greenblatt's critique has nevertheless held sway. On one hand, the notes or lists of works cited in recent essays on early modern culture suggest that psychoanalytic methodology, especially the work of Freud and Lacan, has had a significant impact on critical discourse. It has become *de rigueur* to gesture toward the unconscious, desire, and the signifier in discussions of history, gender, and sexuality, perhaps because, as many critics recognize, psychoanalysis 'opens the way to a concept of sexuality and sexual difference which is alive to the body, aware of social relations, but sensitive to the importance of mental activities' (Weeks 128). As the new historicist emphasis on power has given way to a wider deliberation on a feminist and queer micro-politics of the body, Greenblatt's earlier rejection of psychoanalysis has been superseded by its utilization by critics such as Valerie Traub, Barbara Freedman, and Elizabeth Bellamy. On the other hand, Greenblatt's suspicion of psychoanalytic essentialism has left its mark, in that the Freud and Lacan to whom these critics appeal are often rigorously historicized. Valerie Traub, for instance, locates her often trenchant readings of early modern sexualities within the space between Lacan and Foucault so as to escape the 'false dichotomy' set up between the psychic and the material (7). Inspired by Foucault's social constructionism, Traub attempts to correct psychoanalytic essentialism, or the ontology of desire, with a greater emphasis on material practices (8). In a similar move Elizabeth Bellamy, arguing that when psychoanalysis casts the subject as a 'blank spot' political agency becomes unthinkable, concludes: 'The incompatibility that can result from overlapping (and overdetermined) subject-positions *may* or *may not* be present to consciousness at any given moment ... and it is this (real) indeterminacy that serves as the discursive space of a psychoanalytic politics' (36). For Bellamy, this indeterminacy is real because it is material, materiality (the register of political action) again being opposed to signification or representation. Bellamy wants to preserve the possibility of a psychoanalytic politics, but she implicitly assents to recent historicist accusations that psychoanalysis is insufficiently political because it is insufficiently material and overly idealist.

Greenblatt's view that psychoanalysis imposes a normative and historically specific narrative upon forms of experience that elude it remains influential within criticism of Renaissance texts. Despite the various orthopaedic enhancements that would produce a psychoanalytic discourse that is more sensitive to historical and cultural difference, what is produced, beyond a precarious syncretism that often ignores the very real differences between theorists, is the rejection of psychoanalysis in its entirety. I would argue, moreover, that the suspicion of psychoanalysis is a symptom of a larger suspicion of theory in general. Greenblatt reiterates what has, I think, become a founding gesture of the historicism that has come to dominate many critical endeavours, whether they be historical, feminist, or queer: the wholesale rejection of a theory, of which psychoanalysis is perhaps the primary exemplar, which is variously declared to be normative, repressive, totalizing, and universalist. For it is my contention that the new historicism, as a methodology first elaborated in the reading of early modern texts, and practised with great efficacy by critics such as Greenblatt, Louis Adrian Montrose, Leonard Tennenhouse, Jonathan Dollimore, Alan Sinfield, Karen Newman, Jean E. Howard, and others, is part and parcel of the recent resurgence of a historicism underlying many critical orientations that would not label themselves 'new historicist' at all. The term 'historicism' refers to methodological approaches to the acquisition of knowledge that are not necessarily limited to explicitly historical discourse or to the writing of history. The origins of historicism in post-Kantian Germanic historiography point towards its extension as a general philosophy: as an approach to writing the history of political institutions, historicism originated in part in a German nationalist reaction to French Enlightenment conceptions of natural law (see Iggers 7–11).[1] Initially, the relativism of the historicist rejection of inherent value or right was kept in check by faith in a locus of objectivity, including the Christian God and the myth

---

1 According to Iggers, the combination of historicist methodology and the German sacralization of the state proved deadly, since patriotic adherence to the state provided the only coordinates, the only legitimation, for an ethical understanding devoid of natural right. In part, then, Iggers's history of historicism reads like a relentless philosophical march towards the Final Solution.

of the state. Gradually, however, as the human sciences became consolidated in German thought, historicism as a methodology that privileges historical process came to dominate a number of disciplines that were not explicitly historical. Karl Mannheim, proclaiming the intellectual triumph of historicism's general influence on all of the human sciences, wrote in 1924 that 'we have historicism only when history itself is written from the historic *Weltanschauung*' (85). In other words, historicism is an epistemological position, or more properly, an anti-epistemological position, which promotes the thesis that knowledge is totally immanent to a specific sociocultural field or moment, and thus that 'objectivity' or transcendental reason is impossible. As Hilary Putnam suggests, epistemic notions are reducible to non-epistemic ones (290). Richard Rorty defines epistemology as 'the attempt to render all discourses commensurable by translating them into a preferred set of terms ...'; but, as he consistently argues, we can have no knowledge that this preferred vocabulary is not simply the result of historical contingency, that is, the triumph of the victors (349). Historicism, however, is not a scepticism. Scepticism merely encodes within itself the complete and total failure of universal knowledge. The sceptic desires knowledge of the unconditioned, hence unconditional knowledge; but if the acquisition of knowledge fails in some way, then all knowledge becomes impossible (Cavell 4). The historicist position is not that we can know nothing, but that our knowledge is irremediably limited by the empirical location, or the particular socio-historical position of the knower. Historicism rejects the totalizing epistemology of a universal subject, as well as its sceptical negation, in favour of an epistemology limited by circumstance.

Historicism leads to the rejection of epistemology, and therefore of theory, despite the appropriation of much French poststructuralist thought which, while targeting metaphysical presupposition, also resists the empiricism into which, as I will argue, much North American historicist work has fallen. The new historicism distinguishes itself from the old historicism prevalent in literary studies in part by embracing conclusions implicit in much of the poststructuralist theory that descended upon the United States academy after 1964: a greater awareness of how symbolic systems produce the experience of 'reality'; the deconstruction of historical objectivity; a general dismissal of the so-called 'master narratives' by which history is given purpose and meaning. Although the new historicism has been represented primarily as a discourse about power (most famously, about the ways in which power produces and contains subversion), its primary successes have come, I would argue, from its application of these poststructuralist theories to a historically informed criticism of early modern texts. These theories, moreover, are not limited to new historicism: we have witnessed, within a great deal of criticism, the general triumph of historicism, which joins poststructuralist theses to historical and cultural specificity, regardless of the immediate allegiance of the particular approach, be it Marxist, feminist, or queer.

Nevertheless, historicism carries with it, and virtually requires, the repudiation of a theory that it invariably characterizes as metaphysical, universalist, and hence normative. The most recent versions of historicism have mounted a wide-ranging attack upon essentialist conceptions of the subject and subjectivity, in favour of a 'social constructivist' emphasis on historical variation, local knowledge, and differential subject-positions. In the historicist moment, 'man' or the subject is reduced to a fundamentally empirical entity, a product of positive historical and cultural forces. This retreat from essentialism has also resulted in a retreat from 'theory,' in that historicism privileges history as the ground or foundation of all phenomena, including the concepts, methodologies, and theories through which phenomena are comprehended. Thus, objectivity, essence, and reason are all shown by the historicist to be products of a particular socio-historical moment. Historicism's rejection of the master narratives has been influenced by a political obligation to limit the subject of knowledge, whose exercise of a reason defined as primarily instrumental subordinates all phenomena to its own imperatives. The universal subject, the subject that supposedly subtends totalizing 'theory,' is presumed to mask political and cultural domination. The preferred targets have become the Enlightenment and its progeny: natural right, transcendental Reason, the mirror of nature, the universal, man, the subject. In the reaction against a philosophical tradition for which Hegelian self-reflection, which defined the object of knowledge as an Other reflecting the subject back to itself (Gasché 21), constitutes the dominant paradigm, historicism has sought to limit the use of reason, often by suggesting that the subject lay down its weapons and give itself over to the Other. The recent politicization of the academy, under the influence of feminism, anti-racism, queer theory, Marxism, and other forms of materialism, has endowed an abstract anti-Hegelianism with renewed urgency. The Other is no longer simply an object of knowledge; now Others are the victims of racist, sexist, and homophobic political systems that mask their oppressive exploitation through claims to objectivity.

Despite the valuable reincorporation of politics into criticism, as well as the important challenges posed to an essentialism that too often legitimates political conservatism, historicism as currently practised has led to an impasse that, I would argue, threatens the viability of political thought. Following Rorty, most historicists resist attempts to ground their thinking in a theory or epistemology that would be presumed to exist prior to both politics and experience; in fact, the entire notion of ground or foundation has come under attack. But what has replaced this attack upon ground or foundation is the reliance on a self-evident politics, whether liberal-democratic or radical-socialist. Moreover, this politics does not lack epistemological underpinnings, since the justification (if any) that is proffered for the political position adopted often rests on a materialism or empiricism whose implications remain undeveloped. For example, Valerie Wayne writes in her introduction to *The Matter of Difference*, a collection of materialist-feminist essays, that 'the application of materialist feminism to studies of Shakespeare and Renaissance literature at this time also offers a potentially radical alternative to the depoliticising tendencies of some new historicist practice and to the idealised or essentialised effects of some feminist criticism' (11). Despite Wayne's cogent discussion of theoretical trends within Marxism, especially as it has inflected feminist thought, 'materialist feminism' is implicitly defined by two tendencies: the enumeration of subjectivity through subject-positions, and the reading of early modern culture through the empirical facts of material life.

The historicist repudiation of idealization and de-politicization too often results in an empiricism (often labelled 'materialism') that attempts to forestall an undue theoretical reliance on the symbolic or signification. Judith Butler, for example, critiques theory (and psychoanalysis) for exercising an epistemological domination that totalizes and hence violates the others who have become the objects of knowledge. In this case, anti-essentialism translates into anti-foundationalism; for, to establish a foundation is to establish a universal norm, which cannot help but be exclusionary or repressive of a multiplicity of pre-existent stories, subjectivities, and positions. Butler writes: 'It seems that theory posits foundations incessantly, and forms implicit metaphysical commitments as a matter of course, even when it seeks to guard against it; foundations function as the unquestioned and the unquestionable within any theory. And yet, are these "foundations," that is, those premises that function as authorizing grounds, are they themselves not constituted through exclusions that, taken into account, expose the

foundational premise as a contingent and contestable presumption?'
('Contingent Foundations' 7). Butler rejects the kind of scepticism that
asserts the impossibility of knowing, but she also denies the possibility
of a renewed universalism, since such a universal would always remain
exclusionary. Instead, she calls for an incessant positing and calling into
question of foundations, so that any posited universal does not exclude,
and hence inflict violence on, any claims not mandated by the universal.
But both the target of critique and the solution rest on a problematic
understanding of the relation between the subject and the social. In a
discussion of Gayatri Spivak's call for a strategic essentialism, Butler
invokes a kind of nominalism, in which universals are linguistic signs
that nevertheless fail to reflect the empirical particulars whose recovery
has become the task of feminist politics: 'She [Spivak] knows that the
category of "women" is not fully expressive, that the multiplicity and
discontinuity of the referent mocks and rebels against the univocity of
the sign, but suggests it could be used for strategic purposes' ('Performative Acts' 280). Although Butler has repeatedly been charged with
linguistic idealism, she here employs a linguistic theory of reference that
assumes too readily that there is a strict correlation between the terms
'universal,' 'necessary,' and 'substantial.' In other words, her critique
of theory rests on the equation of the (universal) concept with the
(universal) essence, which reinforces an identity between the subject
and the social, an identity that promotes the intelligibility of social space
to the subject. But the subject cannot retain this essentially positive and
productive relation to reality, since that relation once again raises the
spectre of a self-reflective epistemology that transforms the Other into
the mirror of the self. Butler converts the intelligibility of the social
into an excess of intelligibility, an excess of sense, as if social space
were constituted by a plurality of signifiers that escape the subject's
normative epistemology. To the subject's construction and imposition
of a universal – the rationality of reality – she opposes a reality that
exceeds reason. Ultimately Butler's historicism remains, in a sense, *too*
referential.

Historicism seems inextricably caught up with an empiricism with
which it attempts to forestall the totalizing theory that it opposes. Both
Greenblatt's anti-essentialism and Butler's anti-foundationalism are
open to the charge of promoting naïve empiricist claims for the particular. In the final analysis, they insist on the priority (and the purity)
of facts over theory: the particular, or the local, is assumed to exist 'out
there,' anterior to and subversive of a totalizing theory or a substantive

universal. For example, in a critique of Lyotard's inappropriate attention to epistemological concerns of 'proof,' Greenblatt identifies 'history' as ontologically and temporally prior to 'theory': 'The Faurisson affair is at bottom not an epistemological dilemma, as Lyotard claims, but an attempt to wish away evidence that is both substantial and verifiable. The issue is not an Epicurean paradox ... but a historical problem' ('Towards a Poetics of Culture' 4). In the end, Greenblatt rejects History, the master narrative that literally masters the other, in favour of 'histories – multiple, complex, refractory stories' that form networks that 'fashion our experience of the past, of others, and of ourselves' ('Psychoanalysis' 138). Despite the new historicism's initial and fruitful unsettling of our understanding of the relations between text and context, individual and society, and politics and aesthetics, the questions it has raised have been sidelined in favour of a renewed empiricism, located in either the subject or object of knowledge, in order to correct the new historicism's deficiencies. In order to ground its readings, historicism has resulted in two instances of empiricism: an empiricism of the subject-position, which often conflates social structure with individual experience; or an empiricism of the object – the historical fact. In a cogent overview of new historicism, for example, Jean Howard calls for greater contextualization of the 'literary' within networks of power relations. But she concludes by urging that 'the historically-minded critic must increasingly be willing to acknowledge the non-objectivity of his or her own stance and the inevitably political nature of interpretive and even descriptive acts' (43). Critics following Howard's lead have attempted to extend new historicism's concern with power as it inflected early modern culture beyond the somewhat simplistic subversion/containment model. In so doing, early modern subjectivity, and the critical subject producing knowledge, have been reconceived, along the lines suggested by Teresa de Lauretis (2), as the product of positions defined by the axes of race, class, and gender. The trick has now become to read the subject correctly, through a process whose interminability is marked by the 'etc.' that usually follows these formulations. In this model, historicist criticism has often taken the form of unmasking another critic's indifference to difference, especially differences of race, class, and gender. In contrast with the dispersal of the subject along primarily empirical concentrations of power, the new historicism has also produced a criticism dedicated to the empirical fact, whose very facticity provides resistance to the critic's synthesizing powers. Once again, the critic's role in the construction of empirical fact is denied in favour of faith in the inherent intelligibility and significance of historical fact. In either case, criticism suffers from too much or too little politics.

A final example of historicist criticism will illustrate the link between empiricism and 'immanentism,' and the loss of the possibility of critique that the latter promotes. Neo-pragmatism attempts to escape the theoretical critique of historicism by defining knowledge as a belief produced through practice. Pragmatism takes practice, as opposed to theory, as the guide or foundation for its conclusions. It posits an epistemological position immanent to the field of knowledge, resulting in the collapse of the distinction between empirical and theoretical knowledge. For example, Steven Knapp and Walter Benn Michaels argue the neo-pragmatist case *vis-à-vis* literary interpretation, and in the process deny that there is a metalanguage or a discourse by means of which one can adjudicate opposing claims to speak the truth. To de Manian theory, which locates an internal limit to any interpretation within the rhetorical register of language, Knapp and Michaels oppose the pragmatic fact that interpretative practice inescapably presumes authorial intention: theory becomes impossible, since the attempt to theorize commits us to the futile project of attempting to discover objective knowledge about that of which we can only have belief (24–30). Knapp and Michaels bolster their premise by appealing to a thought experiment, in which a poem by Wordsworth mysteriously appears written on the sand. Even though the poem's author is unknown, the reader must necessarily posit an intentional author; only if one treats the poem as mere marks on the sand (or pure signifiers), which only accidentally resemble language, can one imagine that it is authorless. Knapp and Michaels conclude that the attribution of intentionality is empirical, not theoretical, for as soon as one experiences diacritical marks as meaningful, one assumes intentionality, that is, the intentionality of a particular individual. Meaning *just is* intentionality.

In a sense, Knapp and Michaels are correct when they argue that meaningful statements (meaningful beyond simple diacritical marks) involve attributions of intentionality; they err, however, in suggesting that intentionality is necessarily located in an empirical author. The author is not necessarily empirical, although the reader tends to locate what Foucault called the '"author-function"' (125) in empirical persons. That the search for the author-function is different from that for the empirical author is demonstrated by those cases in which we attribute intentionality, but in which the author becomes corporate or multiple, such as, for example, occurs in the cinema, where the author-function involves producers, directors, screenwriters, and cinematographers. Attributions of authorship are structural rather than empirical, although Knapp and Michaels's commitment to the identity of knowledge and belief would guard against such a conclusion. Since an individual act of reading presumes that the Other is the source of meaning, the Other, who in this case is the author, must be the source of that meaning. What Knapp and Michaels call intentionality is what psychoanalysis calls transference: the attribution of knowledge to a subject (what Lacan calls the subject supposed to know) who is supposed to have access to and control over signification. In this context, therefore, Knapp and Michaels repeat the historicist tendency to locate meaning externally to the subject attempting to know – in the Other – as if a single Other or a whole collection of Others were the source of an intelligibility whose realization becomes the subject's duty.

In denying theory and upholding empiricism, Knapp and Michaels deny the possibility of any transcendence from one's particular empirical location. They then flag this impossibility with a rhetorical appeal to identity that 'just is.' In effect, it would be impossible for Knapp and Michaels to demonstrate this identity, since to do so would require taking seriously the possibility that meaning and intentionality are different. Their historicism thus generates a fundamental problem that remains unsolved, and that is irresolvable from within the historicist domain: if one is locked into one's particular socio-historical moment, then how can one know that this is a relative, contingent position rather than a universalist position? In other words, the historicist judgment rests parasitically on an absolutist claim that it disavows; it implies a split, or an internal distance from one's culture, the possibility of which it then denies. The historicisms that prevail within the academy attempt to limit the knowing subject's exercise of instrumental reason, so as to escape the lures of a totalizing knowledge that would subordinate all phenomena to itself. This limitation is empirical: subjects are conceived of as the products of a particular socio-historical moment, and epistemological claims regarding truth are reduced to the product of power relations or ideology. At the same time, most historicists reject the relativism that logically follows. They retain some form of political project that refuses relativism; yet the historicist methodology cannot articulate the epistemology that founds this position, since epistemological claims about the social are conceived of as products of the social. Historicism is therefore left with no ground or foundation for its ethical and political claims. Although the resurgence of most recent forms of historicism has been accompanied by rousing calls to political action, historicism leads, I would argue, to the demise of critique, and hence to the impossibility of politics.

II

Despite the often rigorous critique mounted by historicists against essentialism, their epistemological categories remain influenced by many essentialist assumptions. First and foremost is the assumption that the relation between the subject and the social is essentially *positive*: that the subject is a product, whether of biological essence or of social forces, and that the subject's knowledge of these relations is hence positive. But as Joan Copjec has repeatedly demonstrated, the problem that afflicts the notion of the subject as it relates to the social is the conflation of *production* with *realization*, whereby the subject fulfils social imperatives ('Cutting Up' 237–42). Psychoanalysis differs from sociology (a term with which I designate attempts to cast the subject as merely the product of social construction) in that it recognizes forces that interfere with the seamless union of the subject and the social. Something, namely the unconscious, gets in the way of this process. The term that Freud gave to his chief discovery, the *un*conscious, should alert us to the epistemological problems introduced by the negation of consciousness. The term 'unconscious' has both a descriptive and a systematic application: it describes those thoughts that are 'unconscious' but capable of becoming conscious, as well as those representations that remain repressed. More important, and more problematically, the unconscious denotes a register of experience not located in the empirical world, and that nevertheless is not pure 'fiction.' Within the psychoanalytic field, the unconscious does not lead to a rank subjectivism. As Laplanche and Pontalis point out, this very difficulty with the unconscious led Freud to 'lose' the concept repeatedly: 'There are therefore three kinds of phenomena (or of realities, in the widest sense of the word): material reality, the reality of intermediate thoughts or of the psychological field, and the reality of unconscious wishes and their "truest shape": fantasy. If Freud, again and again, finds and then loses the notion of psychical reality, this is not due to any inadequacy of his conceptual apparatus: the difficulty and ambiguity lie in the very nature of its relationship, to the real and to the imaginary, as is shown in the central domain of fantasy' (8). Laplanche and Pontalis go on to demonstrate that the necessity of grounding psychical reality, of articulating it as a structure, led to

Freud's scientistic search for origins, whether those origins might lie in the species' phylogeny or in primal myth.

Knowledge of the unconscious cannot therefore be measured according to standard criteria of empirical proof, meaning that unconscious representations cannot be assumed to be impressions or traces of real events. Critics of Freud, such as Jeffrey Masson, have read Freud's rejection of the seduction hypothesis, which holds that neurosis is caused by a real event that the patient remembers and that can be corroborated by other forms of proof, as a result of Freud's investment in the patriarchal family. In other words, psychoanalytic truth is reduced to the warped product of its founder's ideological biases (Masson, passim). But Masson remains imprisoned within philosophical categories of 'real event' versus 'unreal fantasy,' categories that psychoanalysis challenges. Freud's adoption of Oedipus was not dependent upon the rejection of 'real' (that is, empirically verifiable) incidents of childhood sexual abuse, for he recognized throughout his career that such abuse (or 'seductions' as they were then termed) did occur. The discovery that laid the foundation for psychoanalysis was prompted by Freud's realization that individuals are miserable even when no empirically verifiable traumatic event can be isolated; they are miserable in addition to, and even in spite of, real traumas (Rose, 'Feminism and the Psychic' 12–14; 'Where Does the Misery Come From?' 89–98). Despite this recognition, Freud always insisted that psychoanalysis was a science, not a mythology. In 'The Unconscious,' Freud attempts to prove that the unconscious exists and that it affects mental functioning; he does so by appealing to standard scientific procedures, including the citation of manifold proofs of its existence (116–17). Implicitly, knowledge of the unconscious is an issue both for the analysand, for whom a recognition of unconscious processes is necessary for a successful analysis, as well as for the analyst, who must incorporate the disruptive effects of the unconscious into a scientific apparatus. Contrary to irrationalist appropriations of psychoanalysis, Freud asserts the scientific character of psychoanalysis against what he designates intellectual anarchism or relativism, which denies the possibility of truth (see 'Question of a *Weltanschauung*' 155).

The essence of Freud's discovery, which is irreducible to psychoanalysis, lies in the articulation of a field that escapes both biologism and sociologism. But as its history demonstrates, psychoanalysis is constantly in danger of collapse into either position. Given the recent resurgence of historicist opposition to essentialism, of which biologism is the most noteworthy example, the current danger lies in the assimilation of psychoanalysis to social constructionism. The tendency to collapse psychoanalysis into sociology is evident even within Louis Althusser's readings of Lacan, who has been especially influential on recent Anglo-American appropriations of psychoanalysis. Lacan's challenge to Anglo-American ego-psychology, with its emphasis on normality and 'adjustment,' as well as his rigorous reformulation of Freudian discoveries of signifying systems, renders Lacanian psychoanalysis, Althusser believed, potentially harmonious with French Marxism, which was deeply suspicious of the bourgeois prejudices of traditional psychoanalysis. Althusser was especially attracted to the Lacanian concept of the Imaginary (one of the triad including the Symbolic and Real), which provides, as he argued, a means of rethinking the misrecognitions that consolidate the subject's relation, as formulated by ideology, to real conditions of existence ('Freud and Lacan' 219). Althusser recast the Lacanian subject, which for Lacan is always a subject *of the unconscious*, as the product of interpellation: a hailing (literally, a 'Hey you!') of the individual by the symbolic order, and the subsequent transformation of that individual into a subject, who of course accepts that she is the one hailed ('Ideology and Ideological State Apparatuses' 170–7). Lacanian psychoanalysis posits a subject that is radically decentred, whose lack (imaged as castration) marks it as having no content, no essence, no nature. Essentialism, or the belief that the subject has a pre-existent content (a 'being' or 'nature') that destines it for certain social roles or mandates, becomes the ideological strategy *par excellence*, since the subject's acquiescence to the process of interpellation hinges on the (mis)recognition that it was in her nature to be thus hailed. But the subject, as an effect of language, is cut off from what we might designate as being or nature. In order to assent (retroactively) to interpellation, the subject experiences a series of identifications, imaginary and symbolic, that allow her to assume certain mandates of the symbolic order, and that then endow the subject with a content.

Althusser, however, assumes that the process of interpellation is always successful. For Althusser, exploiting the double meaning inherent in the term *subject*, elides the grammatical subject with the political one, who is subjected to large-scale political and governmental institutions. In this way, the subject of the unconscious is both politicized and given positive content. It becomes the product of subjection to ideo-logical apparatuses rather than the limit upon which these apparatuses stumble. As Slavoj Žižek has pointed out, psychoanalysis rests on the thesis that the process of interpellation always fails, to a greater or lesser degree, since the hailing of the individual by the symbolic order is unmotivated by any pre-existing content supposedly belonging to or constituting the subject (*The Sublime Object of Ideology* 110–17). The man-date, position, or role conferred upon the individual by the symbolic order has no reference to the individual's essence or capacity, although the subject later accepts that something in her nature has caused her to be interpellated thus. The slippage between the unmotivated nature of interpellation and the ideological fiction of essentialism opens the space for doubt, that is, for the posing of the subject's hysterical question to the Other: 'Why are you saying what you're saying I am?' By reason of this slippage Moustafa Safouan characterizes the primary relation between the subject and the social, which returns to the subject the image of a being that is permanently placed off-limits, as a question or interrogation: 'once caught in the web of language, the relationship between the organism and its environment is transfigured into the re-lationship between the speaking subject and what is called his being; which being is not presented to him in the constitutive images of his *Umwelt* or even in his own image. In other words, there is nothing trans-parent to him about this being; as a result, the relationship between the subject and being is an interrogation' (275). The Foucaultian emphasis on subject-positions, a concept designed to capture the various modes by which the individual is traversed and positioned by an almost limitless series of discursive formations (sex, race, class, sexual orientation), hides the fundamental rupture between the subject and the social. It is only because subjectivity, which the historicist problematically theorizes as the product of a variety of subject-positions (one notes the exhausted 'etceteras' following the familiar litany of race, sex, and class), is not totalizable, that psychoanalysis speaks of an unconscious that skews the fullness or plenitude conferred by the sum total of one's subject positions. Contrary to recent new historicist work on subjectivity, the subject is not the product of interpellation; the subject is occasioned by the *failure* of interpellation.

Freud's discovery of a subject of the unconscious puts into question the positive relation between subject and social, subject and object, that underwrites recent historicisms, and necessitates a rethinking of representation. That his discovery of the unconscious warps a positivist epistemology in which representations correspond to external objects became increasingly evident to Freud, who nevertheless tried to adhere to a correspondence theory of truth. In his essay 'Negation,' Freud elaborates on the negative relation between knowledge and the perception of reality. He begins by noting that, paradoxically, repression is not necessarily an unconscious process, if we equate the latter with ignorance. A repressed representation can actually become conscious and remain repressed so long as it is negated. Freud goes on to generalize the function of negation as the prototypical judgment, itself the most fundamental intellectual activity. Judgment has two forms: judgments of attribute and judgments of existence. Judgments of attribute are ultimately based on the primordial activity of introjection and ejection: what is good is incorporated, and what is bad is ejected. But judgments of attribute, dependent as they are on the distinction between internal and external, are themselves based on the prior judgment of existence.[2] Freud defines this judgment as 'a question ... of whether something which is present in the ego as an image can also be re-discovered in perception (that is, in reality)' ('Negation' 183). Freud's strange parenthetical equation of reality with perception should alert us to the difficulties that follow. The question will become: what is the ontological and epistemological status of the rediscovered object? Initially, judgments of attribute are aligned with judgments of existence: what is internal is subjective and unreal; what is external is objective and real. But this distinction is pre-psychoanalytic, for it neglects Freud's greatest innovation, the introduction of psychical reality, a register of experience that is not reducible to the subjective or objective. In fact, psychical 'reality' introduces a profound disjunction between the objective and subjective, which calls into question the validity of perception as a guide to reality, and an epistemology (empiricism) that assumes the integrity and accessibility of the object.

Freud must therefore complicate the relation of judgment to 'reality,' as well as the relation of one type of judgment to the other. 'Experience,' he writes, 'has taught that it is important not only whether a thing (an object from which satisfaction is sought) possesses the 'good' property, that is, whether it deserves to be taken into the ego, but also whether

2 Martin Thom suggests that this priority becomes significant only after castration / primal repression: prior to this point, when the distinction between interior and exterior is hypothetically non-existent, judgments of attribute assume sole importance (169–70).

it is there in the external world, ready to be seized when it is wanted'
('Negation' 183–4). Freud here introduces a disjunction between the
two types of judgment, signalled by his use of 'but.' Despite the logical
priority of the judgment of existence, the judgment of attribute may,
in a sense, 'trick' the subject, for the rush to enjoy the object may take
precedence over the necessity of locating the object in reality. Freud suggests that this occurs as a result of 'the faculty which thought possesses
for reviving a thing that has once been perceived, by reproducing it as
an image, without its being necessary for the external object still to be
present' (184). Surprisingly, the capacity to hallucinate the object of satisfaction creates the disjunction between interior and exterior, subjective
and objective, even as it disrupts these distinctions by provoking the
subject's suspicion that the object of perception is in fact a hallucination.
Freud posits a primordial object that pre-exists the subject's own coming
into existence, and that pre-exists the categories into which experience is
divided. For Freud, intellectual judgment, or the ability to negate, arises
in relation to a disjunction between perceptible reality and the object
of desire: 'Thus the first and immediate aim of the process of testing
reality is not to discover an object in real perception corresponding to
what is imagined, but to *re-discover* such an object, to convince oneself
that it is still there' ('Negation' 184). Negation is the originary judgment
because the process of rediscovering lost objects requires that the object
be lost or negated. As Žižek writes, 'In a sense, we could say that "absolute knowledge" implies the recognition of an absolute, insurmountable
impossibility: the impossibility of accordance between knowledge and
being ... we could say that no object is ever "true", ever fully "becomes
what it effectively is". *This discord is a positive condition of the object's
ontological consistency ...*' (*For They Know Not What They Do* 68). In Freud's
best-known example of negation, the object to be negated takes positive
form as the mother. In *Beyond the Pleasure Principle*, the *fort/da* game that
the child plays to master his mother's absence results in the mother's
ejection in her singularity, and her elevation to the status of a universal.
Although this process nullifies the mother, in a sense, it also endows her
with a stability that subtends and survives her contingent comings and
goings (Thom 170–2). The subject's desire for what has been lost always
exceeds the representation of objects, thus leading to the capacity for
judgment. Knowledge is enabled rather than disabled by the loss of the
object.

The subject of psychoanalysis is a limited subject, not through its
placement within a positive and particular socio-historical moment, but

through the loss of a primordial object that creates the locus of the unconscious. But unlike the historicist's subject of knowledge, for whom the limit is prohibitive, the psychoanalytic limit is productive; knowledge is possible only because the process of subjectivation or interpellation has produced a permanent alienation or splitting, thereby putting into question the relation between the subject and the social. This splitting is defined as, above all, a split between the subject and the object. But the object is not an empirical object; rather, it is the object that had to be rejected, even abjected, for the subject to constitute itself within the symbolic order. For this reason, Lacan reclaims the Cartesian *cogito* as the philosophical turn necessary for the psychoanalytic subject. After experiencing radical (and hysterical) doubt, Descartes reformulated the *cogito* as a determinate void in the symbolic order, which then served as the ground for the set of qualities or attributes imputed to the subject (Copjec, 'The *Unvermögender* Other' 31). But Lacan also introduces an important caveat: the *cogito* does not imply the immediacy of thinking and being, of knowledge and reality, but rather their disjunction, their necessary separation (*Four Fundamental Concepts of Psycho-Analysis* 36). The psychoanalytic subject is beyond representation, not because it denotes a depth or meaning that eludes representation, but because it marks a redoubled failure of representation. Representation tempts us to a beyond, a behind-the-veil to which it can only gesture; for, as Lacan suggests, there is really nothing beyond. The trick lies not in what cannot be represented, but in the very impression that there is something, a thing-in-itself, that lies behind and beyond the representation (*Four Fundamental Concepts* 103; 111–12).

Psychoanalysis introduces a disjunction between representation and the object, which nevertheless remain mutually implicated. Psychoanalysis therefore denies a theory of truth that would seek to ground truth by reference to an empirical real. The object is not the Other, the socio-symbolic order of representations, concepts, and universals; nor does the Other possess the object. As a consequence of the mutual exclusion of Other and object, meaning and enjoyment, Lacan strenuously resists ego-psychology's promotion of the analysand's identification with the analyst, since what that identification accomplishes is the mapping of the subject's enjoyment onto the meaning(s) proffered by the analyst. In other words, the subject strives to enjoy according to the analyst's strictures, and analysis becomes a sociology of adjustment. In opposition to this, Lacan proposes as the end point of analysis the disjunction of the object from the Other, the analyst, the subject presumed to know, with the result that the subject comes to realize the split between knowledge (Other) and being (object) (*Four Fundamental Concepts* 272–6). What ends an analysis is an impasse, the point at which antagonism between analyst and analysand is suddenly revealed (Miller 1–2). Analysis demonstrates that the relation between the subject and the social, as presented in the relation between the analysand and the analyst, is essentially negative. Historicism, on the other hand, locates the object in the Other, restoring the Other as the positive source of meaning, which we become ethically obligated to read correctly. Greenblatt's infamous and much contested subversion/containment model of early modern political relations reveals historicism's inner logic, for what is the recuperation of subversion if not the restoration of the Other? On a political level, Greenblatt enforces transference, the same transference that Knapp and Michaels practise in 'Against Theory.' For historicism, the Other has all the answers, which leads to its increasingly problematic empiricism.

Psychoanalysis, as practice and as theory, insistently asks what type of knowledge is possible once the failure of representation has been recognized. The subject of the unconscious disrupts the network of signifiers; historicism, which is the preferred methodology of the human sciences, attempts to suture that gap, to fill in the causes, and hence to produce a totalized and totalizing human subject.[3] Like historicism, psychoanalysis, as a science of failure or lack, challenges essentialism and a reference theory of truth, without falling into the trap of a nascent

---

3 Freud thus relied on the admittedly undeveloped notion of the disposition in order not to delineate an uninterrupted chain of cause and effect. For Freud, the psychic disposition determines the effects of the sociological identification, rather than the identification determining the disposition of the psychical. Disposition marks that which is not assignable to nature or culture. Judith Butler argues that the disposition is the trace of socially determined sexual prohibitions, ideologically disguised as evidence of a natural urge (*Gender Trouble* 60–5). I would argue that the disposition manifests Freud's attempt to preserve the specificity of the psychoanalytic field, by not reducing the subject of a case study to the effect of biological tendencies or social events. The function of the 'disposition' or 'constitution' is to mark a limit to Freud's explanatory procedures; he has recourse to the concept of 'disposition' when he wishes to mark a cause that is not reducible to either sociology or biology. In other words, Freud resists an interpretation that would produce a continuous or interminable series of causes, because to do so would reduce the case history to an exercise in sociology, and relegate the unconscious to the product of external forces, whether biological or sociological. It appears that psychoanalysis inscribes this limit within its own practice via its utilization of the concept of 'disposition.'

empiricism, by rethinking the relation between knowledge and being, between theory and the limits of knowledge. Lacan opens *Television*, originally broadcast as an interview on French television in 1973, by citing the impossibility of truth: 'I always speak the truth. Not the whole truth, because there's no way, to say it all. Saying it all is literally impossible: words fail. Yet it's through this very impossibility that the truth holds onto the real' (3). Like historicism, psychoanalysis denies the validity of universalist theory, but the Lacanian claim resists reduction to relativism because it does not, conversely, conceive of truth as immanent within discourse. The unconscious escapes symbolization and resists scientific formalization, but its symptoms continue to deform or limit knowledge. The subject of psychoanalysis marks a limit to our ability to enumerate the causes of behaviour, whether sociological or biological, at the same time making knowledge possible, since all knowledge is predicated upon its lack. This lack marks not only our knowledge *of the* subject, but our knowledge *as* subjects: the unconscious marks an internal limit to our attempts to theorize the subject and subjectivity.

Rethinking subjectivity in relation to the social field, both as it is thematized within early modern texts and as it operates within criticism itself, remains one of our most important tasks. Doing so according to a psychoanalytic paradigm will not undermine political criticism, but may, in fact, provide its necessary foundation. By overly stressing the embeddedness of the subject within the social, recent political criticism has left itself with no clear method to distinguish between competing political claims, even within anti-sexist and anti-racist movements. A self-evident politics has filled the gap, but we have been left with no justification for why specific political positions should be adopted. This has led to a problematic split, in which other critics are subject to critique based on their subjectivist biases, while an implicit objectivity is claimed for the critic conducting the critique. The most epigrammatic historicist claim, namely, that 'the personal is the political,' was necessary for various identity-politics movements to surmount the traditionally liberal private/public split; it was crucial in determining that there was indeed a sexual politics, a micro-politics of the body profoundly influenced by and implicated within large-scale ideological apparatuses. But we have been left with no limit, internal or external, to the political, no space to reflect upon the specific forms that resistance should take. The response has been either too much or too little politics. Recognizing the disjunction between the subject and the social preserves the space for critique and theoretical reflection that is necessary for any politics.

WORKS CITED

Althusser, Louis. 'Freud and Lacan.' *Lenin and Philosophy and Other Essays.*
Trans. Ben Brewster. New York: Monthly Review P, 1971. 189–219.
– 'Ideology and Ideological State Apparatuses (Notes towards an
Investigation).' *Lenin and Philosophy.* 127–86.
Bellamy, Elizabeth J. 'Discourses of Impossibility: Can Psychoanalysis be
Political?' *diacritics* 23.1 (1993): 24–38.
Butler, Judith. 'Contingent Foundations: Feminism and the Question of
"Postmodernism."' *Feminists Theorize the Political.* Ed. Judith Butler and Joan
W. Scott. New York and London: Routledge, 1992. 3–21.
– *Gender Trouble: Feminism and the Subversion of Identity.* New York and London:
Routledge, 1990.
– 'Performative Acts and Gender Constitution: An Essay in Phenomenology
and Feminist Theory.' *Performing Feminisms: Feminist Critical Theory and
Theatre.* Ed. Sue-Ellen Case. Baltimore and London: Johns Hopkins UP,
1990. 270–82.
Cavell, Stanley. *Disowning Knowledge in Six Plays of Shakespeare.* Cambridge:
Cambridge UP, 1987.
Copjec, Joan. 'Cutting Up.' *Between Feminism and Psychoanalysis.* Ed. Teresa
Brennan. New York and London: Routledge, 1989. 227–46.
– 'The *Unvermögender* Other: Hysteria and Democracy in America.' *New
Formations* 14 (1991): 27–41.
Foucault, Michel. *Language, Counter-Memory, Practice: Selected Essays and
Interviews.* Ed. Donald F. Bouchard. Trans. Donald F. Bouchard and Sherry
Simon. Ithaca: Cornell UP, 1977.
Freud, Sigmund. 'Negation.' *Collected Papers.* Ed. [and trans.] James Strachey. 5
vols. London, 1957, 5: 181–5.
– 'The Question of a *Weltanschauung.*' *New Introductory Lectures on
Psychoanalysis.* Ed. and trans. James Strachey. 1933. Rev. ed. New York:
Norton, 1965. 158–82.
– 'The Unconscious.' *General Psychological Theory.* Ed. Philip Rieff. New York:
Macmillan, 1963. 116–50.
Gasché, Rodolphe. *The Tain of the Mirror: Derrida and the Philosophy of Reflection.*
Cambridge, MA: Harvard UP, 1986.
Greenblatt, Stephen. 'Psychoanalysis and Renaissance Culture.' *Learning to
Curse: Essays in Early Modern Culture.* New York and London: Routledge,
1990. 131–45.
– 'Towards a Poetics of Culture.' *The New Historicism.* Ed. H. Aram Veeser.
New York and London: Routledge, 1989. 1–14.

Howard, Jean E. 'The New Historicism in Renaissance Studies.' *English Literary Renaissance* 16.1 (1986): 13–43.

Iggers, Georg G. *The German Conception of History: The National Tradition of Historical Thought from Herder to the Present.* Rev. ed. Middletown, CT: Wesleyan UP, 1983.

Knapp, Steven, and Walter Benn Michaels. 'Against Theory.' *Against Theory: Literary Studies and the New Pragmatism.* Ed. W.J.T. Mitchell. Chicago and London: U of Chicago P, 1985. 11–30.

Lacan, Jacques. *The Four Fundamental Concepts of Psycho-Analysis.* Ed. Jacques-Alain Miller. Trans. Alan Sheridan. New York: Norton, 1977.

– *Television.* Ed. Joan Copjec. Trans. Denis Hollier, Rosalind Krauss, and Annette Michelson. New York and London: Norton, 1990.

Laplanche, Jean, and Jean-Bertrand Pontalis. 'Fantasy and the Origins of Sexuality.' *Formations of Fantasy.* Ed. Victor Burgin, James Donald, and Cora Kaplan. New York and London: Routledge, 1989. 5–33.

Lauretis, Teresa de. 'The Technology of Gender.' *Technologies of Gender: Essays on Theory, Film, and Fiction.* Bloomington: Indiana UP, 1987. 1–30.

Mannheim, Karl. 'Historicism.' *Essays on the Sociology of Knowledge.* London: Routledge & Kegan Paul, 1952. 84–133.

Masson, Jeffrey Moussaieff. *The Assault on Truth: Freud's Suppression of the Seduction Theory.* New York: Farrar, Straus and Giroux, 1984.

Miller, Jacques-Alain. 'Another Lacan.' Trans. Ralph Chipman. *Lacan Study Notes* 1 (1984): 1–3.

Putnam, Hilary. 'Beyond Historicism.' *Realism and Reason: Philosophical Papers.* Vol. 3. Cambridge: Cambridge UP, 1983. 287–303.

Rorty, Richard. *Philosophy and the Mirror of Nature.* Princeton: Princeton UP, 1979.

Rose, Jacqueline. 'Feminism and the Psychic.' *Sexuality in the Field of Vision.* London and New York: Verso, 1986. 1–23.

– '"Where Does the Misery Come From?" Psychoanalysis, Feminism, and the Event.' *Why War? – Psychoanalysis, Politics, and the Return to Melanie Klein.* Oxford: Basil Blackwell, 1993. 89–109.

Safouan, Moustafa. 'Is the Oedipus Complex Universal?' *The Woman in Question.* Ed. Parveen Adams and Elizabeth Cowie. Cambridge, MA: MIT Press, 1990. 274–82.

Thom, Martin. '*Verneinung, Verwerfung, Ausstossung*: A Problem in the Interpretation of Freud.' *The Talking Cure: Essays in Psychoanalysis and Language.* Ed. Colin MacCabe. London: Macmillan; New York: St. Martin's, 1981. 162–87.

Traub, Valerie. *Desire and Anxiety: Circulations of Sexuality in Shakespearean Drama.* New York and London: Routledge, 1992.

Wayne, Valerie. Introduction. *The Matter of Difference: Materialist Feminist Criticism of Shakespeare*. Ed. Valerie Wayne. Ithaca: Cornell UP, 1991. 1–26.

Weeks, Jeffrey. *Sexuality and Its Discontents: Meanings, Myths, and Modern Sexualities*. London, Melbourne, and Henley: Routledge & Kegan Paul, 1985.

Žižek, Slavoj. *For They Know Not What They Do: Enjoyment as a Political Factor*. London and New York: Verso, 1991.

– *The Sublime Object of Ideology*. London and New York: Verso, 1989.

7

Donne's Odious Comparison: Abjection, Text, and Canon

NATE JOHNSON

When thy *Loose* raptures, *Donne*, shall meet with Those
That doe confine
Tuning, unto the Duller line,
And sing not, but in *Sanctified Prose*;
How will they, with sharper eyes,
The *Fore-skinne* of thy phansie circumcise?
And feare, thy *wantonnesse* should now, begin
Example, that hath ceased to be *Sin*?

And that *Feare* fannes their *Heat*; whilst knowing eyes
Will not admire
At this *Strange Fire*,
That here is *mingled with thy Sacrifice.*

Thomas Browne (1633)

This was for youth, Strength, Mirth, and wit that Time
Most count their golden Age; but 't was not thine.
Thine was thy later yeares, so much refind
From youths Drosse, Mirth, & wit; as thy pure mind
Thought (like the Angels) nothing but the Praise
Of thy Creator, in those last, best Dayes.

Izaak Walton (1635)

I am indebted to the participants in the 1991 seminar held at Cornell, 'Conduct, Identity and Discovery,' for ideas and encouragement in the early stages of this project, and in particular to Barbara Correll. The panel on 'Defamiliarizing the 17th-Century Canon' held at the 1993 MLA convention in Toronto was also useful in helping me refocus and re-articulate some of the main ideas.

Walton's revisionary epigraph to the second edition of Donne's *Poems* appears almost as if in reply to Thomas Browne's question in the first. Browne's verse, dedicated 'To the deceased Author, Upon the *Promiscuous* printing of his Poems, the *Looser sort*, with the *Religious*' (376), quickly fell victim to the sort of editorial circumcision it prophesied, replaced in 1635 by Walton's pious defence. Since the 1635 edition, editors have generally arranged Donne's poems to fit Walton's chronology – profane poems first, religious ones last.[1] The printer of the first edition,[2] however, called the book 'A Peece which who so takes not as he findes it, in what manner soever, he is unworthy of it, sith a scattered limbe of this Author, hath more amiablenesse in it, in the eye of a discerner, then a whole body of some other' (sig. A1^v).

Unlike the 'self-crowned laureates' of Richard Helgerson's influential study, Donne has been 'crowned' – given his literary authority – primarily by others. The printer's dedication to the 1633 edition presents not Donne's 'whole body,' or unified literary 'I,' but instead, a miscellany of 'scattered limbe[s],' or what Lacan might call a 'fragmented body' (4) that has yet to construct a serviceable fiction of identity. One of the primary effects of more than three hundred years of Donne criticism has been to extract from a formally and substantively heterogeneous collection of verse, attested by an even more heterogeneous 'body' of widely circulated, divergent, often questionably attributed manuscript and print versions, the unifying principle of 'John Donne.' Donne experiences the mirror stage, but posthumously, as the scattered limbs of the early manuscript and print versions eventually evolve into (or are deposited within?) Cleanth Brooks's 'well-wrought urn.' In the ordered schema that emerges, 'The Canonization' becomes a synecdoche not only for Donne's ultimate coherence and poetic mastery, but also for the principle of literary canonicity itself.

Influenced in part by the contextualizing impulse of the new historicism, some Donne scholars, most notably Arthur Marotti, have been re-emphasizing the social and material processes of transmission and

---

1 Although this practice has retained the status of received wisdom (see, for example, R.G. Cox's essay in *The New Pelican Guide to English Literature*), Annabel Patterson and Richard Strier have mounted what seem to me successful challenges. Perhaps the real issue is not the historical validity of Walton's epigram, but the motives for emphasizing it.
2 Probably Miles Fletcher (see Grierson 2: lix).

reception that culminate in the contemporary Donne.[3] Likewise, recent textual scholarship, especially in the wake of Jerome McGann's *Critique of Modern Textual Criticism*, has productively complicated and destabilized the notion of a stable authorial text.[4] But despite the destabilizing effects of poststructuralist and of new historicist criticism and the new textual scholarship, the implications of the continuity between text and context, work and reception have yet to be fully realized. The subject of Donne scholarship still consists of a hierarchical body of edited texts whose order and signifying coherence remains naturalized *in practice* even as theoretical and historical studies expose their contingency. To cite a good example of the divergence between revisionist theory and conventional practice, Dayton Haskin, in an article on 'The Canonization,' points out that the challenges readers such as Jonathan Culler and Arthur Marotti have posed to Cleanth Brooks's reading served only to entrench further that text at the centre of the Donnean canon.[5] Often, however, textual scholarship remains segregated from other forms of criticism.[6] Ted-Larry Pebworth, one of the editors of the forthcoming Donne Variorum, persuasively articulates the performative nature of seventeenth-century coterie poetry and the consequent 'flexibility and impermanence' (62) of poetic texts. Pebworth nevertheless distinguishes

3 In addition to Marotti's *John Donne, Coterie Poet* and 'John Donne, Author,' see also Ted-Larry Pebworth, Richard Strier, Annabel Patterson, and Achsah Guibbory. In response to some of the stronger claims that historically oriented critics such as Marotti and Pebworth have made about the ephemeral nature of coterie poetry and manuscript circulation, Richard Wollman has defended a strong version of Donne's manuscript authority. From the opposite corner, Howard Felperin, in a chapter in *The Uses of the Canon*, performs a provocative deconstruction of the new historicists' reliance upon 'context' as the arbiter of the Donnean text.

4 See also Thomas Tanselle's balanced articles, 'Historicism and Critical Editing' and 'Textual Criticism and Deconstruction,' and the essays in *Textual Criticism and Literary Interpretation*, ed. Jerome McGann. Stephen Orgel's 'What Is a Text?' and Peter Stallybrass's 'Shakespeare, the Individual, and the Text' and 'Editing as a Cultural Formation: The Sexing of Shakespeare's Sonnets' offer productive materialist readings of textual editing.

5 To this list one might also add Howard Felperin (89–90) and John Guillory (161–75), both of whom expose the historical contingency of Brooks's reading.

6 The most striking example of this segregation is perhaps the controversial textual scholarship of Stanley Wells and Gary Taylor on the new Oxford Shakespeare, in which the complex, often destabilizing traces of the editorial work are quarantined in the separate, 671-page *Textual Companion*, which most readers will never see. The edited text, on the other hand, is probably the most visually pristine, monumental *Complete Works* ever produced.

between the neo-Levitical function of the textual editor, whose job it is to 'separate out ... any and all authorial and non-authorial variations,' to 'make possible the delineation of individual talent' and the literary critic's responsibility to 'be alert to the history of the particular text under examination' (71), a history often obscured by the separating function of the textual editor.

The division of labour between editors and critics implies that the selection, ordering, and cleansing of texts should and can precede the act of critical reading. Browne, on the other hand, presents the distinction between 'Strange Fire' from 'Sacrifice' as the responsibility of the 'knowing' reader. The 1633 printer also makes such pseudo-editorial 'discerning' a primary interpretive task. For at least these two seventeenth-century readers, establishment of the coherence or incoherence of Donne's authorial 'I' is a possible, but not inevitable, *product* of 'knowing' or 'discerning' study. For most subsequent critics, the coherence of the 'I,' implied in the clean, orderly editions of the *Poems*, is assumed as a starting-point.

In the remainder of this essay, I employ a strategy of reading textual instability and critical practices partly informed by Julia Kristeva's work on language and abjection in *Powers of Horror*; I begin by considering what has been excluded, or 'abjected,' in order to arrive at the narrative coherence of Donne as both subject and object of critical representation. Although I often find helpful the language of contemporary psychoanalytic theory, it is not, however, absolutely necessary to the reading that follows. Most important, Elegy 8, 'The Comparison,' on which I primarily focus, provides a negative picture of signification and authorial control that serves as a powerful antidote to the self-propagating mythology of 'The Canonization.' The conflicting strategies of the narrative voice[s] of 'The Comparison,' when confronted with the breakdown of boundaries between the clean and the unclean, are mirrored by criticism's conflicted appropriation of Donne as a canonical poet. 'The Comparison,' I argue, suggests its *own* methods of reading the Levitical underpinnings of critical and editorial practice, in particular the idealization of the 'authorial' text.

I

Of the poems attributed to Donne, 'The Comparison' is clearly among the 'Looser sort' that Walton retrospectively assigns to 'youth's Drosse,' and that, in the first edition, threatens the idea of an author who thinks 'nothing but the Praise / of [his] creator.' 'The Comparison' is not, however, unrepresentative. Going beyond conventional Renaissance licentiousness, the poem's 'looseness' is not only a matter of content, but also of rhetorical style and textual status. Following Browne, we might say that the diverse manuscripts and early printed texts are themselves 'promiscuous'; from a textual critic's standpoint, they are 'contaminated' or 'infected' from having passed through too many hands.[7] In the passages I quote, I attempt visibly to destabilize the text by indicating some of the cruxes within brackets, including punctuation where it significantly affects the sense. The first alternative given is the one chosen (or invented) by Sir Herbert Grierson in his 1912 edition; the others are alternatives he rejects:

> As the sweet sweat of Roses in a Still,
> As that from which chaf'd muskats pores doth trill,
> As the Almighty Balme of th'early East,
> Such are the sweat drops of my Mistris breast,
> And on her <brow/necke> her skin such lustre sets,
> They seeme no sweat drops, but pearle <coronets/ carcanets/carolettes>.
> Ranke sweaty froth thy Mistresse's brow defiles,
> Like spermatique issue of ripe menstruous boiles,
> Or like the skumme, which, by needs lawlesse law
> Enforc'd, Sanserra's starved men did draw
> From parboild shooes, and bootes, and all the rest
> Which were with any soveraigne fatnes blest,
> And like vile <lying stones/stones lying> in saffrond tinne,
> Or warts, or wheales, <they hang/it hangs> upon her skinne.   (1–14)

'The Comparison' immediately confronts the reader with a powerful set of sexual and religious taboos. By inverting his analogy in Holy Sonnet 13, comparing his mistress's 'sweat drops' with the 'Almighty Balme of th'early East' (presumably alluding to the crucifixion and Christ's blood), Donne places the secular and the sacred in disturbingly close contact. He also raises the spectre of specific Levitical prohibitions against semen, menstruation, contagious sores, and fat (Lev. 3,

---

7 Marotti provides an interesting account of the social conditions and circulation of Donne's poetry. Vast numbers of early texts are involved. See also Grierson's descriptions of major manuscripts and editions (2: lvi–cxxiv) and Sullivan's bibliography of Donne's uncollected printed verse in the seventeenth century.

13–15).[8] Browne's concern about the *'Strange Fire, /* That here is *mingled with thy Sacrifice'* (11–12) is especially appropriate to the 1633 volume, in which the transgressive religious and sexual content of 'The Comparison' is in grave danger of 'infecting' the nearby 'Psalm 137' or the adjacent 'Obsequies to the Lord Harrington.' By moving 'Divine Poems' to the end of the volume and the 'Elegies' to somewhere near the beginning, subsequent editors re-enact a ritual Old Testament quarantine of sacred space.

The quarantine of 'The Comparison' has extended to commentaries on the poem, which critics have generally tended to avoid. Sometimes the silence has been particularly loud, as in Alexander Grosart's comment on line 8: 'In this horrible line, 'menstruous' is probably = polluting or filthy, a latinate sense. The old medical writers yield elucidations, but I mind not quoting' (1: 186). Subsequent editors have not been more helpful. One of Herbert Grierson's glosses is inadvertently revealing because, if true, it would hardly bear stating: 'Article by article, as in an inventory, Donne contrasts his mistress and his enemy's' (2: 74). Helen Gardner, only slightly more usefully, glosses the poem as a combination of the Petrarchan and anti-Petrarchan traditions.[9]

Although the first lines might appear to bear out either editor to some extent, 'The Comparison' has little of the rhetorical coherence of the conventional Petrarchan lyric or of its Renaissance parodies, such as Shakespeare's 'dark lady' sonnets. The affective force of the language, as critics have recently noted (Fish 223; Guibbory 816; Marotti 48–9), becomes increasingly ambiguous, rendering easy distinctions such as Gardner's or Grierson's impossible:

8 Throughout Elegy 8, analogies that appeal to secular or profane values are also underwritten by other Levitical prohibitions concerning corpses (26, 31), molten idols (40–1), and perhaps sodomy (26, 41–4, 48).

9 Gardner is correct with respect to some of the specific words and images, but she misses the poem's radical syntactic, rhetorical, and textual *incoherence*. To support her interpretation, Gardner never refers to 'The Comparison,' but to an anonymous 'mid-seventeenth-century imitation.' By contrast, however, this 'imitation' ends up demonstrating the structural qualities the 'original' lacks; predictable four-line stanzas devote a couplet each to the two mistresses, 'mine' and 'thine' never allowing for a moment of ambiguity. The poem is also a useful counterpoint to Grierson's gloss. At the most banal level, the conclusion, in which the speaker asks the addressee to veil his mistress's face, makes more sense, on its own misogynist terms, than the exhortation to his 'enemy' to 'Leave her' in 'The Comparison.' See 'Laugh not fond foole cause I a face' (Cutts 211).

Round as the world's her head, on every side,
Like to the fatall Ball which fell on Ide,
Or that whereof God had such jealousie,
As, for the ravishing thereof we die.
Thy *head* is like a rough-hewne statue of jeat,
Where marks for eyes, nose, mouth, are yet scarce set;
Like the first Chaos, or flat seeming face
Of Cynthia, when th'earths shadowes her embrace.   (15–22)

Without clearer rhetorical pointers, the antecedent of 'her' in 'Round as the world's her head' depends upon the value one places on cranial rotundity. The other terms in which one expects a clear contrast – 'the fatall Ball which fell on Ide,' the 'flat seeming face / Of Cynthia' – are similarly ambivalent.

Yet a blurring of distinctions between the two mistresses in the poem is not enough to explain the breakdown of language and signification that parallels the rhetorical dismemberment of bodies in the remainder of the poem. The distinctions that dissolve are those that, in a psychoanalytic narrative, ground the identity of the speaking subject: self/other, subject/object, male/female:

Like Proserpines white beauty-keeping chest,
Or Joues best fortunes urne, is her faire brest.
Thine's like worme eaten trunkes, cloth'd in seals skin,
Or grave, that's <dust/durt> without, and stinke within.
And like that slender stalke, at whose end stands
The wood-bine quivering, are her armes and hands <,/.>
Like rough bark'd elmboughes, or the russet skin
Of men late scurg'd for madnes, or for sinne,
Like Sun-parch'd quarters on the citie gate,
Such is thy tann'd skins lamentable state.
And like a bunch of ragged carrets stand
The short swolne fingers of <thy/her> gouty hand<./;>   (23–34)

The Boschian nightmare vision of corpses and limbs has been severed from any stable morphology. No semblance remains of the parallel structure one expects to find in a 'comparison.' Bodies and the language used to describe them have become fragmented and incomplete.

The contaminating effects of the poem spread quickly to every party involved. Although editors simply gloss the use of 'thy' as a 'contraction' of 'thy mistress's' (19, 32, 34) it seems an odd 'shortcut.'[10] The disagreement between manuscript and printed sources at line 34 produces a similar confusion: whose gouty hand are we talking about? The conflation of the addressee and his mistress and, by extension, the speaker, raises the spectre of a hegemonic, contaminating female sexuality that continues to spread as the poem continues:

> Then like the Chymicks masculine equall fire,
> Which in the Lymbecks warme wombe doth inspire
> Into th'earths worthlesse <durt/part> a soule of gold,
> Such cherishing heat her best lov'd part doth hold.
> Thine's like the dread mouth of a fired gunne,
> Or like hot liquid metalls newly runne
> Into clay moulds, or like to that Ætna
> Where round about the grasse is burnt away.   (35–42)

If line 35, 'Then like the Chymicks masculine equall fire,' follows from the preceding lines, the 'best lov'd part' (38) being described would belong to the same woman as do the 'short swolne fingers' at line 34. Here, too, the text creates syntactic distance between the two elements of the alchemical analogy, making it unclear whether the 'cherishing heat' (38) is like that of the 'warme wombe' (36) or, rather, of the 'masculine equall fire.' The genders imply the former, but only the latter works grammatically. The genital analogies that occur a few lines later – 'that Ætna,' 'the dread mouth of a fired gunne' – can apply equally to a vagina, a penis, an anus, or to any combination of those. Like the 'her/thy/her' slippage, the references to genitals that might serve to fix the gender and identity of poet, addressee, and the 'mistresses' instead create further ambiguity. The vehement misogynist invective backfires when, like the two mistresses, the two genders dissolve into one – the gender of the other – and threaten both masculine identity and authorial control.

Although critics have recently been more willing to acknowledge the interpretive problems 'The Comparison' presents, they have tended to elide its textual difficulties. Yet it is towards these specific, mechanical difficulties that one of Arthur Marotti's figurative assessments di-

10 See Grierson 2: 75; Gardner 121; Grosart 186.

rects us: 'the language of vilification contaminates that of praise' (*John Donne* 48). Marotti echoes the language of textual criticism, positing a non-existent ideal text of 'praise' that has been 'contaminated' by a corrupt text of 'vilification.' Likewise textual editors (including Donne's) generally assume a non-existent ideal text, representing the author's 'pure' intention. The interpretive and textual dilemmas the elegy imposes on the reader are indistinguishable from its textual 'corruptions.' The careful reader and the textual critic are confronted with similar questions: Who is being described? Which adjectives describe which modifiers? How do the constituent parts fit together – or do they? Yet in so far as critical readers and textual critics are attempting to pinpoint the author's (or even the speaker's) subject position *vis-à-vis* the text, they will both inevitably fail. The linguistic slippage that results in a tableau of ownerless 'scattered limbs' cannot be resolved, as Grierson and Gardner have attempted to do, by mere choice among textual variants or even by cautious emendation. Nor can critics, even those as agile as Fish or Marotti, entirely resolve the issue by locating the slippage authorially (or in a specific, unified text) when the 'textual' corruptions of the poem so closely resemble those 'corruptions' presumed to be 'authorial.'

Grierson illustrates the difficulty with a justification of one of his rare conjectural emendations. Puzzled by the fact that most manuscripts place the 'pearle coronets' (6) around the woman's *neck*, he replaces them on her *brow* in order to match the other woman's brow in line 7. (A quick look at the rest of the poem shows just how many body parts would need to be similarly rearranged for this process to become the 'article by article' comparison Grierson desires.) In justifying his emendation, Grierson admits the difficulty of locating the source of the error: 'The explanation of the error is, probably, that an early copyist passed in his mind from breast to neck more easily than to brow ... Possibly Donne himself in the first version, or a copy of it, wrote "neck", meaning to write "brow", misled by the proximity and associations of "breast"' (2: 74). With this speculation Grierson, whose edition appeared about a decade after the publication of Freud's *Psychopathology of Everyday Life*, wanders into the grey area between textual criticism and psychoanalysis. Implicit in Grierson's statement, however, is a common assumption underlying textual criticism that is fundamentally at odds with psychoanalytic interpretation. In *Textual Criticism and Scholarly Editing* G.T. Tanselle articulates the common view of the editor's project as 'an effort to come as close as possible to the text intended by the author,'[11] adding in a footnote: 'One cannot simply say "written by the author," since the author's manuscript may have contained slips of the pen, and the critical editor is aiming for an ideal that may not ever have been realized in any document, even the author's own manuscript' (302–3). From a psychoanalytic perspective, this 'critical editor' is aligned not with the historical 'author' but with a particular psychic function that Tanselle here redefines as a kind of author-ideal. But if the author is defined by the ideal, rather than by the act of writing or by what is written, who or what is it that *writes*?

II Errours endlesse traine

> This is the wandring wood, this *Errours den*,
> A monster vile, whom God and man does hate ...

(Spenser, *The Faerie Queene* 1.1.13)

> Her vomit full of bookes and papers was.

(*FQ* 1.1.20)

Psychoanalysis has its own idiosyncratic variety of textual criticism. In *Leonardo da Vinci and a Memory of His Childhood* Freud points out that Leonardo repeats the time of his father's death, 'à ore 7,' twice in the same sentence:

It is only a small detail, and anyone who was not a psycho-analyst would attach no importance to it ...

The psycho-analyst thinks differently. To him nothing is too small to be a manifestation of hidden mental processes. He has learnt long ago that such cases of forgetting or repetition are significant, and that it is the 'distraction' which allows impulses that are otherwise hidden to be revealed (11: 119).

Where the textual scholar sees error, the psychoanalyst sees a symptom.

---

11 In light of recent critiques such as McGann's, Tanselle in his introduction backs away slightly from his assertion of the universality of this assumption.

However, Freud's general intuition – that slips of the tongue or pen are symptomatic of certain hidden processes – is more compelling than many of his laboured readings of particular lapses.[12] Sebastiano Timpanaro, in *The Freudian Slip: Psychoanalysis and Textual Criticism*, which is perhaps the most important encounter between textual criticism and psychoanalysis, provides a necessary sceptical counterweight to Freud's non-verifiable speculations in some of the well-known examples from *Psychopathology of Everyday Life*: the Signorelli/Botticelli slip (Freud 6: 1–7; Timpanaro 63–81) and the bungled Virgil quotation (Freud 6: 8–14; Timpanaro 29–48). Timpanaro's critique, however, stops short of refuting Freud's general principle, as stated in his commentary on Leonardo, nor does he provide convincing alternative explanations. Rather than resorting, as Timpanaro does, to hypotheses such as 'banalization,' which defer or displace the theoretical problem without resolving it, we might instead address the particular limitations of Freud's analysis, in particular his inadequate theorization of the psychoanalytic function of language.

If symbolic functioning, as post-Freudian analysts such as Kristeva and Lacan have suggested, engages the emergence and structuring of nascent subjectivity, then one might expect to find in lapses of symbolic functioning a corresponding failure of the mechanisms of subjective self-constitution. In *Powers of Horror*, Kristeva links cultural and religious taboos with (pre)subjective identity formation and the subject's traumatic initiation in language. The primary, pre-symbolic difference that precedes symbolic functioning is between self and not-self, and initially established in the always incomplete abjection of the 'maternal':[13] 'The abject confronts us … with our earliest attempts to release the hold of *maternal* entity even before ex-isting outside of her, thanks to the autonomy of language. It is a violent, clumsy breaking away, with the constant risk of falling back under the sway of a power as securing as

---

12 For further examples of what Freud does, for better or for worse, with 'errors' in speech and language, see chapters 1–6 of *Psychopathology of Everyday Life* (6: 1–133) and his discussion of parapraxes in *Introductory Lectures on Psychoanalysis* (15: 15–82).

13 One has to be careful, perhaps more than Kristeva herself is, with language such as this. The 'maternal' is a retrospective, and loaded, association of a symbolic category with the undifferentiated pre-symbolic from which it emerges. One could argue that the particular choice (of all symbolic objects) of 'mother' or of women generally to figure this state is itself a symptom of linguistic failure – although perhaps a revealing one.

it is stifling' (13). The paradox in discussing abjection is that language, including Freud's, Kristeva's, or my own, requires an already constituted system of symbolic difference, of discrete objects. The 'objects' of abjection are abject precisely because they are not yet constituted as objects – the hazy forms, neither self nor other, that constantly trespass the boundaries of signification: milk, excrement, blood, corpse, mother.

Although the abject is by definition that which defies signification, its traces may appear in those places where signs break down, where, in Kristeva's words, language 'gives up' and 'object and sign ... tumble over into non-sense' (11). Abjection appears as a problem or an anomaly in speech and writing rather than as a sign. In another of Kristeva's formulations, the abject manifests itself in certain forms of poetry and, though less visibly, in all language: 'Does one write under any other condition than being possessed by abjection, in an indefinite catharsis?' (208). The real danger of certain forms of poetic language, or of a 'lapse' of the kind discussed here, is that it will undermine language's ideology, the lie that allows it to function. Yet the abject also has a set of associations in the subject's early history and in cultural taboo, providing a lexicon of terms that defensively displaces the abject within language.

In 'The Comparison' the failure of language is enacted physically as the conflation and dismemberment of women's bodies, and particularly as a threatening female sexuality; the apparent lapses and gaps in the text of the poem should be read as continuous with the misogynist thematic. The variant readings of 'her' and 'thy,' the conflation of 'thy' with 'thy mistresse,' and the displacement of body parts are the traces of a symbolic order not fully constituted. If Grierson's gloss is taken seriously (as indicative of either Donne's symptom or his own), the 'breast' that 'distracts' the author momentarily *becomes* the author, erasing a complex symbolic relation (brow/coronet) in favour of an asymbolic contiguity (breast/neck). The association of the breast with early childhood would also link the breast, in a Kristevan narrative, with the female figure or figures in 'The Comparison' who fade constantly into one another, into the addressee of the poem, and into the subject position of the author, conjuring visions of an abject 'maternal' against which language always struggles to constitute the subject.

The textual critic's project is similar: to construct pure authorial intention against encroaching, entropic forms of contamination implicitly and sometimes explicitly gendered female. Paul Maas writes that in textual genealogies, available manuscripts 'are related to the original somewhat as the descendants of a man are related to their ancestor. One might perhaps illustrate the transmission of errors along the same lines by treating all females as sources of error' (20). Maas's analogy, like the patrilineal cultural context on which it depends, attempts to conceal heterogeneity by setting the 'female' outside of signification as abject, asymbolic 'error.'[14] Like any system of taboo, it creates its own violations.

Some of the best evidence for the relationship between a misogynist system of cultural taboos and linguistic abjection at the level of textual error is inadvertently provided by Timpanaro. Of the seven examples of authorial lapses or 'banalizations' he cites to explain Freud's confusion of Boltraffio/Botticelli with Signorelli (65–9), no fewer than four of the elisions concern women, with associations that threaten distinct ego-boundaries.[15] Citing Cicero's confusion of Ulysses' wet-nurse, Euryclea, with his mother, Anticlea, Timpanaro argues that 'the equal number of syllables, the rhyme … [and] the affinity in role between the two characters … are more than sufficient to account for the "slip"' (65). In another instance, Heine mistakenly writes 'Käthchen' when he intends Goethe's 'Gretchen,' the object of powerful sexual taboos in *Faust*. Gretchen's brother, Valentine, predicts as he is about to die that 'all good folk will shun you / And step around you, lifting their feet, / As at infected carrion-meat' (3751–3). (One might say that Heine violates Valentine's curse by calling Gretchen/Käthchen a 'charming creature' [cited in Timpanaro 66].) The Italian critic Domenico Comparetti misquotes 'Cynthia' for 'Trivia' in a line from Dante's *Paradiso*: 'Cinzia/[Trivia] ride fra le ninfe eterne' [Cynthia/(Trivia) smiles mid nymphs eternal] (Timpanaro 67). According to Timpanaro, Cynthia and Trivia are simply versions of the same name. But 'Trivia' – which Comparetti forgets – is more closely associated with darkness, the underworld, sorcery (Zimmerman); both names, moreover, carry strong connotations of female sexual taboo, of that which is 'off-limits.'

---

14 For an excellent discussion of the 'gender' of literary texts, see Carolyn Dinshaw's introduction to *Chaucer's Sexual Poetics* 3–27.

15 Not to mention the Austrian's error with respect to Dido's speech in the *Aeneid*. One need not follow Freud's longish route to arrive at a connection between Dido's powerful curse (*'hanc vocem extremam cum sanguine fundo'* [4.621]) and the departing traveller's tryst with the Italian woman, even down to the specific concerns about menstruation and childbirth.

Finally, Timpanaro cites the fascist critic Barna Occhini, who mis-wrote 'Armida,' the sorceress in Tasso's *Jerusalem Delivered*, for Ariosto's 'Alcina.' Both figures are symptomatic of the Renaissance tendency to demonize women's sexuality as a form of witchcraft.[16] But Alcina, in *Orlando Innamorato* and *Orlando Furioso*, is a particularly threatening shape-shifter, a prototype of the unstable body in 'The Comparison,' whose seductive beauty conceals the worst corruption and decay. And, like the subject-object of 'The Comparison,' Alcina reduces to silence the men who discover her secret:

> And lest that they about the world might go
> And make her wicked life and falsehood known,
> In diverse places she doth them bestow
> So as abroad they shall not make their moan,
> Some into trees amid the field that grow,
> Some into beasts, and some into a stone.   (*Orlando Furioso* 141)

Thwarted by the tongue-tying powers of Ariosto's misogynist fantasy, Occhini becomes one of Alcina's victims.

That so many examples of Timpanaro's 'banalization' turn out to be banalizations of the names of such threatening, sexually charged creations of the male literary imagination indicates that banalization may not be an answer to the problem of textual slippage, but a deferral of the problem. But what, precisely, is the *problem*? For Timpanaro and most textual critics, the problem is error as such. Yet as my readings have suggested, the 'error' may be in the definition of error. The common as-sumption is that language and texts are parthenogenetic, that is, 'derived … from a single original' (Greg 1), and that incongruencies, elisions, and variations are pathological. But poems like 'The Comparison' and the anomalies Freud and Timpanaro *both* raise demonstrate a plurality of voices within language – the voices of the 'other,' the un-self within the self.

Perhaps the commonplace association of women and women's sex-uality with error, contamination, and disease should be read not as a symptom or result of error, but as one of its sources. The literary fantasy of encroaching pollution or of threats to signification in the

16 Spenser's Duessa is in many ways a knock-off of Alcina (see esp. *Faerie Queene* 1.8.47–8). Duessa, along with Error (*FQ* 1.1.13–25), and Milton's Sin (*Paradise Lost* 2.725–870), are among the more egregious examples.

form of sexually charged female figures may recall for the writing subject a pre-symbolic state in which threats to the emergent ego are linguistically undifferentiated and abjected indiscriminately, in which language does not yet function. Alcina, as a misogynist fantasy, may be self-fulfilling – a threatening female sexuality with the power to compel, alter, or silence the parthenogenetic 'male' text: 'Leave her, and I will leave comparing thus, / She, and comparisons are odious' ('The Comparison' 53–4).

III The Cracked Urn[17]

The poem is an instance of the doctrine which it asserts; it is both the assertion and the realization of the assertion.

Cleanth Brooks (16)

The task confronting the speaker in 'The Comparison' and the critic who approaches the poem, a task at which both are destined to fail, is to separate the clean from the unclean, to distinguish between beauty and ugliness, health and corruption, the sacred and the profane. What is originally presented as an aesthetic choice between two female figures becomes by the end of the poem a choice between defilement and silence. As outlined earlier, many of the substances and acts the poem places in front of the critic – semen, menstrual blood, leprous boils, sodomy, corpses, excrement – are the focus of powerful biblical and pre-biblical taboos.[18] The speaker's final gesture might then be understood as a gesture of atoning self-sacrifice or self-abjection that exchanges the poem itself for a temporary reprieve from impurity.

Such gestures of exclusion are also, at least in part, what create and preserve a literary canon, in spite of the mystifying assertions of literary self-propagation in poems like 'The Canonization,' for example, or Shakespeare's widely anthologized Sonnet 55 ('Not marble, nor the guilded monuments'). The conclusion of 'The Comparison,' a gesture of self-abjection, begins the process that Browne, Walton, and

---

17 With apologies to Professor Brooks.
18 The literature on this topic is extensive. In addition to Mary Douglas and Julia Kristeva, N. Kiuchi, David Wright, and Emanuel Feldman have written usefully on the biblical significance of pollution.

the seventeenth-century printers continue. Although many early critics, including Joseph Spence and David Hume, rejected Donne altogether, critical judgment generally either followed Walton in dividing Donne in two and offering part of the author as sacrifice (or foreskin) to preserve the other, or Dryden, who called Donne 'the greatest Wit, though not the best Poet of our Nation' (3), distinguishing 'poetry' from 'wit,' excluding Donne from the former while admitting him to the latter. An anonymous article entitled 'A Poetical Scale,' published in 1758 in *The Literary Magazine*, for example, included a chart ranking twenty-nine English poets. Donne is excluded from the 'scale'; and in the arbiter's explanation of the criteria for inclusion or exclusion of particular authors, Donne is dealt with summarily, in the final sentence, in terms that recall Dryden's comment: 'Dr. *Donne* was a man of wit, but he seems to have been at pains not to pass for a poet' (8). The fallible process of distinction and definition through which 'The Comparison' struggles, repeats itself in criticism as literary 'canonization.' Donne is excluded in order to sustain a consistent definition of 'poetry,' yet the very statement that excludes or abjects him is also, implicitly, a form of inclusion. Donne, exiled to the last sentence, becomes the ultimate limit of the implied canon – the problematic, permeable boundary of discourse.

The critical fate of 'The Comparison' itself is exemplary. In general, the poem has been widely ignored. Yet Samuel Johnson, who held 'metaphysical' poetry generally in contempt, and discussed Donne only in his *Life of Cowley*, quotes the first seven lines of 'The Comparison' as part of a sequence of negative examples of the metaphysical style. Johnson prefaces the excerpt only with 'This is yet more indelicate' (32). Contravening all sense of good Augustan versification, Johnson breaks off the quotation not only in mid-sentence but in mid-couplet, and concludes with a period, as if the subsequent line, which contains the worst offences against Levitical taboos, is too offensive even for a discussion of Donne's faults.[19] Johnson's treatment of Donne illustrates a retreating series of exclusions, the purpose of which is finally to purify the hallowed ground of English poetry. The exclusions can be interpreted as follows: (1) The 'metaphysical' poets are unnatural and

---

19 An anonymous review of Johnson's *Works of the English Poets*, published in *The Monthly Review* in 1779, seized upon exactly those seven lines as an example of Donne's poor taste and Dr Johnson's good judgment and 'singularly happy' choice of excerpts.

offensive; read Pope instead; (2) If you do read metaphysical poetry, read Cowley, not Donne; (3) If you must read Donne, at least don't read 'The Comparison'; and (4) If you can't avoid 'The Comparison,' whatever you do don't read past the seventh line. The possible boundary of the canon is being pushed farther and farther back, settling eventually at the seventh line of 'The Comparison' and excluding the Levitical contamination in line 8.

The operation of cultural taboos and their effect on the production and dissemination of texts is not difficult to see at the institutional level, especially in overt forms such as censorship, or in the compiling of lists such as that in *The Literary Magazine*. In a much-needed demystification of the idea of canonicity, John Guillory has insisted on the *imaginary* nature of the 'canon,' and suggested that in place of naïve conspiracy theories of canon formation, critical discussion should refocus on a 'sociology of judgment' (xiv) that would take into account the specific institutional sites where decisions 'with canonical force' (29) take place: the syllabus, the list, the curriculum. To these I would add *the texts themselves*, since, like the canon, the ideal text is an imaginary entity, an 'ideology' in the Althusserian sense, which covers for the cultural work of its actual, social manifestations.[20] The contingency of certain specific *texts* challenges the strict line Guillory draws between the two senses of 'representation.' Forms of judgment that determine the status of representation *within* a particular text are not easily separated conceptually from the judgment that determines that text's representation within (or outside of) a syllabus or list.

Guillory's major achievement is the dismantling of the assumption, shared by cultural conservatives and liberals alike, that the connection between content and canon is always as transparently conspiratorial as it is in certain forms of censorship or propaganda. But I am suggesting a different connection, which can be expressed in either a weak or a strong form. At a minimum, it appears that both forms of representation are organized around systems of pollution and purification, which

20 The obvious chasm between my essay and Guillory, Althusser, or Bourdieu is my lack of attention to class. It would not be difficult, however, to see how the pure/impure distinctions in textual criticism, for example, translate into class terms, especially in their constructions of genealogies. The notion of texts as requiring constant editorial mediation has fairly obvious ideological implications, given rather brutal force, for example, in A.E. Housman's assertion that 'textual criticism, like most other sciences, is an aristocratic affair, not communicable to all men, nor to most men' (3: 1069).

share formal characteristics and which can take either a subjective or a social form. The stronger hypothesis, which would require further elaboration and documentation, finds in abjection a causal or logical connection between texts and canons, a mutually determining relationship in which 'aberrant' textuality emerges from social codes gone awry, and slippages in institutional or critical judgment result from the gaps in and transgressions of the text.

WORKS CITED

Ariosto, Lodovico. *Orlando Furioso*. 1516. Trans. Sir John Harington. 1591. Ed. Rudolf Gottfried. Bloomington: Indiana UP, 1963.

Brooks, Cleanth. *The Well Wrought Urn*. New York: Reynal and Hitchcock, 1947.

Cox, R.G. 'The Poems of John Donne.' *The New Pelican Guide to English Literature*. Ed. Boris Ford. Rev. ed. 9 vols. Vol. 3. London: Penguin, 1982.

Cutts, John P., ed. *Seventeenth-Century Songs and Lyrics*. Columbia: U of Missouri P, 1959.

Dinshaw, Carolyn. Introduction. *Chaucer's Sexual Poetics*. Madison: U of Wisconsin P, 1989. 3–27.

Donne, John. *Poems*. London, 1633.

– *Poems*. London, 1635.

Douglas, Mary. *Purity and Danger: An Analysis of the Concepts of Pollution and Taboo*. New York: Praeger, 1966.

Dryden, John. Dedication. *Eleonora*. London, 1692.

Feldman, Emanuel. *Biblical and Post-Biblical Defilement and Mourning: Law as Theology*. New York: Yeshiva UP, 1977.

Felperin, Howard. *The Uses of the Canon: Elizabethan Literature and Contemporary Theory*. Oxford: Clarendon P, 1990.

Fish, Stanley. 'Donne and Verbal Power.' *Soliciting Interpretation*. Ed. Elizabeth D. Harvey and Katharine Eisaman Maus. 223–52.

Freud, Sigmund. *The Standard Edition of the Complete Psychological Works of Sigmund Freud*. Ed. and trans. James Strachey. 24 vols. London: Hogarth, 1953–74.

Gardner, Helen, ed. *John Donne: The Elegies and the Songs and Sonnets*. Oxford: Clarendon P, 1965.

Goethe, Johann Wolfgang von. *Faust*. Ed. Cyrus Hamlin. Trans. Walter Arndt. New York: Norton, 1976.

Greg, Walter Wilson. *The Calculus of Variants: An Essay on Textual Criticism*. Oxford: Clarendon P, 1927.

Grierson, Herbert J.C., ed. *The Poems of John Donne*. 2 vols. Oxford: Clarendon P, 1912.

Grosart, Alexander B., ed. *The Complete Poems of John Donne, D.D.* 2 vols. London, 1872–1873.

Guibbory, Achsah. ' "Oh, Let Mee Not Serve So": The Politics of Love in Donne's *Elegies.*' *ELH* 57.4 (1990): 811–33.

Guillory, John. *Cultural Capital: The Problem of Literary Canon Formation.* Chicago: U of Chicago P, 1993.

Harvey, Elizabeth D., and Katharine Eisaman Maus, eds. *Soliciting Interpretation: Literary Theory and Seventeenth-Century English Poetry.* Chicago: U of Chicago P, 1990.

Haskin, Dayton. 'A History of Donne's "Canonization" from Izaak Walton to Cleanth Brooks.' *Journal of English and Germanic Philology* 92.1 (1993): 17–36.

Helgerson, Richard. *Self-Crowned Laureates: Spenser, Jonson, Milton, and the Literary System.* Berkeley: U of California P, 1983.

Housman, A.E. *The Classical Papers of A.E. Housman.* Ed. J. Diggle and F.R.D. Goodyear. 3 vols. Cambridge: Cambridge UP, 1972.

Johnson, Samuel. 'Life of Cowley.' *Lives of the English Poets.* 3 vols. Vol. 1. Dublin, 1779. 3–77.

Kiuchi, N. *The Purification Offering in the Priestly Literature: Its Meaning and Function. Journal for the Study of the Old Testament.* Supplement Series 56. Sheffield: Sheffield Academic P, 1987.

Kristeva, Julia. *Powers of Horror: An Essay on Abjection.* Trans. Leon S. Roudiez. New York: Columbia UP, 1982.

Lacan, Jacques. 'The Mirror Stage as Formative of the Function of the I as Revealed in Psychoanalytic Experience.' *Écrits: A Selection.* Trans. Alan Sheridan. New York and London: Norton, 1977. 1–7.

Maas, Paul. *Textual Criticism.* Trans. Barbara Flower. Oxford: Clarendon P, 1958.

Marotti, Arthur F. 'John Donne, Author.' *Journal of Medieval and Renaissance Studies* 19.1 (1989): 69–82.

– *John Donne, Coterie Poet.* Madison: U of Wisconsin P, 1986.

McGann, Jerome. *A Critique of Modern Textual Criticism.* 1983. Charlottesville: UP of Virginia, 1992.

– ed. *Textual Criticism and Literary Interpretation.* Chicago: U of Chicago P, 1985.

Milton, John. *Complete Poems and Major Prose.* Ed. Merritt Y. Hughes. New York: Macmillan, 1957.

Monthly Review 61 (July–Dec. 1779): 4.

Orgel, Stephen. 'What Is a Text?' *Staging the Renaissance: Reinterpretations of Elizabethan and Jacobean Drama.* Ed. David Scott Kastan and Peter Stallybrass. New York and London: Routledge, 1991. 83–7.

Patterson, Annabel. 'All Donne.' *Soliciting Interpretation.* Ed. Elizabeth D. Harvey and Katharine Eisaman Maus. 37–67.

Pebworth, Ted-Larry. 'John Donne, Coterie Poetry, and the Text as Performance.' *SEL: Studies in English Literature 1500–1900* 29.1 (1989): 61–75.

'A Poetical Scale.' *The Literary and Antigallican Magazine for January, 1758. The Literary Magazine: Or, Universal Review.* 3 (Jan.–Aug. 1758): 6–8.

Spenser, Edmund. *Spenser: Poetical Works.* Ed. J.C. Smith and E. De Selincourt. 1912. Oxford: Oxford UP, 1970.

Stallybrass, Peter. 'Shakespeare, the Individual, and the Text.' *Cultural Studies.* Ed. Lawrence Grossberg, Cary Nelson, and Paula A. Treichler. New York and London: Routledge, 1992.

Strier, Richard. 'Radical Donne: "Satire III."' *ELH* 60.2 (1993): 283–322.

Sullivan, Ernest W. *The Influence of John Donne: His Uncollected Seventeenth-Century Printed Verse.* Columbia: U of Missouri P, 1993.

Tanselle, G. Thomas. 'Historicism and Critical Editing.' *Studies in Bibliography: Papers of the Bibliographical Society of the University of Virginia* 39 (1986): 82–105.

– 'Textual Criticism and Deconstruction.' *Studies in Bibliography* 43 (1990): 1–33.

– *Textual Criticism and Scholarly Editing.* Charlottesville: U of Virginia P, 1990.

Timpanaro, Sebastiano. *The Freudian Slip: Psychoanalysis and Textual Criticism.* Trans. Kate Soper. London: NLB, 1976.

Virgil. *The Aeneid of Virgil.* Ed. R.D. Williams. 2 vols. Basingstoke: Macmillan, 1972.

Wells, Stanley, and Gary Taylor, eds. *William Shakespeare: The Complete Works.* Oxford: Clarendon P, 1986.

– *William Shakespeare: A Textual Companion.* Oxford: Clarendon P, 1987.

Wollman, Richard B. 'The "Press and the Fire": Print and Manuscript Culture in Donne's Circle.' *SEL: Studies in English Literature* 33.1 (1993): 85–97.

Wright, David P. *The Disposal of Impurity: Elimination Rites in the Bible and in Hittite and Mesopotamian Literature.* Atlanta, GA: Scholars P, 1987.

Zimmerman, J.E. *Dictionary of Classical Mythology.* New York: Harper & Row, 1964.

8

Marginal Man: The Representation of Horror in Renaissance Tragedy

SUSAN ZIMMERMAN

In recent decades, critical interest in the representation of horror has concentrated on cultural productions of the past three centuries, from the eighteenth-century Gothic novel to twentieth-century fiction, drama, and film. This body of scholarship, despite its size, has for the most part excluded important early modern antecedents of horror, in particular English tragic drama. One reason for this oversight may be the preoccupation among scholars of the early modern theatre with the tragedies of Shakespeare, and with the differences between his plays and those of his contemporaries. The blood and gore, mutilations, lunacy, rapes, and incest regularly featured on the English Renaissance stage appear in Shakespeare's plays (with the possible exception of *Titus Andronicus*) in limited and marginal ways. In comparison to Shakespeare, the sensationalism of other dramatic texts of the period, particularly of the so-called revenge tragedies, has often seemed crude or 'decadent.' Such distinctions, however, obscure the fact that from approximately 1588 to 1630, drama showcasing horror was a persistent phenomenon on the English stage; this drama involved most major playwrights, and was performed in both public and private theatres, as well as at court. Collectively, the audiences for these plays represented a sizeable cross-section of London society in terms of class, gender, age, and education. Thus an understanding of the widespread theatrical representation of horror is crucial to our analysis

I should like to thank Catherine Belsey and Peter Stallybrass for their customary generosity in offering helpful suggestions and alternative perspectives during the preparation of this essay.

of the theatrical industry in early modern London and of early modern cultural production in general.

My project here – albeit limited in terms of the scope of the subject – is to offer a theoretical paradigm for problematizing early modern horror, and to demonstrate its relevance to the analysis of (non-Shakespearean) theatrical texts. Section I of the essay addresses the basic question: What *is* horror? What constitutes the raw material on which early modern theatrical conventions depend, or which, in effect, they resist? I approach this question by means of the anthropological theories of Georges Bataille and Mary Douglas, whose analyses of ritual and taboo locate horror, and desire, in the subject's recognition of interstitial being. But anthropological theory, although richly suggestive, fails to account for the psychic mechanisms that construct the interstitial as that which the subject both dreads and desires. Because such mechanisms are the material of psychoanalysis, I borrow from Lacanian theory, specifically Lacan's analysis of the structure of desire, to undergird the anthropological concepts of my paradigm.

Examining representative plays in Section II, I put the theoretical model to work in the service of a materialist analysis. Elsewhere, I have argued that the disjunction in criticism between psychoanalytic and materialist criticism is a false one, that psychoanalysis is itself a material theory in that it is inscribed in the operation of language (see introduction, *Erotic Politics*, esp. 1–5). In this paper, I attempt to identify what is distinctive about the representation of horror in early modern tragedy by measuring this representation *against* a paradigm that lays claim, at least structurally, to transhistorical legitimacy. That which is thrown into relief by the discontinuities between paradigm and practice – the synchronic determinants of the culture – is precisely what I am concerned with discovering. My study suggests that one such synchronic variable in the theatrical representation of horror concerns the function of woman. By reconfiguring the paradigmatic position of woman so as to implicate man in her symbolic function, early modern tragedy uniquely showcases the problematic nature of sexual division.

I

Among postmodern theorists, Georges Bataille and Mary Douglas, considered jointly in terms of major areas of affinity, provide the most fully formulated anthropological theory of horror, one that assumes the interdependence of violence and taboo. According to Bataille, the taboo represents the human subject's refusal to participate in nature's unimaginable 'orgy of annihilation' (61). The taboo, in other words, seeks to deny the excessive violence that constitutes the natural process of death and renewal. Because the transformative drive of the natural order leads to the void – the cancellation of all discontinuous, or individuated selves – the taboo disrupts or forestalls the unconfined, terrifying continuity of reproduction and death, nature's 'virulent activity of corruption' (56). Based, then, on the denial of disequilibrium, the taboo for Bataille serves as the organizing principle for social constructs, in particular those dealing with sexuality and death. By inspiring fear, disgust, and horror in the subject, the taboo seeks to regulate primary forms of human violence, and thereby to defy the larger scheme of radical instability that constitutes the subject's world.

In Bataille's paradigm, however, the taboo also serves as conduit for the subject's desire for death. Because violence can 'never be anything but partially reduced to order' (40), the taboo is always subject to transgression. It cannot, in fact, function as taboo unless it *is* transgressed, the need for taboo implying the subject's underlying acceptance of violence. Thus the 'counterpoise of *desire*' (37, emphasis added) gives the taboo its deepest significance. Against the subject's insistence upon discontinuous (individuated) being, he/she opposes a desire to approach the void: 'desire originates in its opposite, horror' (59). What both fascinates and repels is continuity itself, the fusion of living forms (death) in the proliferation of life. For Bataille, 'eroticism opens the way to death' (24) because it leads to an exultant union of discontinuous beings, a union that seems liberating, whether it be that of lovers (orgasm as 'the little death'), or of mystical experience (ecstasy transcending the need for an object). But if eroticism is exuberant, it is also horrific. The 'blending and fusion of separate objects' (25) is synonymous with the generative power of corruption and decay, that which the taboo would hold at bay.[1]

The body's own structure, moreover, suggests the linkage between erotic experience and death. Bataille puts it graphically: 'the sexual channels are also the body's sewers'; there are 'unmistakable links between excreta, decay, and sexuality.' The 'mingled horror and fascination' aroused in the subject by the 'stinking putrefaction' of a corpse is akin to abhorrence of the body's by-products: excrement, menstrual

---

1 Douglas's formulation of similar principles deals with taboo in terms of pollution rituals, which inevitably cluster around sex and death: 'Formlessness is ... an apt symbol of beginning and of growth as it is of decay' (161).

blood (56–8).[2] For Bataille and Douglas, the threat of putrefaction is the absence of recognizable form, of identity (menstrual blood, for example, viewed as a human being *manqué* [Douglas 96]). Marginal, indeterminate being – that is, being that escapes logical categorization (what Douglas calls 'dirt') – evokes the horror of (and desire for) originary formlessness, Bataille's void.[3]

In patriarchal cultures, the subject's struggle with the opposing forces of desire and repulsion is inscribed in the female body, whose sexual and reproductive functions serve as the chief locus of taboo. As Douglas demonstrates, the eroticism and fertility of the female govern most pollution rituals. These rituals are aimed, on the one hand, at rendering the female body sexually pure, an 'unchanging lapidary form' that functions as the enemy 'of ambiguity and compromise' (162), and on the other, at protecting the social order against the death implicit in the 'dirt,' or indeterminacy, of the female body's by-products, particularly menstrual blood (see esp. 140–58). But because the creative potency of the female, a potency that connects with 'the powers inhering in the cosmos' (Douglas 161), ultimately cannot be fully harnessed by taboo, the female body comes to symbolize the horrifying danger and attractiveness of marginality itself.

2 Bakhtin, in his theory of the grotesque/carnivalesque, is also concerned with the connections between reproductive and excretory functions, and with the continuum of death, decay, and rebirth. Carnival provides a means of transgressing physical and social boundaries through inversion and bodily excess: 'the essence of carnival lies in change, in death-rebirth, in destructive-creative time' (Todorov 79). For Bakhtin, however, carnivalesque transgression represents a form of communal transcendence, of gaiety; Bakhtin's grotesque is not horrific (see 'Rabelais in the History of Laughter' and 'The Grotesque Image of the Body and Its Sources,' in *Rabelais and His World* 59–144; 303–67).

3 In *Powers of Horror* Kristeva also describes the perverse attraction of marginal forms:

A wound with blood and pus, or the sickly, acrid smell of sweat, of decay, does not *signify* death ... refuse and corpses *show me* what I permanently thrust aside in order to live. These body fluids, this defilement, this shit are what life withstands, hardly and with difficulty, on the part of death. There, I am at the border of my condition as a living being. My body extricates itself, as being alive, from that border ... If dung signifies the other side of the border, the place where I am not and which permits me to be, the corpse, the most sickening of wastes, is a border that has encroached upon everything ... The corpse ... is the utmost of abjection. It is death infecting life ... It is thus not lack of cleanliness or health that causes abjection but what disturbs identity, system, order. What does not respect borders, positions, rules. The in-between, the ambiguous, the composite (3–4).

Although Bataille and Douglas refer only incidentally to Freud, his essay on 'The Uncanny' provides a psychoanalytic underpinning to their analyses of the female body as site of horror. For Freud, the uncanny appears as a 'harbinger of death,' a '"double"' (235) that connects disturbingly to 'what is known of old and long familiar' (220). As such, the uncanny is manifested as the in-between; both familiar and concealed, it exists in the margins of consciousness. Although an experience of the uncanny can be triggered either by an infantile repression or by the revival of an animistic belief that has been previously surmounted, the fear of castration/death, often symbolized by female genitalia, is common to both situations. The uncanny aspect of female genitalia is the repressed, (un)familiar body of the mother, the intrauterine existence (symbol of life and death). Thus the 'ghostly harbinger of death' manifests itself through the generative potencies of the female/mother, and leads the subject 'back' to the creative formlessness of life/death.[4]

The exclusion of psychoanalytic theory from the anthropological paradigm for horror suggests a fundamental conceptual problem: the paradigm would describe psychic phenomena and their effects without a theory of psychic processes. Although Freudian concepts of female sexuality, repression, and the unconscious are implicit in anthropological concepts of transgression and desire, anthropology fails to account for the internal processes that structure 'desire' for the human subject. These processes are precisely what Lacan, reformulating Freud, elucidates.

For Lacan, the human subject enters into consciousness, and simultaneously the unconscious, through the agency of language, and in so doing experiences a fundamental split or division: the subject, both more and less than its own conscious identity, is defined by difference, absence, and a sense of the loss of organic being.[5] Further, in the fissure or gap of the radical split, and by virtue of its negation (I am *not* synonymous with my consciousness), desire is born: desire to possess that

4 In 'The Theme of the Three Caskets,' Freud discusses the function of ancient female deities as dual symbols of love and death, and in this context examines the interdependence of the 'three inevitable relations that a man has with a woman': his relation to 'the woman who bears him, the woman who is his mate and the woman who destroys him,' namely, Mother Earth (522).
5 Several of the key Lacanian concepts outlined here are discussed in 'The signification of the phallus' (*Écrits* 281–91). See also Freud, 'On the Universal Tendency to Debasement in the Sphere of Love' (394–400).

which is always absent, closed to signification – the imaginary wholeness of the pre-discursive condition, a fantasy of organic being.

The subject's induction into what Lacan terms the symbolic order (language and the Law) means that all of the mental impulses prohibited by the symbolic order must be repressed; this is the function of the unconscious, and the reason why the conscious and the unconscious take shape simultaneously. In Lacan's system, that which the subject constructs as the source of meaning and prohibition within the symbolic order, that which names and differentiates the subject, the locus of language itself, is called the Other. The Other appears to hold the 'truth' of the subject, and would supposedly provide access to the pre-symbolic, the pre-discursive, to the lost *objet a* that underpins symbolization itself. But since the Other is language itself, it cannot; there is nothing but lack in the place of the Other.[6] Thus desire is impossible because it always reaches beyond its object in search of the Other; desire for originary oneness is inevitably structured as an endlessly repeated process of substitution and deferment. The 'unutterable residue' of desire, the excess over what can be experienced as pleasure, or spoken in language – Lacan's *jouissance* – indicates lack; and 'the missed meaning in the (absent) place of the Other' prompts the re-enactment of substitution and deferment (Belsey, 'Desire's Excess and the English Renaissance Theatre' 86). By virtue of its repetitive structure, desire is thereby implicated in what Freud terms the death drive.

In Freudian theory, the death drive operates beyond the economy of pleasure; implicit in Freud's elaboration of the *fort/da* game in *Beyond the Pleasure Principle*, it is the purest form of the compulsion to repeat. The symbolic construction of desire as a process of substitution and deferment serves as symptom of, or substitution for, this drive. Slavoj Žižek describes the Lacanian formulation of this principle: '*desire itself is a defence against desire*: the desire structured through fantasy is a defence against the desire of the Other, against this "pure" trans-phantasmic desire (i.e., the "death drive" in its pure form)' (118). If we *traverse* the

---

6 In naming, language supplants what it constitutes, whether objects or human subjects: 'the symbol manifests itself first of all as the murder of the thing' (*Écrits* 104). Moreover, the linguistic sign is arbitrary and unfixed; meaning *circulates* in language. Thus the human subject's effort to attribute omnipotence to the Other, to render the Other as site of full presence, is a delusion: 'there's no such thing as an Other of the Other' ('Desire and the Interpretation of Desire in *Hamlet*' 25).

fantasy, we find what Lacan terms the Real, namely, the inaccessible impossibility that escapes symbolization but that 'exercises a certain structural causality' on symbolization: 'it is precisely this impossibility which is to be grasped through its effects' (Žižek 163). *Das Ding*, a kind of primal pleasure in the Real, connected with the fantasy of organic being, occupies a position between our fantasy of death (our symbolization of it) and natural death (the obliteration of the signifying network itself).[7] *Das Ding* is thus the primal pleasure *beyond* fantasy that the human subject seeks through the death drive, and that leads to the void – the dead end of desire.[8]

Although the projects of Bataille/Douglas and Freud/Lacan are fundamentally different, their theoretical affinities serve to conceptualize horror: that is, Lacan's theory of psychic process, of *desire* as it connects to *death*, undergirds the anthropological paradigm for horror. In both paradigms, violence gives birth to the human subject: for Bataille, in the violence of nature's 'orgy of annihilation' and renewal; for Lacan, in the radical, inaugural split, which Kristeva describes as the 'murder of soma' (*Revolution in Poetic Language* 75). Further, Lacan's symbolic order, which represses all that cannot be accommodated by the Law, includes the prohibitions of Bataille's taboo; and the Lacanian subject's desire for originary oneness, inseparable from the desire for death, resonates in the desire for continuity that threatens the discontinuous self of Bataille's subject. Moreover, that which cannot be categorized or described, which escapes the symbolic order (for Bataille and Douglas, the marginal and indeterminate; for Lacan, *jouissance* – ultimately

7 In a translation by Wlad Godzich of the Russian text of an essay on Dostoevsky (published in Moscow in 1977; cited in Todorov 98), Bakhtin makes a similar distinction: '"But there exists no death from the inside; it exists for no one ... it has absolutely no existence [31.315]. The absence of a conscious death (death-for-oneself) is as objective a fact as the absence of conscious birth. Therein resides the specificity of consciousness" (31.316).'

8 Lacan's brilliant essay on Hamlet, 'the man who has lost the way of his desire' (12), takes up Freud's notion of the uncanny to illustrate the imbrication of death in desire, and of the Real in the symbolic. During moments of 'subjective disorganization' Hamlet experiences depersonalization ('the imaginary limits between subject and object change' [22]). At these moments, Hamlet's fantasy of his identity decomposes; this, for Lacan, is the experience of the uncanny. Ultimately, 'what is rejected from the symbolic register reappears in the real,' but the fatal signifier 'can be purchased only with [Hamlet's] own flesh and [his] own blood' (38). The subject must be eclipsed 'at the precise point where the object *a* attains its greatest value' (29).

Das Ding) figures, for all, the dreaded and desired void. In fact, that which makes Bataille's void 'unimaginable' is precisely what Lacan is concerned with demonstrating, namely, the grounding of symbolization in the unconscious.

There are also important affinities in psychoanalytic and anthropological theory with respect to the positioning of woman as primary site of destabilization. Lacan's controversial statement, 'The woman does not exist' ('God and the *Jouissance* of The Woman' 144), refers to woman's status as fantasy with respect to the symbolic order, her cultural construction as the symptom for man, that is, the privileged site of his prohibitions, the embodiment of his repressions and idealizations. As we might expect of theories produced in a patriarchal culture, woman's 'identity' consists of shiftings between contradictory significations: she carries dual signification as 'the midwife of individuation' (the radical split, original experience of absence and loss), and as its idealized opposite, 'the impossible union in life with the lost primordial' (Bronfen 33). Moreover, in her function as erotic object, woman mediates sexuality (physical union, an exultant form of dissolution) and death (ultimate formlessness). Finally, in the marginality of her (non)'identity,' woman figures marginality itself – Douglas's dirt, Bataille's horrific.

In sum, then, horror may be conceptualized by means of these theorists as the interstitiality – the in-betweenness, the marginality – at the nexus of sexuality and death. In accordance with this concept, representations of horror can be expected to foreground marginal states of being (for example, bodily deformities and mutilation, madness, dead but uncorrupted flesh), as well as transgressions of taboos (incest, murder) that protect the symbolic order against the destructive power of subversive desire. In both types of representation, woman serves as the primary locus of destabilization.

II

When considered in light of the psychoanalytic/anthropological paradigm, the representation of horror in early modern English tragedy requires a reconfiguration of terms. The crux of the problem concerns the positioning of woman as the locus of destabilization. The paradigm contains an implicit binary in the opposition of the shifting significations of the *female* to the *male* authority of the symbolic order: that is, in the establishment of the marginality of woman as the *other* of man, phallocentrism necessarily finds social expression in binarism, in the construction of categories that are differentiated as opposite.[9] However, a large corpus of recent scholarship, following Foucault's lead, has challenged this assumption with respect to early modern sexuality.[10] Although a plethora of early modern patriarchal discourses – religious, legal, and political – insists upon the division of the sexes in the regulation of the social order, other discourses, most notably in the areas of medicine and biology, render this division problematical.[11] In early modern England, the theatre serves as a site for the exploration of this problematic: sexual 'identity' is represented on the stage as fluid and shifting rather than categorically (and biologically) fixed. As a result, no female figure in a play is ever consistently or unproblematically 'female' because theatrical conventions themselves interrogate the meanings of 'male' and 'female.'

Not surprisingly, the convention of the boy actor, or theatrical transvestism, serves as the foremost signifier of discontinuous sexuality.[12] As Peter Stallybrass has persuasively argued, the cross-dressed boy actor stages two contradictory fixations or fantasies of sexuality: what is visible and prosthetically suggestive of the 'essential' marks of female sexual identity (breasts, vagina); and what is absent and imagined – the body beneath the prosthetic fantasy, which may be imagined as

9 As Elizabeth Bronfen argues, Lacanian theory itself 'evades essentialism ... woman's proximity to radical Otherness does not exclude anatomical males'; it is thus possible to cross over between anatomically prescribed categories of masculine and feminine. 'Lacan ... never loses sight of the fact that these constructions, operating with notions of sexual lack, do so as a superimposition on to a ubiquitous, non-gendered split of death's presence in life' (211). For a discussion of the symbolic construction of woman, see Lacan, 'God and the *Jouissance* of The Woman.'

10 For a representative collection of this scholarship, see *Erotic Politics*, ed. Susan Zimmerman. Queer theory has recently mounted an even more radical challenge to the imposition of modern heterosexual norms in the analysis of early modern sexuality. See Jonathan Goldberg's *Sodometries* and his collection of essays, *Queering the Renaissance*.

11 Although Thomas Laqueur's argument, in *Making Sex*, for the dominance of the fungible, one-sex model in the early modern period has been challenged, the model itself has not been displaced as a major hegemonic discourse. Interestingly, Laqueur's model has recently been invoked in a contemporary context by Carol J. Clover in her excellent study of sexual positioning in the slasher film. According to Clover, slasher films foreground the uncertainty of sexual identity, or 'one-sex reasoning,' by feminizing the male killer and phallicizing the Final Girl or heroine (*Men, Women and Chainsaws* 15).

12 Despite its awkwardness, the contemporary term 'transvestism' has been widely adopted in studies of early modern sexuality.

either male or female ('Transvestism and the "Body Beneath,"' passim). Transvestism thus requires the simultaneous awareness of contradictions: it is a presence that speaks of absence. To foreground absence is to 'play' with liminality in a *self-conscious*, overt fashion. As Catherine Belsey puts it, on the early modern stage 'it is possible ... to speak from a position which is not that of a full, unified, gendered subject ... A male actor *and* a female character is speaking' ('Disrupting Sexual Difference' 180–1). Referring to Kristeva's poststructuralist definition of difference as '"itself the ground of meaning, *within* identity, including sexual identity,"'[13] Belsey notes that 'the effect will be to bring out "the multiplicity of every person's possible identifications" [Kristeva, 'Women's Time' 35] ... in the margins of sexual difference, those margins which a metaphysical sexual polarity obliterates' (188–9).[14]

Because transvestism is foregrounded in all dramatic performances of the English Renaissance, it is central to any analysis of the theatrical representation of sexuality. But I would argue that the multiplicity of possible identifications to which Belsey alludes may also be suggested by actors who are not cross-dressed, that transvestism is the most accessible (and intractable) symptom of a far-reaching interrogation of sexual categories on the Renaissance stage. Contradictory fixations also emerge, for example, in tragedies whose male protagonists become so invested in the obsessive demonization of females that they themselves accede to the status of that which they would violently expel or obliterate: they become men/women. Because transvestism is the *sine qua non* of every English Renaissance play, it always intensifies the representation of this obsession, but does not always do so directly. Transvestism is, in effect, the primary symptom of a complexly configured fascination with sexual liminality. Horror hyperbolizes this fascination; it raises the ante, as it were. Thus the tragedies that foreground woman as locus of horror make possible male identification with that which is most

---

13 Belsey is quoting from Kristeva's essay on 'Women's Time,' *Signs* 7.1 (1981): 13–35; 34.

14 The viewpoints of Stallybrass and Belsey are not identical. Whereas Stallybrass argues that the early modern theatre stages a multiplicity that is both historically and semiotically prior to what we now call sexual difference, Belsey contends that sexual indeterminacy in the theatre arises from the blurring of sexual categories that are inscribed in various hegemonic discourses that the theatre interrogates. Belsey's position accords more closely with Lacan's principle that sexual division begins with language and as such is always already inscribed in human consciousness by the symbolic order.

alien to the symbolic order. If it is the marginality, the non-identity, the 'dirt' of woman that opens the way to the void, and her sexuality in particular that mediates sexuality and death, then male complicity in the representation of 'woman' radically contravenes the sexual binarism that reifies the phallic principle. In such instances, the male is overtly implicated in female marginality: male/female occupies the 'absent,' liminal space in which horror resides.

Accordingly, theatrical representations of horror that insistently show-case the female *body* – as erotic object, as reproductive centre, or as corpse – distinctively enable the interrogation of sexual identity. Two such plays from the Jacobean period, Middleton's *The Revenger's Tragedy*[15] and Webster's *The Duchess of Malfi*, exemplify the ambiguities implicit in theatrical attempts to instantiate horror in the female.

In *The Revenger's Tragedy* three violated female bodies serve as emblems of sexuality and death: the corpse of the raped and suicidal wife of Antonio; the incestuously lustful body of the Duchess; and the skull of the poisoned virgin Gloriana. These emblems signify interdependently in the play. For example, on one level Antonio's wife, as a suicide, and Gloriana, as blanched bones, function respectively as symbols of the radically cleansed and transcendently pure. Yet they also represent horrific states of marginality. The fully-fleshed corpse of Antonio's wife, centrepiece of her own wake, remains erotically powerful in its interstitial state. Even more grotesquely threatening is the 'fleshed out' figure of Gloriana – the skull at-tired – which arouses the Duke's lust and poisons him with a kiss. Mediating between these two ambiguous emblems of death is the transgressively depraved body of the living Duchess.

As dual symbols of purity and putrefaction, skull and corpse figure the oppositional extremes in the patriarchal symbolization of woman. Bataille argues that the decomposing human corpse, the flesh as food for worms, serves as anguishing reminder of 'the sickening primary condition of life,' whereas 'whitened bones' close the disgusting connection with decomposition, 'draw the first veil of decency and solemnity over death' (56). The clean, hard surface, the 'very ragged bone' (1.1.18) of

---

15 For a brief review of the controversy surrounding the authorship of *The Revenger's Tragedy*, see the Penguin text, ed. Bryan Loughrey and Neil Taylor (xxv–xxix). Most scholars now accept Middleton's authorship; the play will be included in the forthcoming edition of Middleton's works to be published by Oxford University Press.

Vindice's 'bony lady' (16) – the hollow sockets of her skull once held eyes like 'diamonds' (19) – fix Gloriana in a defleshed, decontaminated (and virginally uncontaminated) state. As skull, she can safely represent the woman as Other, the 'truth' of the uncorrupted male subject.[16] But Vindice's 'fleshing' of the skull in the murder scene stages sensationally the fatal potency that the bones would mask. Here, Gloriana's erotic attractiveness and the putrefaction of her body are inseparable. No longer clean, the skull is situated at the intersection of sexuality and death.

The corpse of Antonio's violated wife – 'That virtuous lady!' (1.4.6), 'precedent for wives!' (7), 'As cold in lust as she is now in death' (35) – has similarly ambiguous signification. Not yet pared of its flesh, and displayed with Latin prayer-book pointing to a maxim on deathless honour, the beautiful corpse would be inscribed by Antonio and his colleagues with a timeless stability that denies the violence of the rape: her body 'merits a tomb of pearl' (70). But as Elizabeth Bronfen has argued, any representation of the female corpse as a 'triumph over disseverment and facticity' (11) is bound to contain its own failure. In looking *over* the dead beauty, the male gaze would use her as 'mediatrix [with] the absolute' (49), a form of exteriorization that is inevitably disrupted by the 'decay, disease and fatality' (11) invested in the female genitals. In fact, Antonio's graphic description of his wife's public rape – 'He [Junior, the Duchess's youngest son] harried her amidst a throng of panders / ... And fed the ravenous vulture of his lust' (1.4.42, 44) – dominates the scene; the still and prostrate body, 'alive' in its beauty, perversely invites the imaginative re-enactment of the frenzied crime. Thus violence disrupts the apotheosis of the corpse: the scene ends with a plan to bathe 'the ruins of so fair a monument / ... in the defacer's blood' (67–8).

That which the emblems of skull and corpse would pre-empt or foreclose is hyperbolized in the unleashed potencies of the Duchess. Symptomatic of an uncurtailed corruption that saturates the court, the Duchess's sexual destructiveness is invariably linked to images of conception, reproduction, and maternity. She sees no cause for censure

16 In her chapter 'Sacrificing Extremity' (181–204) Bronfen argues that 'women are often culturally associated with ... decomposition, with first burial (they are the prime mourners, they wash and guard the corpse)' (199), whereas bones and tombs, the secondary, unpolluted symbols of death, are appropriated by males. In the bones of a female corpse, the female is reborn as masculine sign.

when Antonio's wife is raped by her 'youngest, dearest son' (1.2.103), and persuades Spurio that incest is no worse a perversion than 'to live a bastard, / The curse o' the womb' (159–60). Transgression of the primary taboos is power: 'Who but an eunuch would not sin?' (165). In responding to the nihilistic dynamism of the Duchess, Spurio perversely constructs his 'appetite' for her from images of his own reckless conception:

> *Spurio.*   … some stirring dish
> Was my first father, when deep healths went round,
> And ladies' cheeks were painted red with wine,
> Their tongues as short and nimble as their heels,
> Uttering words sweet and thick …
> …
> I was begot in impudent wine and lust.
> Step-mother, I consent to thy desires …   (1.2.179–91)

Although the maternal seducer is not mentioned in Vindice's castigation of incest, the Duchess's lascivious conduct with Spurio (as manifested in their repeated kissing, for example) gives visible shape to it:

> *Vindice.*   O Dutch lust! Fulsome lust!
> Drunken procreation, which begets so many drunkards.
> Some father dreads not (gone to bed in wine)
> To slide from the mother, and cling the daughter-in-law;
> Some uncles are adulterous with their nieces,
> Brothers with brothers' wives. O hour of incest!
> Any kin now next to the rim o'th'sister
> Is man's meat in these days …   (1.3.58–65)

The mother-lover who provokes her bastard stepson, her 'love's true-begot' (1.2.111), to 'double' and 'heap,' who publicly flouts the primary taboos, unambiguously threatens the symbolic order: she is what any woman not already rendered as skull or corpse might become.[17]

---

17 Peter Stallybrass, in 'Reading the Body and the Jacobean Theater of Consumption: *The Revenger's Tragedy* (1606),' examines images of eating and of the kiss as signifiers of 'the symbolic burden that women are forced to bear … when they are conceptualized as mapping both an ideal enclosure and its impossibility, both the negation of and the figures for eating/being eaten, corrupter/corrupted' (218). Such imagery,

If the significations of these three bodies on the Jacobean stage accord with woman's contradictory status in the symbolic order, their modes of representation simultaneously threaten the security of the phallic principle. The body beneath the corpse of Antonio's wife, showcased so as to act as sexual stimulant, is that of a male actor. Antonio's reconstruction of her rape, in full view of her corpse, further heightens this ambiguity. The physicality that underwrites the incest theme, and the emphasis on wombs, conception, and reproductive power in the representation of the Duchess/boy actor, produce similarly multi-layered sexual valences. And when Vindice metatheatrically 'dresses up' Gloriana, he directly constructs her sexual debasement according to his own obsessively misogynist view of woman, thereby investing himself in the destruction of her 'ideal' self, and in the corrosive potency of her sexuality.

The death of the Duke is fully horrific.[18] He mistakes the cosmeticized skull for the 'bright face' (1.1.16), the 'life and beauty' (17) of a maid like the original Gloriana. The Duke refuses to recognize death in beauty, whereas Vindice talks of little else throughout the play. Gloriana's skull, an unpolluted symbol, should evoke an idealized memory of her beauty; but as Vindice progressively develops the *memento mori* as emblem of the corrupting power of female sexuality, he effectively erases this memory:

Advance thee, o thou terror to fat folks,
To have their costly three-pil'd flesh worn off
As bare as this ...   (1.1.45–7)

Does every proud and self-affecting dame
Camphor her face for this? ...

---

which foregrounds the mouth, also figures prominently in the representation of the Duchess, and of Gloriana as agent of death.

18 My use of 'horrific' in the context of my theoretical paradigm does not exclude other tonalities in the scene, such as, for example, its comic aspects. Part of the larger study in which I am currently engaged focuses on pre-realistic theatrical practices that yoke conflicting tonalities in the representation of horror. In addition to transvestism, these include the juxtaposition of the comic and tragic; the hyperbolization of effects, as in the parodic use of the court masque for multiple murders at the conclusion of plays; the mixture of allegorical and non-allegorical dramaturgical modes; the shifts in focus occasioned by the proliferation of tangential 'sub-plots'; and the prevalence of metatheatrical allusions. In aggregate, these practices situate theatrical horror in an artifice that is distinctive to the early modern period, and that contrasts markedly with neo-realistic genres (including Clover's slasher film) of later centuries.

...

Here might a scornful and ambitious woman
Look through and through herself; see, ladies, with false forms
You deceive men but cannot deceive worms.   (3.5.83–97)

In Vindice's obsessive imagery, 'pure' and 'impure' (or cosmetic) female beauty become finally indistinguishable. Both are subject to corruption, but, more dangerously, are themselves corrupting, death-dealing to men. The 'ideal' Gloriana whom Vindice is supposedly devoted to avenging is no longer separable from the 'quaint piece of beauty' (3.5.53) that he serves up to the Duke. More fundamentally, in converting bones to flesh, Vindice eschews the sanitized (male) symbol for the dead female in favour of a direct investment in its opposite.

Further, through Gloriana's poison, Vindice transforms the Duke's head into a spontaneously putrefying piece of flesh, an incipient skull. The Duke's teeth fall out, his tongue starts to rot, and Vindice longs to 'tear up his lids / And make his eyes like comets shine through blood' (3.5.198–9). Part of what Hippolito calls the 'quaintness of [Vindice's] malice' (3.5.108) is to render the dying Duke as a hideous counterfoil to the instrument of Vindice's murder. Thus the poisoned Duke provides a visual emblem in another register for the destabilization of sexual distinction: female skull and male head, both produced by Vindice, link as interstitial images of corruption and death.

In this scene and indeed throughout the play, Vindice's manipulation of events traverses symbolic boundaries. Ostensibly following a moral imperative, Vindice is imaginatively invested in sexual depravity and taboo.[19] By recreating morbid versions of the evils he abhors (the staging of the Duke's death mimics the Duke's attempted seduction and murder of Gloriana), Vindice ironically incorporates that which he would destroy. Vindice's descriptions of Piato, himself in disguise, are revealing in this connection. Shortly after presenting an idealized image of the skull of Gloriana at the outset of the play, Vindice conjures Piato in similar terms: 'Strike thou my forehead into dauntless marble, / Mine eyes to steady sapphires' (1.3.8–9), the sapphire eyes evoking Gloriana's diamond eyes, and the incorruptible pearl of Antonio's wife's tomb. But by the end of the play, after Vindice has contaminated the whitened bones, that is, *sexualized* them in the service of death, he renounces

19 For the corruption implicit in Vindice's relationship with his sister, Castiza (which has an implicitly incestuous dimension), and with his mother, Gratiana, see Stallybrass 210 and passim.

Piato, and does so in terms usually reserved for women: "'Tis well he died; he was a witch' (5.3.119).

Thus the horror implicit in the marginality of the female bodies in *The Revenger's Tragedy* is inscribed not only in woman but in man as well, and in a double sense. In so far as one term of any binary is always implicit in its opposite, woman as Other will always represent the repressed desires and fears of the (male) symbolic order. But in the context of the unconscious, repression is precisely the point: the death drive is what *lies behind* the process of desire, the categories of 'male' and 'female' working to occlude the repressed connections between sexuality and death. In contradistinction to these mechanisms, early modern theatricality seems deliberately to 'play' with the very liminalities that the categorization would occlude, and in so doing to implicate man overtly in his own demonization of woman. Indeed, it might be argued that the more extreme the symbolic demonization appears to be, the more radically dual its signification. Vindice is the worst of misogynists, but he is also a witch.

In *The Duchess of Malfi* the investment of Ferdinand in the body of the Duchess is an even more complex example of the disruption of male/female positioning in the representation of horror. The body of the Duchess, its physical transformations, serve as organizing principle for the play's action, which is defined in terms of male responses to these transformations. First presented as lover, the Duchess moves through pregnancy and childbirth to maternity, and from maternity to death. Her private world, as Susan Wells has argued, is domestic: 'She is the "sprawling'st bedfellow"; she vomits; she eats apricots greedily; she calls out in childbirth; her hair turns grey' (66); she playfully teases and kisses her husband, and in her last moments she worries about cough syrup for her children. The insistence upon the Duchess's corporality/maternity simultaneously underscores her femaleness and the prosthetic fantasy of her femaleness: the Duchess's body, in all of the avatars made possible by her reproductive functions, is inhabited by a boy actor.

But in the play such contradictory fixations serve to underline the murkiness and confusion of Ferdinand's sexual obsession. Consumed by an incestuous desire that he would displace onto the body of his twin sister, Ferdinand is obdurate in resisting the Duchess's representation of herself as chaste. Insisting upon a celibate ideal, one that might cleanse his own diseased imagination, he demonizes her body as corrupt and contaminating. The violence he levels against her is thus justified in

terms of his prerogative to control the degradation of female sexuality. Throughout the play, Ferdinand's overwrought desire simultaneously conjures the Duchess's beauty and its rankness: '... her fault and
beauty / Blended together, show like leprosy, / The whiter, the fouler'
(3.4.61–3). He fantasizes her promiscuity in self-tormenting detail –
'... with some strong-thigh'd bargeman; / Or one o'th' wood-yard /
... or else some lovely squire' (2.5.43–5) – which feeds his 'wild-fire' (48)
rages. He would 'bequeath' his handkerchief to the Duchess's 'bastard'
in order 'to make soft lint for his mother's wounds, / When I have
hewed her to pieces' (2.5.29–30); or he would '... dip the sheets [the
lovers] lie in, in pitch or sulphur, / Wrap them in't, and then light
them like a match' (70–1). In wanting to envelop the lovers in fire at the
moment when they are wrapped sexually, Ferdinand would consume
both his own desire and his abhorrence of it.

   This is, of course, Ferdinand's purpose in finally having the Duchess
murdered, but he first attempts to wrench her from her domestic happi-
ness into the nightmare of his own despair. The sadistic tortures of the
madmen, the wax tableau of the Duchess's 'dead' husband and 'cubs'
(4.1.33), as Ferdinand calls her children, the severed hand proffered
in greeting, invite her to enter the transgressive, interstitial spaces of
taboo. These torments represent a perverted declaration of Ferdinand's
desire: he wants 'to bring her to despair' (4.1.114) in order to reassert
his power over her outside of the confines of the symbolic order.

   But Ferdinand can neither subjugate the Duchess nor escape his prohibited desire; even her murder fails to 'fix her in a general eclipse'
(2.5.80). The serene beauty of the Duchess as corpse confuses him:
'Cover her face. Mine eyes dazzle' (4.2.263). The corpse would deny
Ferdinand's image of the Duchess's body as a conduit for the pestilent
infection of 'whore's milk' and 'whore's blood' (2.5.48, 49). Instead, it
presents Ferdinand with a physical emblem of the female ideal that he
has tried to impose on the living Duchess: beautiful but self-possessed,
whole and incorruptible – in Lacanian terms, the 'truth' in the place of
the Other.

   Ferdinand's idealization is of course incompatible with the demonization that is its opposite, both originating in his own duality. Ferdinand is
the Duchess's twin; the 'witchcraft' that 'lies in her rank blood' (3.1.78)
and that inevitably disrupts the false apotheosis of her purity is the
counterpoise of his own. The incestuous infection of his own blood
has created the Duchess as witch. In the end, his body, linked with
hers in blood, cannot be independently differentiated. His grotesque

refusal (lycanthropy) to accept the Duchess's 'not-being,' his compulsion to assume the shape of a wolf in order to 'scrape ... up' dead bodies (4.2.307), would connect him to her corpse and to the confusion of its dual signification.[20] The nightmare of his sexual obsession has given way to the horrific marginality of the wolf/man: literally enmeshed in the (female) generative power of corruption and decay, Ferdinand importunes his friends to 'rip up his flesh' (5.2.19).[21]

If woman, in Middleton's and Webster's tragedies, is to be found at the nexus of sexuality and death, the site of horror, so is man. The interplay of contradictory fixations made possible by theatrical trans-vestism would appear to have encouraged on the Renaissance stage a profoundly unsettling exploration of the complicity of death in desire. Here, representation foregrounds rather than forecloses marginality, challenging the protective sexual categories of the symbolic order, and, in so doing, pointing horrifically at the originary oneness that figures the void.

WORKS CITED

Bakhtin, Mikhail. *Rabelais and His World.* Trans. Hélène Iswolsky. Bloomington: Indiana UP, 1984.

Bataille, Georges. *Erotism: Death and Sensuality.* Trans. Mary Dalwood. San Francisco: City Lights Books, 1957.

Belsey, Catherine. 'Desire's Excess and the English Renaissance Theatre: *Edward II, Troilus and Cressida, Othello.' Erotic Politics: Desire on the Renaissance Stage.* Ed. Susan Zimmerman. New York and London: Routledge, 1992. 84–103.

20 Lycanthropy also connects Ferdinand to the Duchess's murdered children, whom he has consistently degraded: 'The death / Of young wolves is never to be pitied' (4.2.257–8).

21 Bosola's relationship to the Duchess also has sadistic and erotic features, but Bosola's nihilism, unlike Ferdinand's fanaticism, substitutes cynicism for passion. The *pas de deux* of the execution scene (Bosola's growing sympathy for the Duchess only intensifies the sadism of his proffered 'comfort' [4.1.85]) culminates in the necrophiliac moment when he attempts to restore 'fresh colour' (4.2.343) to the 'pale lips' (342) of her (presumed) corpse. It is a breakthrough moment in that for once Bosola is able to imagine the possibility of goodness. But the recognition does not change him. Like Ferdinand, he is unable to reconcile the 'ideal' Duchess with his loathing for the 'rottenness' of female sexuality, or to find a shape of his own, amid his many shifts and disguises, in relation to that ideal.

- 'Disrupting Sexual Difference: Meaning and Gender in the Comedies.'
  Alternative Shakespeares. Ed. John Drakakis. London and New York: Methuen;
  Routledge, 1985. 166–90.
Bronfen, Elizabeth. *Over Her Dead Body: Death, Femininity and the Aesthetic.*
  Manchester: Manchester UP; New York: Routledge, 1992.
Clover, Carol J. *Men, Women and Chainsaws: Gender in the Modern Horror Film.*
  Princeton: Princeton UP, 1992.
Douglas, Mary. *Purity and Danger: An Analysis of the Concepts of Pollution and
  Taboo*. 1966. London: Routledge, 1991.
Freud, Sigmund. 'On the Universal Tendency to Debasement in the Sphere
  of Love,' 'The Theme of the Three Caskets,' and 'Beyond the Pleasure
  Principle.' Trans. James Strachey. *The Freud Reader*. Ed. Peter Gay. New York
  and London: Norton, 1989. 394–400; 514–22; 594–626.
- 'The "Uncanny."' *The Standard Edition of the Complete Psychological Works of
  Sigmund Freud*. Vol. 17. Ed. and trans. James Strachey. London: Hogarth,
  1968. 218–56.
Goldberg, Jonathan. *Sodometries: Renaissance Texts, Modern Sexualities*. Stanford:
  Stanford UP, 1992.
- ed. *Queering the Renaissance*. Durham, NC and London: Duke UP, 1994.
Kristeva, Julia. *Powers of Horror: An Essay on Abjection*. Trans. Leon S. Roudiez.
  New York: Columbia UP, 1982.
- *Revolution in Poetic Language*. Trans. Margaret Waller. New York: Columbia
  UP, 1984.
Lacan, Jacques. 'Desire and the Interpretation of Desire in *Hamlet.*' *Literature
  and Psychoanalysis: The Question of Reading: Otherwise*. Ed. Shoshana Felman.
  Baltimore and London: Johns Hopkins UP, 1982. 11–52.
- *Écrits: A Selection*. Trans. Alan Sheridan. New York and London: Norton,
  1977.
- 'God and the *Jouissance* of The Woman. A Love Letter.' *Feminine Sexuality:
  Jacques Lacan and the École Freudienne*. Ed. Juliet Mitchell and Jacqueline
  Rose. New York: Norton, 1985. 138–48.
Laqueur, Thomas. *Making Sex: Body and Gender from the Greeks to Freud.*
  Cambridge, MA: Harvard UP, 1990.
Middleton, Thomas. *The Revenger's Tragedy. Five Plays: Thomas Middleton*. Ed.
  Bryan Loughrey and Neil Taylor. London: Penguin, 1988. 71–160.
Stallybrass, Peter. 'Reading the Body and the Jacobean Theater of Consumption:
  The Revenger's Tragedy (1606).' *Staging the Renaissance: Reinterpretations of
  Elizabethan and Jacobean Drama*. Ed. David Scott Kastan and Peter Stallybrass.
  New York and London: Routledge, 1991. 210–20.

- 'Transvestism and the "Body Beneath": Speculating on the Boy Actor.' *Erotic Politics: Desire on the Renaissance Stage.* Ed. Susan Zimmerman. New York and London: Routledge, 1992. 64–83.
Todorov, Tzvetan. *Mikhail Bakhtin: The Dialogical Principle.* Trans. Wlad Godzich. Theory and History of Literature 13. Minneapolis: U of Minnesota P, 1984.
Webster, John. *The Duchess of Malfi. John Webster: Three Plays.* Introduction and Notes by D.C. Gunby. Middlesex: Penguin, 1972. 167–292.
Wells, Susan. *The Dialectics of Representation.* Baltimore: Johns Hopkins UP, 1985.
Zimmerman, Susan. Introduction. *Erotic Politics: Desire on the Renaissance Stage.* Ed. Susan Zimmerman. New York and London: Routledge, 1992. 1–11.
Žižek, Slavoj. *The Sublime Object of Ideology.* London: Verso, 1989.

PART FOUR
POLITICAL ENGAGEMENT AND PROFESSIONAL
DISCONTINUITIES

9

Academic Exchange: Text, Politics, and the Construction of English and American Identities in Contemporary Renaissance Criticism

BARRY TAYLOR

When New Historicism plays with history to enhance the text, its enhancement is like the colorizing of old movies for present consumption. The denial and defacement of the black and white originals prevents the possibility of cultural critique ... To learn political lessons from the past we need to have it in black and white.

Jane Marcus (133)

I start with Jane Marcus's statement because it opens up in a particularly emphatic fashion a number of oppositions regarding the relations between history, writing, and politics, relations that I hope to problematize in what follows. I am particularly concerned with the opposition announced by Marcus between the 'political,' and the 'play' of a historical writing that is relegated to the position of a more or less frivolous textuality. The binarism – politics/textuality – is closely involved with another binarism that has structured a number of accounts of the history of critical work on the Renaissance since 1980, and that persists, in different ways, in recent books by Alan Sinfield and Francis Barker – namely, the oppositional pairing of a

I should like to thank Robin Durie, Andrew Lawson, Duncan Webster, and Susan Wiseman for their comments and suggestions.

('textualist') American new historicism, and a ('political') English cultural materialism.[1]

It is in some ways surprising, to elaborate upon my epigraph, to be told that the past is in black and white, this black-and-whiteness serving so clearly as a sign of reality over against the supplementary enhancement, the playing around with originals, with which new historicism is charged. The demand for politics, and the identification of a deficiency of the political in new historicism, is involved here with the demand for a past that rests, in its black and whiteness, outside of the supplementary 'play,' the 'enhancement' of writing. One of my central concerns is with the assertion of the grounding of a politics (in the case of Marcus a certain version of feminism) in a place outside of the field identified as that of textuality, and the mounting from that place of critiques of modes of writing that are deemed to stay within 'textuality' and therefore to resist, ignore, or trivialize 'politics.' My own uncertainties about such an account of the relation between politics, history, and textuality prompt one of this essay's guiding questions: Was the past in black and white when it was the present?

Brits in Struggle, Yanks in Suits: 'Politics' vs. 'Professionalism'

Paraphrasing Howard Felperin's contribution to the 'Essex Symposia' volume, *Uses of History: Marxism, Postmodernism and the Renaissance*, Francis Barker and his fellow editors, all from the University of Essex, describe the differences between the two critical 'schools' of American new historicism and British cultural materialism in the following way: 'The British model perhaps lacks the sleekness of its United States counterpart but at least runs in the tracks of a well-established historical materialist tradition, allowing it to display quite openly its commitment to political change' (15). This little fable, of the stolid but dependable British puttering along behind their smart but meretricious American

---

1 Where I continue to use the terms 'England,' 'America,' 'English,' and 'American,' it is to signal their deployment within the structure of oppositions that I am questioning here. While my focus in this essay is necessarily more upon the displacement of the dominant 'English' term in this key binarism, I am aware of the importance of many of the criticisms that have been levelled against the practices and theoretical implications of new historicist work. My purpose is not to reinstate the binarism by elevating the subordinated 'American' term, but to retrieve a sense of the heterogeneity of critical positions and the difficulty of thinking the relationships between history, politics, and textuality on both 'sides' of the Atlantic.

competitors, a fable with its resonances of homely tortoises and flash Yankee hares, is one that surfaces in different versions in a number of histories of recent Renaissance criticism. Whatever their specific inflections and emphases, all of these variants share in a binary tropology – announced here in the opposition of rough reliability to the sleek and slippery – that reveals the fable to be the localized enunciation of a much longer-established and more widely articulated narrative of Englishness vs. Americanness.[2] One aspect of that larger narrative that is re-articulated here is the association of 'Britain' with *tradition*, with its implied opposition to a historically deracinated U.S.A. The Essex variant is of interest in its linking of a particular kind of tradition, 'historical materialist,' to an *explicit* politics, a politics that can be 'display[ed] quite openly' (15). This linkage is commonly found in the recent histories of new historicism, including some by United States scholars. In Louis Montrose's 'Professing the Renaissance: The Poetics and Politics of Culture,' for example, politics in the work of 'American male academics' is seen as being safely displaced into and confined by 'the English past that is presently under study' (26), while British work is said to be marked by a forging of continuities between the politics of the past under study and a present in which 'the coercive pressure of the state upon educational institutions and practices is now conspicuously direct and intense' (27). For Montrose that engagement of British criticism with a more explicit and more *present* politics than its U.S. counterpart (one more conspicuous, direct, intense) is once again linked to a situation, unlike that in the U.S., in which 'radical politics and radical discourses enjoy stronger tradition' (27).

As in many narratives of the presentness of a presence, this one, through the trope of tradition, grounds presence in the continuity of a singular history. In some accounts, this superior presence of the political in British work accrues to itself a quasi-mystical language of communion, of the English academic's at-oneness with his or her (but it is usually his) radical heritage. In Felperin's '"Cultural poetics" versus "cultural materialism"' we are told, for example, that 'whereas cultural poetics inhabits a discursive field in which Marxism has never really been present, its British counterpart inhabits one from which Marxism has never really been absent ... Its practitioners seem to have been born

---

2 One episode in that longer history that is relevant to the metaphorics of the Essex quotation is the 'streamlining controversy' over the Americanization of English and European design, and particularly car design, discussed by Dick Hebdige (45–76).

into this continuing discourse of history in something of the way the rest of us were born into our native language' (88). The implication here is that U.S. scholars inhabit a space cut off from the organic continuity of old-world history, a state of historical depthlessness where politics cannot take root. The implication relates to the more general cultural thematics of American *belatedness* that is at play when Graham Holderness states, in the same collection, that 'American "political" critics seem to think of their ideology as having been formed in the environment of 1960s campus radicalism ... where their British counterparts are at least as likely to have imbibed their ideological formation from the free milk and orange juice of the post-war socialist reconstruction' ('Production' 157–8). Here the nurturance of the immemorial socialist Mother is set against the belated faddishness of 'campus radicalism'; the latter, by implication, is learned rather than 'imbibed,' generated in the academy, and, according to Holderness, bears its withered fruit in the depoliticized academicism of current American critical practice: 'New Historicism has no sense of a ... political legacy, and takes its intellectual bearings directly from "post-structuralist" theoretical and philosophical models' ('Production' 157).

By these accounts, then, American new historicists appear to be denied, by their very historical displacement and belatedness, any access to that continuity of 'history' that brings with it – along with the free milk and orange juice – 'a class politics that exercises something like a gravitational force' (Cohen 27). What, then, *are* American scholars of the Renaissance supposed to have, in this post-historical, post- (or is it pre-) political vacuum they inhabit? One thing, as the last quotation from Holderness suggests, is 'theory.' In his reference to a 'direct,' 'intellectual' taking of bearings in U.S. criticism, Holderness implies that the influence of 'theory' is a matter of a closed circuitry of academic discourses that is sealed off from the arena of 'politics.' 'Cultural materialism,' on the other hand, 'is much more concerned to engage with contemporary cultural practice' ('Production' 157). Academic theory/political practice: a familiar opposition that is deployed here as one key element in a scenario of American academic 'professionalization' that is set against that of British politicization.

The histories of new historicism frequently invoke the destruction or recuperation of 'politics' by the structures and protocols of the American academy. Montrose, for example, refers to new historicism's 'almost sudden installation as the newest academic orthodoxy, to its rapid assimilation by the "interpretive community" of Renaissance literary studies'

(18), while Don Wayne describes 'the condition of the male academic literary critic in the United States' as one of 'institutionally enforced alienation from the actual conditions that lead him to produce scholarship in one or another mode of critical discourse' (58; see also Lentricchia 242; and Felperin 79). In terms of the characterization of new historicist practice, the stress on academicism and professionalization comes through in descriptions of new historicism as confined within a quasi-antiquarian discourse on the past that refuses to make connections with the politics of the present (Holderness, 'Production' 157; Wayne 49), as a Geertzian anthropology that constitutes society and history as entirely discursive (Barker 143–206), as concerned too much with what has been *written*, as opposed to theatrical and other practices (Holderness, 'Production' 158, 164), or as an anthropology whose characteristic use of the anecdote betrays an 'impressionistic *belle-lettrisme*' (Barker 199n58). In all of this, the term 'deconstruction' frequently hovers on- or just off-stage as the bad spirit of textualism, presiding over a critical practice that, in the words of Alan Sinfield, 'often hesitates to develop its political potential. It slides back into old historicism or takes the easy route into the new oblivious formalism of poststructuralist word games' (285).

The image that emerges from such representations, of the white male new historicist as the more or less anguished, more or less complicit academic incarnation of corporation man, is a commonplace of the recent literature, often invoked to explain why American scholars are drawn to the 'containment' or recuperation model of power in their historical analyses – the explanation in terms of '"left disillusionment"' to which Catherine Gallagher refers (38; see also Sinfield 285–90). In a particularly hostile version, it issues in Holderness's Essex Symposium essay in the image of Greenblatt-as-exemplary-new-historicist, the reclaimer of history's marginalized and dispossessed voices, who 'encounters a need simultaneously to adopt a voice capable of contesting power and authority within the apparatus of that very academic institution established to suppress those lost voices. Greenblatt's work has already, significantly, been widely acknowledged as the acceptable face of political criticism; and many a voice crying compellingly in the wilderness has ended up as a voice droning unopposed through the Senior Common Room' ('Production' 158–9). The implication, of course, is that English voices such as Holderness's own resonate more authentically against the surfaces of some extra-academic reality, undeadened by the absorptive walls of the 'academic institution.' The element of overstatement in this construction of the British situation is the focus of my next section.

In diachronic terms, as I have suggested, the commonly invoked 'tradition' of British Marxist cultural critique is supposed to secure for cultural materialism the historical grounding of its contemporary political discourse, and the politicization of its historical analysis. In synchronic terms, the penetration of the walls of the academy by critical discourse, and its authenticating purchase upon an external sphere of political realities, is conjured up by focusing attention upon studies in the ideological reproduction of Shakespeare as the exemplary form of cultural materialist practice. This – the focus of Holderness's *Shakespeare Recycled* and *The Shakespeare Myth*, for example, or of part 2 of Dollimore and Sinfield's *Political Shakespeare* (130–239) – is where the academic analysis of canonical texts can be most dramatically envisioned as entering into unmediated struggle with the state for the definition of English national identity itself. Thus Felperin can refer to 're-readings of the canonical texts of Elizabethan drama' as the means by which 'these critics read and write to change the world, or at least the structure of British society, through the State ideological apparatus of higher education' (88). Or Holderness can less precisely invoke cultural materialism's relation to 'contemporary cultural practice,' which may refer again to the university's role – apparently an exclusively British one – as an ISA, or to then Tory disputes around the role of the English literary canon in the government's National Curriculum for schools, or perhaps to a heated argument about Shakespeare's ideological function on the letters page of the *London Review of Books* in the early nineties (for the latter, see Hawkes 154 and Sinfield 8–9). However vague the formulation, it is nevertheless clear that the 'reproduction of Shakespeare' tendency in cultural materialism is seen as exemplifying a critical practice that enters directly into an embrace with the reality of contemporary politics. From that place the practices and address of American new historicism can be characterized by opposition as apolitical, politically acceptable, politically belated and therefore superficial, or recuperated by the disciplinary machine of the academy.

Tradition and the Individual Militant: The Genealogy of Cultural Materialism

What becomes clear in hostile references to American 'institutional leftwardness' (Felperin 88), 'campus radicalism' or 'the acceptable face of political criticism' (Holderness 'Production' 157, 158) is that rather than an opposition between a political criticism and one without politics, what is being constructed in these narratives is an opposition between two versions of political criticism: one that claims a metaphysically grounded authenticity, and one that, in its inability or unwillingness to assume any such position, is deemed 'not genuinely *historical* or seriously political' (Felperin 86). It becomes important, then, to specify my reasons for describing the founding narrative of English cultural materialist politics as metaphysical or mythological, by considering in more detail one recent version of it.

Chiding Walter Cohen for starting his account of British 'leftist cultural criticism' in 1980, Holderness refers to the achievements of 'British Marxism' in the 1930s and 1950s, which were 'mediated into our modern cultural practice by the work and example of Raymond Williams' ('Production' 159). That continuity is invoked despite the acknowledgment of the 'wholesale revision of earlier variants of Marxism' that intervened in the shape of the British assimilation of Althusser during the 1970s, and the subsequent opening of 'dialectical relations with linguistic, psychoanalytic and feminist theories' (159). Nevertheless, Holderness characterizes 'the revisionist Marxism we are likely to be holding on to today' as 'not so very different from the Marxism we inherited at the end of the 1960s' ('Production' 160). This position is maintained despite Holderness's later acknowledgment that 'Marxism was very much, in the late 1960s and early 1970s, a philosophy in crisis and change' (161). In fact, if we reconsider one or two of the key moments in Holderness's narrative, we can see that crisis and change, rather than the unruffled dialectical unfolding of a tradition, are what the story is about.

If, first, we consider the crucial mediating function of Raymond Williams in Holderness's account, we find a writer whose trajectory marks precisely a series of *dis*continuities in the relation between English Marxism and the critique of culture. Williams's first published entry into the sphere of general cultural analysis, *Culture and Society 1780–1950* (1958) is indeed an attempt to construct a specifically English tradition of cultural critique, but one that alludes to the contributions of English Marxists of the pre-war period, such as West and Caudwell, in order to note their reductionism, economism, or effective non-Marxism (262–75; see also Hall, 'Cultural Studies and the Centre' 25). Indeed, it was precisely the inadequacy of English Marxist thinking about culture that obliged Williams to look, in *Culture and Society*, to a non-Marxist English 'tradition' of cultural critique, and then increasingly in the 1960s and 1970s to a difficult process of negotiation between English 'culturalism,' European Marxist aesthetics, and emerging tendencies in

European 'theory' (see Williams's discussion of his transitional *The Long Revolution*, in *Politics and Letters* 133–74; for this negotiation within cultural studies more generally, see Hall, 'Cultural Studies and the Centre' 26–34, and Clarke 3–4, 12).

If we turn to another crux in Holderness's narrative, the moment of Althusser, we once again find disruption and dispute within the 'traditions' of the post-war British left. Althusser's work, in its assault on conceptions of ideology and cultural production as theorized within the framework of 'expressive totality' or the unproblematized determination of superstructure by economic base, and in its associated themes of contradiction and over-determination, represented a significant break with key positions in existing Marxist cultural theory. At the same time, the theoretical anti-humanism of the British Althusserians, most emphatically articulated in the work of Hindess and Hurst, involved a fiercely oppositional relationship to the humanistic 'culturalism' that Stuart Hall identifies in the earlier work of Richard Hoggart, E.P.Thompson, and Williams himself (Hall, 'Cultural Studies: Two Paradigms' 19–20). In relation to the frequent attacks by cultural materialist and other critics on the 'containment' model of cultural power entertained by Greenblatt and other key new historicists (see, for example, Lentricchia 235–7; and Barker, *Culture of Violence* 197), it is significant that the British dispute centred upon opposing models of the balance between individual agency (an emphasis created by E.P. Thompson in his attack on Althusser) and the structural determination of individual consciousness and action (see Hall, 'Two Paradigms' 19–37; Clarke 12; McGuigan 29–30). The fact that this is a problematic that cannot be conveniently displaced onto U.S. scholars is emphasized by the continuation of the argument, within the British 'tradition,' in the form of recent debates in cultural and media studies around consumption, spectatorship, and populism (see McGuigan 68–79; and Clarke 73–112).

The turn towards Gramsci in the later 1970s, associated initially with Stuart Hall and the Birmingham Centre for Contemporary Cultural Studies, constituted an attempt to find a route via the theory of hegemony out of the hostile debates between the 'structuralist' and 'culturalist' positions (Williams, *Problems in Materialism and Culture* 31–49; Bennett et al. 191–213; Hebdige 203–4). As Dick Hebdige has pointed out, the Gramscian theoretical trajectory is intimately related to the development in the 1980s of work by Stuart Hall and others, loosely grouped around the 'New Times' agenda of the journal *Marxism Today*; that agenda articulates at once the need for a 'postmodern' Marxist politics of alliance that respects the contemporary disarticulation of social identities and categories of oppression, and the impossibility of subsuming such dispersion under the categories of base/superstructure, totality, structure in dominance, or determination (218; 258n16). As John Clarke notes, this theoretical and political problematic *within* the Marxist 'tradition' connects to the already circulating and developing critiques of 'unreformed' Marxism articulated in the 1980s by feminists, as well as by those drawing upon the poststructuralist discourses of Derrida, Foucault, and Lacan (12–15).

It is precisely the challenge that such a complex theoretical con-·juncture presents to the idea of a secure, singular Marxist tradition of cultural critique that makes the narrative construction of cultural-materialist political 'authenticity' untenable. The moment that Jonathan Dollimore characterizes as a happy conjunction and cooperation of ideological housemates – cultural materialism as growing out of the 'convergence of history, sociology and English in cultural studies, some of the major developments in feminism, as well as continental Marxist-structuralist and post-structuralist theory' (Dollimore 3) – is one of the most recently contested moments in the serial crisis (but also the decentred, non-teleological fertility) that is the post-war 'development' of English Marxist cultural politics.

My purpose in rewriting Holderness's genealogy of English Marxist cultural critique in this way is twofold. First, I think it is important to challenge such narratives in so far as they serve to disavow the fundamental disagreements about conceptualization, critical practice, and political strategy that have characterized post-war British leftist theory and politics. Second, this is one way to begin to deconstruct, at both the theoretical and political levels, disabling oppositions between 'textuality' and 'politics,' Marxism and poststructuralism/postmodernism, the academic practices and politics of England and North America. In theoretical terms, the retrieval of this narrative of discontinuity reminds us that the questions posed by 'theory' to Marxism have been central to the development of English radical criticism in the past thirty years, rather than being an academicist diversion from the 'real' business of political critique, and therefore able to be displaced onto the 'depoliticized' North American scene. In political terms, an emphasis upon discontinuity disturbs the vision of a critical discourse grounded in a taken-for-granted British relation to the arena of class politics, and opposed to a deracinated North American politics without Marxism or class struggle. The debates on the British left in the 1980s, debates driven by the hegemonic successes of Thatcherism and the perceived decline of the Labour Party's class base as well as by theoretical imperatives, introduced the 'postmodern' (or 'post-Marxist') issues of decentralization, local activism, alliance, and 'identity' politics, and the specificities of oppression and determination by race, gender, and class, as inescapable questions for any 'reformed' Marxist strategic agenda (Hebdige 204). The fact that a politics obliged to deal on its British home ground with such issues looks remarkably similar to the ritually patronized politics of the North American new left and its successors is another reason why the claim to an English academic radicalism centred upon and guaranteed by 'a class politics that exercises something like a gravitational force' (Cohen 27) cannot and should not be sustained. (For a sympathetic account of this phase in U.S. leftist history, see Gallagher 38–43.) The offloading of a series of problems *within* British Marxism onto a pathologized pre-political, post-ideological, or postmodern 'America' is a way of continuing not to listen to crucial questions about theory and strategy addressed to (and within) English Marxism itself.

In Renaissance studies, one of the results of these political and theoretical disavowals is a downplaying of the heterogeneity and internal uncertainties of British criticism, and the corresponding tendency to conflate cultural materialism with studies in Shakespeare and ideological reproduction. Theoretical heterogeneity is acknowledged in overviews such as Dollimore's and Cohen's, only to be tamed into a spurious unity by explicit or implicit recourse to a Jamesonian totalization. For Cohen, alluding to Dollimore's account, the 'gravitational force' of 'class politics' holds the fissiparous cultural materialist compound of cultural studies, bits of feminism, Marxist-structuralism, and poststructuralist theory together as a single entity that can be deemed to have a singular, authentic politics, even as Cohen notes the hesitancy and provisional nature of its formulations in the work of specific critics (26–7). Rather than being totalizable under the banner of class politics, the uneasy conjuncture of these theoretical forces in the 1970s and 1980s can be more accurately thought of as a sign of the crisis of class politics in any such unexamined, foundational sense.

The Real Dead: Textuality, Politics, and Critical Responsibility

As I have already suggested, one of the principal ways in which English cultural materialism is said to maintain a grasp on the reality of politics is through the work of the 'reproduction' critics. One peculiar result of the recommendation of reproduction studies as the future of an engaged critical practice is that the grounds of its supposed political authenticity – the encounter with Shakespeare at the very ramparts of the dominant ideology of Englishness – are also a guarantee that radical criticism of Renaissance writing will continue to circle around a drastically restricted version of the Shakespeare canon. There is little room for any adequate response to the diversity of Renaissance texts, their intertextual relationships, their ambiguous cultural locations and political affiliations, their complex relationships with a social order undergoing fundamental structural reorganization and rapid conjunctural change, if the true object of political criticism is the limited range of texts that have come to be appropriated by the later hegemonic strategies of the 'dominant.'

A similar restriction of definition underwrites Francis Barker's *The Culture of Violence* (1993), which is not a study in Shakespearean reproduction, but which is structured by this same definition of politics, a study that brings us back again to readings of *King Lear*, *Hamlet*, and *Macbeth*, albeit with excursions into *Titus Andronicus* and the (canonical) politics of the 1640s (Milton and Hobbes). The restriction of range, however, and the circling about a dominant definition of the cultural centre, is structured into Barker's construction of the text as an object of analysis, and of a responsible critical practice. Barker attacks the new historicism of Stephen Greenblatt as a form of postmodernism, and as therefore opposed to 'a properly radical, anti-historicist historicity' (107) that is identified with certain Marxist practices of historiography. Just as new historicism as a 'movement' is conflated with the work of Greenblatt (the only other critic cited is Leonard Tennenhouse, whose *Power on Display* [1986] is described as 'epigonous' [163]), 'postmodernism' is identified with Jean-François Lyotard's *The Postmodern Condition: A Report on Knowledge* (1979), which in turn is conflated with Francis Fukuyama's *The End of History and the Last Man* (1992) (Barker 210n2). This chain of association, 'anchored' finally in a text that can undoubtedly be described as a promotion of U.S. foreign policy by theoretical means, is one of the main strategies by which Barker contrives an association between postmodernism (and therefore its subset, new historicism) and 'America.'

The identification of new historicism with postmodernism rests in the association of the former with a Geertzian anthropology that, according to Barker, dictates that 'interpretation is interminable in principle, and in practice always incomplete,' that 'there is no "ground," no foundation, no fundamental level of social reality at which interpretation stops ...' (161). New historicism is deemed to align itself with 'a variety

of post-modernist interpretative strategies,' including those of deconstruction, whose practitioners 'abolish historical difference in the name
of generalised textuality, without perceiving any problem of theory or
method' (125). A 'properly radical, anti-historicist historicity' is to be
distinguished from historicism old or new by the way that 'it operates
a kind of parallax by which the legitimating circularity of the dominant
historical discourse is interrupted in a dialectical movement between
the history of the present and the difference of the past' (107). Such
a practice, Barker acknowledges, may involve 'some scepticism about
its own groundedness, but this is quite different from beginning in a
programmatic way from that lack of foundation' (107). This seems to
imply, despite the nod to 'theory' in 'some scepticism about ... groundedness,' that the project of a 'radical historicity,' with its commitment
to 'the objective of a full historicisation' (107), will, unlike its postmodernist adversary, realize its political seriousness in its ability to
make contact with the '"hard" structures' of history, 'the ontological
level of the reality of the lived cultural forms ...' (161). Indeed, that
claim is embedded in the very term 'radical historicity,' which passes
off the epistemological problems associated with *any* approach to the
past onto others' 'historicisms,' while conflating its own epistemology
with the ontological status of its object of study. Barker's essay on *Titus
Andronicus* (chap. 2) shows how the objective of 'full historicisation' is
realized in a specific piece of analysis.

In discussing *Titus* Barker focuses initially on the way in which
the influence of Geertz's anthropology 'leads to what in the critical
practice of the new historicism is a signal de-realisation of power' in
its accounts of society and the text (160). The tendency to turn society
'more or less wholly into discourse' (157) is seen as determining the new
historicist concern with power as representation and display, so that 'it
is the language of the aesthetic which provides both the lexicon and
the conceptual repertoire for thinking ... "culture"' (164). In opposition
to this 'aestheticisation of politics' Barker proceeds with a reading of
the play that centres upon the moment in act 4.4 when a Clown, after
delivering a message from Titus to the emperor, is ordered to be taken
and hanged, without explanation. The very casualness and apparent
aesthetic de-motivation of this incident of executive violence stands,
for Barker, in stark contrast to the sadistic excesses for which the play
has commonly been castigated. Barker's response to this passage – 'it is
simply *there*: strange, *unheimlich*, and, I have found, haunting' (168) – is
a sudden shift in his mode of discourse, from meta-theoretical critique

and textual reading to the presentation, in a self-consciously 'flat' and unelaborated way, of 'some historical research' (168).

There follows a painstaking summary of the sources, methodological procedures, and problems involved in calculating the hanging statistics for Elizabethan and Stuart England and Wales. This section then bridges back into the discussion of *Titus Andronicus* and new historicism:

In defence of property and the established social order the Elizabethan and Jacobean crown killed huge numbers of the people of England ... Sometimes the spinal chord was snapped at once; or they hung by their necks until they suffocated or drowned; until their brains died of hypoxeia, or until the shock killed them. Pissing and shitting themselves. Bleeding from their eyes. Thinking ...

But nothing of this is dramatised in *Titus Andronicus* (190).

For Barker, the purpose of the extended section of historical demography is to 'de-occlude' the reality of power's operation by both the text itself and the textualist strategies that would be brought to its reading by the new historicism, through a 'citation of brute and brutal evidence' (203), the 'blank "facts"' (201) of judicial murder. Statistics, in other words, function as the vehicle by which the Real is readmitted, disruptively, into the fabric of the Shakespearean and new historicist texts, which would both otherwise succeed in *representing* violence only in order that its reality – 'the real dead' (192) – may be covered up.

I do not wish to deny or downplay the reality, the extent, or the significance of hanging as an early modern fact, or to doubt the commitment and anger that inform Barker's discussion of his statistics. What troubles me are the models of the text, and of a 'radical historicity' and political criticism, which this mode of argument implies. The charge of *occlusion* laid against *Titus Andronicus*, a term that dominates the final section of Barker's chapter, implicitly involves a return to a reflectionist model of the text. The play is taken to task for 'direct[ing] attention away from, rather than towards, the elimination of huge numbers of the population' (190), and new historicism is seen as complicit with this occlusion in its commitment to a model of representational power that equally diverts attention from the 'brute fact' of hanging. The good text, it appears, would be one that had hangings in it, and the politically responsible critical practice one, like Barker's own, that adequately reflects the reality baldly presented in his statistics (which is why, for Barker, a Greenblatt essay called 'Murdering Peasants'[3] can be grudgingly welcomed as a step in the right direction [203n64]).

I do not intend to revisit the general arguments against a reflectionist aesthetic, although I note that a refusal to recognize the formal and aesthetic economies of the text, together with the relation to them of the specific textual moment and the 'occlusion' that it signals, is readily acknowledged by Barker: 'Nor have I commented interpretatively on the precise nature of the general relationship between the occluded material as such and the text of *Titus Andronicus* ...' (202). The problem with this refusal to interpret is that it is not, in fact, an option. Barker wants his statistics to have the status of a self-declarative reality that insists, shamingly, outside the irresponsible play of interpretation/representation; what he will not acknowledge, however, is that as soon as he decides that *this* textual element will be related to *this* aspect of the context, he is *in interpretation*. The refusal to comment further on the specific relations involved in this decision is merely that, a refusal to do what follows from the initial positing of a relation: to specify and further explore the nature of the relationship between these unlike 'facts' that make it meaningful to bring them together and to privilege this relationship.

Barker deals with the problem of mediation between text and context that confronts *all* interpretative activity, a problem that he identifies in Greenblatt's untheorized use of anecdote and 'local interpretation,' and that he describes as being 'internal to the philistinism of *bourgeois* culture' (199n58), by collapsing it into the demand of a self-evident reality for truthful textual reflection. The discussion of culture and violence in *Titus* resolves into a model of culture as the representational alibi of the reality of systemic violence, and the epistemology of occlusion into a model of the text as either underwriting or contesting 'the signifying practices of the dominant culture' (194) that would keep that violence hidden. The responsibility of the critic in this situation is to unmask the reality of violence that culture works to occlude.

Barker's arguments reveal the dangers involved in the mutually implicated claims to 'full historicisation,' an 'authentic' class politics, and a direct interpretative purchase upon the Real of history. If systemic violence is the occluded Real of all cultural texts, and the task of the political critic is the unmasking of that reality, the work of interpretation is pre-empted, before it begins, by a totalizing gesture that directs all 'political' reading towards a single signified. This undiverted approach

---

3 See Stephen Greenblatt, 'Murdering Peasants: Status, Genre and the Representation of Rebellion,' *Representations* 1.1 (1983): 1–29.

to the Real (which is in fact the isolation of one segment of reality as the ground of an authentic politics) is then established as the standard by which other modes of reading, which are more troubled by problems of epistemology, mediation, and the heterogeneity of cultural texts and their determinations, can be deemed 'not genuinely *historical* or seriously political' (Felperin 86).

As is the case with reproduction studies, the implications of Barker's identification and location of a 'real' politics include the reinforcement of the cultural and political centrality of Shakespeare – and, in practice, the Shakespeare of the tragedies, the histories, and the Roman plays. It is not clear what such a criticism would have to say about the greater number of English Renaissance texts – about lyric poetry, citizen comedy, topographical treatises, satirical tracts, epithalamia – apart from noting their determined occlusion of the judicially murdered peasant. Perhaps more damagingly, it is difficult to know what can be done with an analytical model that admits of only two possible positions within the field of early modern cultural production: the 'underwrit[ing]' of 'the signifying practices of the dominant culture (and by way of that the political and social power of the dominant ...),' or the 'unsettl[ing]' of 'such structures and institutions by transgressing, erasing, confusing, contesting or making "disfunctional" the categories and representations they support and which in turn support them' (Barker 194–5). We are back, ironically, to a version of the containment/subversion opposition that Barker (along with other Marxist critics of new historicism such as Lentricchia and Holderness) castigates in the work of 'bourgeois' American critics. In short, the gesture that secures an 'authentic' politics of reading by a displacement of epistemological difficulty onto ('American') 'historicism,' 'textualism,' or 'deconstruction' does so at the cost of a reductionist account of the cultural formation and a reflectionist model of the text.

Repro-Men: Shakespeare and the Class(room) Struggle

It is significant that 'reproduction' studies, which, as we have seen, tend to be hailed as the model of an authentically political and historical criticism, emerge at precisely the moment in the 1980s of theoretical and political crisis for the British left, a crisis to which Barker's aesthetics/politics of occlusion are so clearly a reaction. In this context, the rhetoric generated around reproduction studies, a rhetoric of direct political struggle between literary academics and the state for the meaning of Englishness, is more convincingly read as compensatory. It is a

reassertion of a direct and clearly legible relation between academic radicalism and 'politics' in its most conventional definition rather than the
latest realization of an untroubled patrimony of revolutionary praxis.

Alan Sinfield's congratulation of Lawrence Levine, Don Wayne, and
Michael Bristol for finally getting the reproduction-of-Shakespeare ball
rolling in the United States (7) emphasizes the relationship between
this tendency and the oppositional construction of England/America,
particularly if we look at the discussion of the new historicist/cultural
materialist relationship in Sinfield's chapter, 'Cultural Imperialism and
the Primal Scene of U.S. Man' (chap. 10, 254–302). Part of Sinfield's
argument revolves around the dangers of the neutralization of radical
politics by the process of academic professionalization, a process that,
he suggests, despite his adoption of a supposedly transnational 'we,' is
far more of a problem in the U.S. than in Britain: 'the professionalized
U.S. discourse ... can probably assimilate politicized criticism without
much strain ["Cultural materialists? Don't we have one of those? –
Hire one!"]' (8). The way out of this entrapment, he suggests, 'is that
academics should reverse the move away from subcultures of class,
ethnicity, gender, and sexuality. We should seek ways to break out of the
professional subculture and work intellectually (not just live personally)
in dissident subcultures' (294). In leading up to this conclusion, Sinfield
refers on a number of occasions to E.D. Hirsch's *Cultural Literacy* and
Allan Bloom's *The Closing of the American Mind* as texts that articulate
a dominant, white, imperialist version of American identity, in which
the cultural capital of English literature plays a key supportive role,
and against which, among its other tasks, the dissident critical practice
of the future must speak out. And as part of the prolegomenon to
that project Sinfield includes his own export version of Shakespearean
reproduction in the United States, critiquing the Bloom/Hirsch position
with his usual scholarly incisiveness and wit.

The only problem with Sinfield's account is that a principal motiva-
tion of the Hirsch and Bloom polemic is an anxious reaction to what
has been termed 'political correctness,' the right-wing scare-term for
precisely the kind of 'dissident' articulation by U.S. academics and
educationalists of 'subcultural' voices and heritages that Sinfield is
advocating.[4] One must ask why *this* ideological struggle over canons

4 For a wide-ranging set of academic responses to Bloom and Hirsch, see Gless and
  Smith, *The Politics of Liberal Education.* See also the references to Bloom, Secretary of
  State William Bennett, and newspaper attacks on leftist academics in Montrose (27–31)
  and Gallagher (45). An associated debate around feminist work on Shakespeare is

and curricula, in a context that advocates educational policy initiatives like those put in place by Christian fundamentalists in Lake County, Florida (see Freeland 10), is less 'political' than the struggle over the place of Shakespeare and the canon in English schools (Macleod 2). The implication that indigenous intellectual activism is either not there, or not 'seriously political,' while the way to introduce politics to the benighted U.S. academy is to import a few more reproduction studies of the second Henriad, is one of the richer ironies of the narrative we have been tracing.

The inaudibility of subcultural voices in such characterizations of the 'American' academy – of work, that is, which is undertaken in an explicit relation to the 'external' agendas of the politics of race, sexuality, and gender – is possible only because of a consistent tendency to conflate all academic activity with that of 'U.S. Man,' to use Sinfield's term. This is true of the rhetoric of the accounts of new historicism by Montrose (26) and Wayne (58) – even where that rhetoric goes against the grain of the argument as a whole – and, in a more extreme reduction, by Lentricchia and Barker, for whom 'U.S. Man' (and new historicism) is 'Stephen Greenblatt.' Where some acknowledgment of other, more 'politicized' versions of American new historicism is made, it is usually feminist scholarship that is identified as an honourable exception to the general sad story of co-optation and professionalization (an exception implied, for example, by Montrose's and Wayne's critical targeting of, specifically, the male U.S. academic). What is not clear is why this exemption does not problematize the original narrowed and exclusive definition of new historicism and its supposed politics: does critical practice stop being new historicist when it becomes feminist and therefore 'political'? Or is the problem in the exclusiveness of the original definition of 'politics'?

Ironically, the vision of U.S. academic professionalization that Sinfield shares with other critics relies upon a 'containment' model of ideology that is precisely the one he and others cite in the work of new historicists as a sign of the hopeless political inertia of the American academic (see Sinfield 285). In hostile critiques of the United States

---

brought together in Kamps: it is interesting that this collection, which is derived from an MLA special session on 'Shakespeare and Ideology' (1989), includes an essay on *Richard II* by Holderness, whose participation in that project coincides with the publication of his 1991 Essex Symposium essay lamenting the depoliticized professionalism of the American academy. The question of why only one of these forums is to be considered 'political' relates centrally to the concerns of this essay.

academy there is often an indecision as to whether the problem is that the academy is an institution with 'no cultural function at all' (Paul de Man, quoted in Sinfield 289) – a political dead zone of ritual professionalism – or one that functions as if it were the cultural ministry of U.S. corporate capitalism. Sinfield's own account oscillates between the two, referencing de Man to shore up the first version, Bloom and Hirsch the second. In either case the image results from a monolithic conception of the relationship between social agents, institutions, power, and ideology that is forcefully, and quite rightly, rejected when it is spotted in new historicist accounts of Shakespeare or Marlowe. If the containment thesis is untenable in relation to Renaissance England – and I would agree that it is – then it is untenable in relation to the late capitalist United States. If it isn't, we can bid farewell to the politics of dissident reading.

In Holderness's narrative of Anglo-American relations, the internal contradictions and weaknesses of British Marxist politics are displaced onto the depoliticized space of 'American' theory and professionalization; in Barker's analysis, problems of mediation are excluded in order to reinstate a reflectionist aesthetic, and are redefined as an issue only within the politically regressive terms of 'American' postmodernism. For Sinfield, the program for a 'politics of dissident reading' is to be defined against 'American' academic professionalization, even while the names of Bloom and Hirsch signal the impact of just such a politics within the U.S. educational system. In all three cases (and, as I have suggested, they are symptomatic of a more widespread tendency), the production of a positive model of authentic politics brings with it, as its inevitable counterpart, the production of blindness – blindness to the internal problems of theory and practice on the British academic left, to the significance and often the very existence of radical work in the U.S. academy, and to the possibilities of a fruitful consideration of the likenesses, as well as differences, in the cultural and political positions of British and American intellectuals. These are some of the dead ends where we are likely to arrive (to keep arriving) if the space between 'England' and 'America' continues to be mapped under the figure of opposition rather than discontinuity.

WORKS CITED

Barker, Francis. *The Culture of Violence: Tragedy and History*. Chicago: U of Chicago P; Manchester: Manchester UP, 1993.

Barker, Francis, Peter Hulme, and Margaret Iversen, eds. *Uses of History: Marxism, Postmodernism and the Renaissance.* The Essex Symposia. Manchester: Manchester UP; New York: St Martin's P, 1991.

Bennett, Tony, Graham Martin et al., eds. *Culture, Ideology and Social Process: A Reader.* London: Batsford Academic and Educational Ltd./Open UP, 1981.

Clarke, John. *New Times and Old Enemies: Essays on Cultural Studies and America.* London and New York: Harper Collins Academic, 1991.

Cohen, Walter. 'Political Criticism of Shakespeare.' *Shakespeare Reproduced.* Ed. Jean E. Howard and Marion F. O'Connor. 18–46.

Dollimore, Jonathan. 'Introduction: Shakespeare, Cultural Materialism, and the New Historicism.' *Political Shakespeare.* Ed. Jonathan Dollimore and Alan Sinfield. 2–17.

Dollimore, Jonathan, and Alan Sinfield, eds. *Political Shakespeare: New Essays in Cultural Materialism.* Manchester: Manchester UP; Ithaca and London: Cornell UP, 1985.

Felperin, Howard. '"Cultural Poetics" versus "Cultural Materialism": The Two New Historicisms in Renaissance Studies.' *Uses of History.* Ed. Barker et al. 76–100.

Freeland, Jonathan. 'Fundamentalist Schools in Florida Introduce the American "Master Race" to the Curriculum.' *Guardian* 16 May 1994: 10+.

Gallagher, Catherine. 'Marxism and The New Historicism.' *The New Historicism.* Ed. H. Aram Veeser. 37–48.

Gless, Darryl J., and Barbara Herrnstein Smith, eds. *The Politics of Liberal Education. South Atlantic Quarterly* 89.1 (1990).

Hall, Stuart. 'Cultural Studies and the Centre: Some Problematics and Problems.' *Culture, Media, Language.* Ed. Stuart Hall et al. 15–47.

– 'Cultural Studies: Two Paradigms.' *Culture, Ideology and Social Process,* ed. Tony Bennett et al. 19–37.

Hall, Stuart, et al., eds. *Culture, Media, Language: Working Papers in Cultural Studies, 1972–79.* London, Melbourne, and Sydney: Hutchinson and Centre for Contemporary Cultural Studies, U of Binghamton, 1980.

Hawkes, Terence. *Meaning by Shakespeare.* London and New York: Routledge, 1992.

Hebdige, Dick. *Hiding in the Light: On Images and Things.* London and New York: Routledge, 1988.

Holderness, Graham. 'Production, Reproduction, Performance: Marxism, History, Theatre.' *Uses of History.* Ed. Barker et al. 153–78.

– *Shakespeare Recycled: The Making of Historical Drama.* New York, London, and Toronto: Harvester Wheatsheaf, 1992.

- Holderness, Graham, ed. *The Shakespeare Myth*. Cultural Politics. Manchester: Manchester UP; New York: St. Martin's P, 1988.

Howard, Jean E., and Marion F. O'Connor, eds. *Shakespeare Reproduced: The Text in History and Ideology*. New York and London: Methuen, 1987.

Kamps, Ivo, ed. *Shakespeare Left and Right*. New York and London: Routledge, 1991.

Lentricchia, Frank. 'Foucault's Legacy – A New Historicism?' *The New Historicism*. Ed. H. Aram Veeser. 231–42.

Macleod, Donald. 'Curriculum Fight Goes on amid Anger at Blueprint for English.' *Guardian* 10 May 1994: 2+.

Marcus, Jane. 'The Asylums of Antaeus: Women, War, and Madness – Is There a Feminist Fetishism?' *The New Historicism*. Ed. H. Aram Veeser. 132–51.

McGuigan, Jim. *Cultural Populism*. London and New York: Routledge, 1992.

Montrose, Louis A. 'Professing the Renaissance: The Poetics and Politics of Culture.' *The New Historicism*. Ed. H. Aram Veeser. 15–36.

Sinfield, Alan. *Faultlines: Cultural Materialism and the Politics of Dissident Reading*. Berkeley, Los Angeles, and Oxford: U of California P, 1992.

Veeser, H. Aram, ed. *The New Historicism*. New York and London: Routledge, 1989.

Wayne, Don E. 'Power, Politics, and the Shakespearian Text: Recent Criticism in England and the United States.' *Shakespeare Reproduced*. Ed. Jean E. Howard and Marion F. O'Connor. 47–67.

Williams, Raymond. *Culture and Society 1780–1950*. 1958. Harmondsworth: Penguin; New York: Columbia UP, 1960.

- *Politics and Letters: Interviews with 'New Left Review.'* London: New Left Books, 1979.

- *Problems in Materialism and Culture: Selected Essays*. London: Verso Editions and New Left Books, 1980.

10

The Status of Class in Shakespeare: or, Why Critics Love to Hate Capitalism

SHARON O'DAIR

In explaining to Roderigo why he continues to serve Othello when he no longer feels 'in any just term ... affin'd / To love the Moor' (*Oth.* 1.1.39–40), Iago distinguishes between two kinds of servants and two kinds of service:

> You shall mark
> Many a duteous and knee-crooking knave,
> That, doting on his own obsequious bondage,
> Wears out his time much like his master's ass,
> For nought but provender, and when he's old, cashier'd,
> Whip me such honest knaves: others there are,
> Who, trimm'd in forms, and visages of duty,
> Keep yet their hearts attending on themselves,
> And throwing but shows of service on their lords,
> Do well thrive by 'em, and when they have lin'd their coats,
> Do themselves homage, those fellows have some soul,
> And such a one do I profess myself ...   (1.1.44–55)

Because of the injury endured in being passed over for promotion, a promotion that 'by the old gradation' (line 36) should have been his, Iago no longer feels bound to love the Moor, and thus redefines his relationship to service and to Othello, casting himself as a fellow with some soul, who serves in order to thrive, to get ahead personally (1.1.58–60).

Iago does not serve for love and duty; several years earlier, however, Shakespeare created a character who, according to Orlando, embodies 'The constant service of the antique world, / When service sweat for duty, not for meed!' (*As You Like It* 2.3.57–8). Old Adam not only warns Orlando of Oliver's evil plottings, thereby putting his own safety in question, but he also offers the impoverished 'younger brother' his entire life's savings to stead Orlando in his escape (2.3.39–46). Adam's unrestrained loyalty, his utter selflessness – indeed, his uncomplaining acknowledgment that the fate Iago abhors is likely to be his – prompts Orlando to lament the 'fashion of these times, / Where none will sweat but for promotion, / And having that do choke their service up / Even with the having' (lines 59–62).

Orlando and Iago describe the kinds of service in the same way – one kind is rooted in duty and the other in self-interest. Similar oppositions occur in other plays. Consider, for example, the contrast in *Timon of Athens* between Timon's loyal servants and the 'base,' self-interested servants of his flatterers (3.1.43–52; 3.4.40–60; and 4.2); or the contrast in *King Lear* between Oswald and Kent: one proves to be 'super-serviceable' (2.2.16) in the effort 'to raise [his] fortunes' (4.6.225), while the other knows how, in seeking service, to recognize authority in the 'countenance' of one he 'would fain call master' (1.4.27–8). All this is not simply a matter of good servants and bad, an early modern lament about the difficulty of finding good help these days. It is a signifier of change in a society in which, as sixty per cent of the population engaged in service at some point, 'one nearly always "belonged" to somebody' (Ariès 396).

Taking a cue from Stephen Greenblatt's analysis of representations of rebellion in Dürer, Sidney, Spenser, and Shakespeare, I would suggest that in Shakespeare's representations of service we find more evidence that, as Greenblatt puts it, 'status relations ... are being transformed before our eyes into property relations' (25). In such representations, Shakespeare responds to a process that, roughly more than two hundred years later with the making of the English working class, finally severs the reciprocal bonds of connection between inferiors and superiors that had organized society (and inequality) before the industrial revolution. Shakespeare responds to a process that slowly transforms service (and labour generally) from a matter of social relations to a matter of economics, a process that Zygmunt Bauman has called a 'de-socialisation' of labour (103).[1]

---

1 Bauman locates this change primarily in the late eighteenth and early nineteenth centuries. The point, he writes, is made with 'rare clarity' in 1845 by the *Westminster Review* in an article 'dedicated to the analysis of the "causes of the present trouble"':

For contemporary Renaissance criticism, at issue here is how to theorize inequality, that is, the relationships between superiors and subordinates within Shakespeare's plays, and not incidentally within early modern England. As Greenblatt asserts, we can detect in the literature of the period evidence of a new concern with personal property – in this case, with the ownership of the servant's labour (25).[2] Yet it is equally clear that a society in which *The Courtier* provides essential information about success is one organized as a network or web of dependencies, of rights and obligations. With respect to service, as Ariès explains, there existed between masters and servants throughout the seventeenth century 'something which went beyond respect for a contract or exploitation by an employer: an existential bond which did not exclude brutality on the one hand and cunning on the other, but which resulted from an almost perpetual community of life' (396). Such a 'perpetual community of life' is quite obvious in Shakespeare's many representations of the master-servant relationship. One thinks of 'servants' whose

---

the *Review*, according to Bauman, argues that 'previous eras associated subjection with protection – either absolutely, as in the case of slavery, or partially, as in the case of a system defined as "feudal vassalage." The new era, however, brings a totally new arrangement, "that of bargain or mutual agreement," in which "simple service is balanced against simple payment" – with, so to speak, no strings attached on either side ... A social relation between classes was to be re-articulated as an economic exchange of a "commodity" (labour) for money (wage)' (101–2). Subordinates could no longer expect or claim from their masters the security, protection, and assistance that had been their due within the feudal relation; neither could masters any longer expect or claim from their subordinates the deference, loyalty, and love that had been their due. The new principle required submission for wages only: subordinates would be required to arrange for their own security out of their wages, and masters would be required to endure the not insubstantial resentments of a free labour force (Bauman 101–2).

2 Marx points out that the worker could sell his labour 'only after he had ceased to be bound to the soil, and ceased to be the slave or serf of another person. To become a free seller of labour-power, who carries his commodity wherever he can find a market for it, he must further have escaped from the regime of the guilds, their rules for apprentices and journeymen, and their restrictive labour regulations. Hence the historical movement which changes the producers into wage-labourers appears, on the one hand, as their emancipation from serfdom and from the fetters of the guilds, and it is this aspect ... which alone exists for our bourgeois historians. But, on the other hand, these newly freed men became sellers of themselves only after they had been robbed of all their own means of production, and all the guarantees of existence afforded by the old feudal arrangements. And this history, the history of their expropriation, is written in the annals of mankind in letters of blood and fire' (875).

positions are not low and who are themselves empowered to command others, such as Malvolio in *Twelfth Night*, the Steward in *Timon of Athens*, Cassio and Iago in *Othello*, Kent and Oswald in *Lear*, or Enobarbus in *Antony and Cleopatra*. One thinks also of servants whose positions are complicated by a location within a family or household (the Nurse in *Romeo*, Grumio in *Shrew*, the twin Dromios in *Comedy of Errors*). Representations such as these approve the period's analogizing of the master-servant relationship to that of the husband and wife, or parent and child (see Cressy 29–44; and Ariès 365–407).

The master-servant relationship in Shakespeare's plays, then, is not defined exclusively or even generally in terms of economic domination and exploitation; as the examples cited above suggest, domination is less abstract, embedded as it is within hierarchies of household and family, of the military or the state. Furthermore, Shakespeare's plays cast as evil those servants who, like Iago or Oswald, wish to break the bonds of a 'perpetual community of life' and redefine service as primarily an economic relationship, as an exchange of labour for resources that allow for personal advancement. We are led to prefer the old Adams and the Kents of the tragedies to the Iagos or the Oswalds, and, in the comedies, to laugh at the brutality that moulds the loyal servant (the beatings endured by a Grumio or a Dromio). For these reasons Shakespeare's plays pose a difficulty for critics who, in addressing the inequality and subordination found in them, look exclusively to Marx and Marxian class analysis for interpretive help or theoretical grounding. Critics must in addition explore the importance of the established and competing model of stratification in the early modern period, that is, as a model revealed in a hierarchy of status, in which an economy of prestige takes precedence over an economy of money.[3]

In an essay that 'ponder[s] the representation of "class"' (276) in *The Taming of the Shrew*, *The Merchant of Venice*, and *Julius Caesar*, Thomas Moisan alludes to this difficulty, opening his discussion by acknowledging the existence of competing models of social stratification, one rooted in status and the other in class. But as the essay proceeds, and as the title suggests, Moisan gives precedence to the latter model, or

3 Weber defines the status order as 'the way in which social honor is distributed in a community between typical groups participating in this distribution' (2: 927 and passim). Stratification by status reveals the distribution of prestige or honour in a society.

at least he allows status to be absorbed by class. Part of my argument (and a point to which I return in my conclusion) concerns exactly such slippage: what are the political and intellectual implications of the general failure of literary critics to distinguish between 'class' and 'status' as concepts? First, though, let me emphasize that stratification based on class is not irrelevant to the early modern period. Class as a principle of stratification is, however, only emerging at this time; the transformation of England into a class society has barely begun,[4] and will take another 150 to 200 years to achieve, during which time elements of the status order remain intact and influential, as some do even today.[5]

4 Certainly debate continues in history, sociology, and literary history about the nature and the timing of the transition to capitalism and to a class society. I find most sensible the positions of those who complicate the process, arguing, as does Fernand Braudel, that the pre-industrial economy is characterized by the coexistence of an inflexible, inert, and slow-moving primitive economy 'alongside trends – limited and in the minority, yet active and powerful – that were characteristic of modern growth' (5). Immanuel Wallerstein recounts that the century between 1540 and 1640 was 'a period of class formation' (256) in which an 'emerging capitalist class [was] recruited from varying social backgrounds' (244), in which enclosure offered opportunities as well as dangers (248), and in which 'there was no across-the-board correlation of social status and adaptability to the demands of capitalist agriculture' (237). With respect to the creation of a proletariat, Wallerstein maintains that this period saw only its initial stages, an assertion supported by Richard Lachmann, who reports that 'at no point before 1567 did more than an eighth of English peasants lack personal bonds to the land. Over the following seventy years, from 1570 to 1640, the portion of English peasants who were proletarianized – that is, who lost their land rights and were forced to work for wages or for poor relief payments, rose to 40 percent' (16).
5 Wrightson observes that 'class was not born at the turn of the eighteenth and nineteenth centuries, any more than hierarchy died' (200). Beynon expands on the latter part of Wrightson's statement, observing that in mid-nineteenth century England, 'aristocratic capitalists were strongly committed to the ideas of paternalism and to a view of society based upon status and obligation' (246). Perhaps even more surprising is the 'considerable evidence' that similar ideas 'were also present within the growing numbers of industrial workers,' especially with respect to occupational cultures (247–8), and thus that we see in the transition a 'social process which is more complex than the "combined and uneven" development of economic forces.' That is to say, 'pre-capitalist forms (and orders) are maintained and reproduced during the process of capital accumulation' (248). Guillory describes exactly this process in his identification of the historical 'function' of intellectuals since the late eighteenth century as 'producing – primarily through the educational system – a cultural distinction between the bourgeoisie and the lower classes. The schools made possible

Indeed, any given social formation that includes market institutions will differentiate by status and by class. Such differentiation coexists, to different degrees and strengths, in differing times and places. The point is not to subsume status by class or to see the relationships between them as 'in conflict' or as emergent and residual, but to assess the relative strength of each, while keeping in mind the tension between them. As John R. Hall has observed, 'the question ... becomes, What is the interaction between markets and groups, between class and status, between economic formations and cultural formations?' (277). To tease out that interaction, Hall insists, it is necessary to 'maintain an analytic distinction between status group and class' (273).[6] What follows is an attempt towards making that distinction, after which I turn to a discussion of *Timon of Athens* and its criticism.

Weber and Marx / Status and Class

Let me repeat that class is a form of stratification that can be distinguished from other forms of stratification, such as those based on kinship, caste, race, status, or degree of political rectitude. All societies are stratified or ranked according to some criterion or another, either alone or in concert; inequality is nothing new and neither is a concentration of power in the hands of a privileged few. Within capitalist or market societies the dominant but by no means exclusive form of stratification is class, a form of stratification in which privilege is determined by one's role in the processes of production, that is, by one's relationship to the means of production of goods. For Marx, class signifies conflict; and, as Bauman points out, while feudal society 'had also its language of

---

a kind of mimetic identification of bourgeois culture with aristocratic culture. The cultural distinction between classes has operated since ... as a mode of ideological domination of the working class, a strategic doubling of the class hierarchy as a status hierarchy' ('Literary Critics' 134–5).

6 A failure to establish that distinction is perhaps evident in Moisan's statement that 'the modern use of class [is] to differentiate social caste and status group' (277n2), a statement that seems to suggest that we moderns use differentiation by class as a substitute for differentiation by caste or status. My argument is that differentiation by class and by status co-exists; and that while one can safely argue, like Berger, that 'under industrial capitalism there has been the progressive displacement of all other forms of stratification by class' (52), this is not to say that status is irrelevant even now or that at some point – 1603 or 1867 – class supplanted status as a principle of stratification.

conflict,' capitalist society moves 'conflict from the murky, shadowy and threatening margins of the social order into the very centre of society; from the scrap heap to the main building site of social order' (39).[7] In Marx's view, such conflict sometimes erupts into active class conflict, which becomes the *primum mobile* of history, since in each epoch two classes are set against each other in a struggle for control of the means of production.

Implicit in this analysis is the notion that economic relations determine social and political development. This notion has been difficult for some to accept, and one of the first theorists to attack Marx on this score was Weber, much of whose sociology is, as Anthony Giddens argues, 'an attack upon the Marxian generalisation that class struggles form the main dynamic process in the development of society' (50). Although Weber agrees with much of what Marx says about class in general and with respect to conflict within industrial capitalism, he takes issue with Marx's insistence that a class – individuals who share economic situations – would necessarily develop class consciousness, move from a 'class in itself' to a 'class for itself,' and thus become principal agents within history. For Weber, '"classes" are not communities; they merely represent possible, and frequent, bases for social action' (2: 927), which may take any of 'innumerable possible forms' or none at all: 'The emergence of an association or even of mere social action from a common class situation [that is, a common market situation] is by no means a universal phenomenon' (2: 930, 929).[8] For Weber, Marx thus exaggerates the role of economic relations in the development of modern societies and in the operations of power within them, the 'political' influencing the structure of power far more than Marx

7 Berger explains that 'class must have a political aspect, in that classes have vested interests in common, interests that must always be pursued *against* other interests' (52). Dahrendorf argues that Marx's analysis of class involves the attempt to understand social conflict or the possibilities for organized action; class is not a model for the description of hierarchy in a society at a given point in time (76). Needless to say, most literary critics are not so strict in their use of Marx.

8 Weber argues that for ' "class action" (social action by the members of a class)' to occur, 'the real conditions and the results of the class situation must be distinctly recognizable. For only then the contrast of life chances can be felt not as an absolutely given fact to be accepted, but as a resultant from either (1) the given distribution of property, or (2) the structure of the concrete economic order. It is only then that people may react against the class structure not only through acts of intermittent and irrational protest, but in the form of rational association' (2: 929).

allows.[9] Fredric Jameson locates 'Weber's most influential legacy to the anti-Marxist arsenal' in precisely this 'strategic substitution, in his own research and theorization, of the political for the economic realm as the principal object of study, and thus, implicitly, as the ultimately determining reality of history' (4).

Weber argues that what is definitive and radical about capitalism is not the emergence of classes but its rationalized production. In this, capitalism follows the lead of the state, itself already rationalized and bureaucratized; indeed for Weber, as Giddens observes, 'the trend towards the expansion of bureaucratisation expresses the integral character of the modern epoch: the rationalisation of human conduct creates a systematised and hierarchical division of labour which is not directly dependent upon the capitalist class structure' (46). Jameson suggests that the Weberian perspective displaces questions of the economy onto political and social history, such that, for instance, 'analyses of capitalism are parried by discussions of political freedom, and concepts of economic alienation and of the commodity system replaced by attacks on party bureaucracy, the "new class," and the like' (4). One might, however, wish to argue *contra* Jameson that the charge of displacement focuses attention inappropriately, thwarting attempts to bring together – or, better yet, to hold in tension – the Weberian 'political' and the Marxian 'economic.' For surely the 'expropriation of the worker' is not solely the consequence of capitalism, but also, as Weber argued, of bureaucratization and the increasing centralization of rational administrative control, which is a seemingly inescapable feature of the modern world, whether socialist or capitalist (see Giddens and Held 11).[10]

---

9 Acknowledging 'the risk of some oversimplification,' Giddens explains that whereas Marx's abstract model of capitalist development proceeds from the 'economic' to the 'political,' Weber's is derived from the opposite process of reasoning, using the 'political' as a framework for understanding the 'economic' (46–7).

10 In *The Class Structure of the Advanced Societies*, Giddens comments that 'the rise of the modern nation-state, with its body of bureaucratic officials, whose conduct is oriented to impersonal norms of procedure rather than to the traditionally established codes associated with patrimonialism, serves as a paradigm case for Weber's analysis of bureaucratisation in general. The rational state, Weber stresses, is by no means merely an "effect" of the formation of modern capitalism, but precedes its emergence, and helps to promote its development' (47). See also Bauman, who argues that the discipline and control characteristic of industrialization prompt class formation: 'the formation of workers into a class was a response to the advent of industrial society;

Norbert Elias points out, and doubtless Weber would agree, that 'what is considered "rational" depends at any time on the structure of society' (110). From the point of view of a class society in general, what is most irrational about the structure of pre-capitalist society is its stratification by status, in which, as Weber observes, a claim to social esteem carries with it certain privileges and is rooted principally in 'a specific *style of life*' (2: 932; see also 935–8). Concerned principally with status, pre-capitalist society focuses not on the production of goods in a competition for wealth, but on 'the *consumption* of goods' in a competition for prestige (Weber 2: 937).[11] Differentiation by class and by status, then, suggests alternate, and often opposed, modes of life. Elias identifies attitudes towards the use of money as perhaps the crucial difference between them. In a class society (or say, for the bourgeoisie) success requires the individual or the family to 'subordinate expenses to income' in order to save for future capital investment. In a status society (or say, for the aristocracy) success requires lavish consumption, public display: the individual or the family must 'make its expenditure dependent not primarily on its income but on its status and rank' (66–7, 285). Such expense is an investment made in the interests of social rather than financial return: for the aristocrat, 'ownership of capital was finally a means to an end. It was significant primarily as a condition for upholding a social "reality", the centrepiece of which was distinction from the mass of people, status as members of a privileged class, and behaviour that stressed this distinction in all the situations of life, in short, nobility as a self-evident value' (96).

Maintaining distance and distinction from the mass of people requires, as Weber explains, 'a monopolization of ideal and material goods or opportunities' (2: 935). In early modern Europe, any number of legal and traditional prerogatives combined to distinguish gentry from commoners, including the rights to bear arms, to wear certain types of clothes, or to possess serfs and bondsmen.[12] Veblen points

---

only obliquely, because of the circumstances of the time and place, can this formation be portrayed as a reaction to the capitalist form of industrial society' (19).
11 Weber sums up the status order as follows: 'Every status society lives by conventions, which regulate the style of life, and hence creates economically irrational consumption patterns and fetters the free market through monopolistic appropriations and by curbing the individual's earning power' (1: 307).
12 Lisa Jardine describes the tension created by bourgeois assaults on such monopolies in her discussion of the flurry of Elizabethan sumptuary legislation. Intended to

out that the 'economic expression of their superior rank' (1) is the prohibition against the gentry's entering into most forms of what Weber calls 'rational economic pursuit, and especially entrepreneurial activity' (2: 936).[13] In feudal societies, élites are customarily 'reserved for certain employments to which a degree of honour attaches ... the rule holds with but slight exceptions that ... manual labour, industry, whatever has to do directly with the everyday work of getting a livelihood, is the exclusive occupation of the inferior class' (Veblen 1–2). Perhaps a freedom from labour or work most distinguishes the aristocracy from the mass of people and sets the stage for its particular style of life. Yet in doing so, it also sets the stage for the deep financial troubles faced by many aristocrats in the late sixteenth and early seventeenth centuries. Aristocratic lifestyles required expenditures of huge sums of money; however, as Bush points out, aristocrats 'stubbornly sought to make ends meet without having to participate in commercial activities' (74). Compelled by social norms on one hand to spend but not to work, and on the other to leave (relatively) undisturbed the customary rents of their tenant farmers, English aristocrats waded through inflationary times, financing their lifestyles by receiving favour from the monarch, by marrying well, or by mortgaging – and sometimes losing – land to merchant-usurers. Not uncommonly, the requirement that aristocratic lifestyles emphasize both consumption and idleness resulted in financial ruin, as Shakespeare demonstrates in *Timon of Athens*. Like Lord Timon – or any number of gallants in Jacobean city comedy – aristocrats discovered that 'the greatest of your having lacks a half / To pay your present debts' (2.2.148–9).

Status and Class in *Timon of Athens*

Rebuffing the Steward's 'sermon' on prodigality, and acknowledging the ruin that his gift-giving has bought, Timon summarizes the tension I have been describing between aristocratic and bourgeois assumptions about economics: 'Unwisely, not ignobly, have I given' (2.2.178). Timon

---

police the border between gentry and commoner, the legislation was doomed to failure, since 'the affluent burghers with ready money to dress like the gentry were also the purveyors of the commodity being legislated about: expensive fabrics' (145).
13 In 1583, Thomas Smith described the English gentleman as any 'who can live idly and without manuall labour ...' (72); in seventeenth-century France, the nobility was legally prohibited from engaging in commerce (Elias 69).

acknowledges his economic foolishness, but he remains confident that his investment will pay dividends appropriate to the assumptions of the status society in which he lives. Timon can turn for help to those of his rank, he assures his steward, and thus can see his debts as 'blessings; for by these / Shall I try friends. You shall perceive how you / Mistake my fortunes; I am wealthy in my friends' (2.2.186–8). At this crucial moment in the play, Shakespeare underscores the assumption of solidarity and reciprocity among the nobility, which Timon had previously emphasized to the crowd of banqueting lords: 'I have often wish'd myself poorer that I might come nearer to you. We are born to do benefits; and what better ... can we call our own than the riches of our friends? O what ... comfort 'tis to have so many like brothers commanding one another's fortunes' (1.2.98–103). Financial crisis allows Timon to test his friends, but what he tests is not primarily their affective ties to him but his status and prestige among them: 'Ne'er speak or think / That Timon's fortunes 'mong his friends can sink' (2.2.234–5).[14]

Sink Timon's fortunes do; all his friends deny him. Failing to reciprocate 'like brothers,' they ignobly but wisely determine, like Lucullus, 'that this is no time to lend money, especially upon bare friendship, without security' (3.1.41–3). It is a scandalous situation, according to the First Stranger, who witnesses Lucius's snivelling refusal of aid, but one that registers again the tension between aristocratic and bourgeois attitudes towards economics: the First Stranger infers from the disagreeable situation that 'Men must learn now with pity to dispense, / For policy sits above conscience' (3.2.88–9), the conscience, that is, requiring the aristocrat to give bountifully to others. People must adapt to changing circumstances; those who do not will be ruined, like Timon, and forsake society in misguided misanthropy.

Such might be distilled from the First Stranger's comment and offered as the germinal seed of Shakespeare's play, save for the fact that the playwright loads the play in Timon's favour. As John Draper put it in 1934, Shakespeare 'clearly expected his audience to sympathise

14 In discussing the importance of etiquette for the aristocracy, Elias suggests that 'social opinion, which constitutes the prestige of the individual, is expressed by reciprocal behaviour within a communal action according to certain rules.' Moreover, 'in this communal action each individual's existential bond to society is directly visible. Without confirmation of one's prestige through behaviour, this prestige is nothing.' The enormous 'value attached to the demonstration of prestige and the observance of etiquette does not betray an attachment to externals, but to what was vitally important to individual identity' (101).

with Timon' (20). Critics have wrestled with what Draper calls the play's 'fundamental paradox' – that Timon is 'a bankrupt wastrel whose downfall we are expected to lament' (21) – principally and logically enough by denying Draper's charge and accepting the play's assertions about Timon's nobility (and especially about the pernicious effects of economic rationality), about a society infused by money and what any number of critics have called the acquisitive principle. As Maurice Charney explains, 'there is general agreement that the world of *Timon* is corrupt and that Athens is a materialistic, money-grubbing city in which virtue is doomed to cynical betrayal' (309).[15]

It is not surprising, therefore, to find in H.J. Oliver's introduction to the 1959 Arden edition of *Timon* the suggestion that 'those twentieth-century critics who have brought to the play their knowledge of the Elizabethan "background" have ... sometimes been blinded by such knowledge – blinded to the facts of the play' (xliv). Oliver finds distasteful the arguments of Draper and of Pettet, who think *Timon* 'a straightforward tract for the times,' (Pettet 321) depicting 'the social chaos consequent ... upon the economic ruin of the nobility' (Draper 28) and thus casting Shakespeare, like some of his creations, as 'a backward-looking lover of the old order' (Pettet 332) who wishes his audiences to sympathize with a 'bankrupt wastrel' (Draper 21). It is difficult to discern whether Oliver dislikes Draper's and Pettet's characterizations of Shakespeare's politics in the play or their sullying of Timon's character, or both. In any event, Oliver clearly thinks Draper's and Pettet's economic and historical analyses have missed the point of Timon's nobility, a nobility that for Oliver, as for many other critics, transcends his stupidity about economics. For Oliver and others, as well as for Timon himself, acting 'unwisely' is acceptable – or at least excusable – as long as 'nobility' is preserved.

My point, and that of Weber and Elias among others, is that economic irrationality largely constitutes nobility as a social reality and defines social differentiation by status.[16] Thus, to the aristocrat or to anyone invested in or sympathetic to seeing social power distributed and regu-

15 See, for example, essays by Chorost, Kahn, Miola, Burke, Muir, Pettet, and Draper.
16 Both Draper and Pettet think Shakespeare clear-headed in *Timon*, and both contrast the play with Shakespeare's earlier consideration of nobility in *Merchant* where, as Cohen observes, 'the concluding tripartite unity of Antonio, Bassanio, and Portia enacts ... interclass harmony between aristocratic landed wealth and mercantile capital, with the former dominant' (772). If *Merchant* suggests a fantasy of reconciliation between these contrasting élites, *Timon* presents an uncompromising vision of the losers in the transition from feudalism to capitalism, from a status society to a class society.

lated by non-market mechanisms – for example, by birth or education – Timon's unwise but noble giving is both understandable and legitimate, even admirable. He becomes the disillusioned philanthropist, cruelly destroyed by a society focused on self-interest. To the bourgeois or to anyone invested in or sympathetic to seeing social power distributed and regulated through markets, Timon's unwise but noble giving is foolish and reveals him to be what Draper calls him, a 'bankrupt wastrel,' not quite the kind of fellow one would wish to see occupy an élite position. To the bourgeois, Timon is misguided, first a prodigal and finally a misanthrope, blaming others for what he has brought upon himself.

My aim is not to suggest that any of these critics is 'wrong' in his analysis of *Timon*. Indeed, if *Timon* does what Draper and Pettet think it does, presenting the cold, hard facts of early seventeenth-century economic life while casting Timon himself as a sympathetic, even tragic, character, then Shakespeare must have constructed the play around 'a critique of money and money-oriented economies,' as Michael Chorost, one of *Timon*'s recent critics, suggests (349). My aim rather is to question the readiness with which critics have embraced Shakespeare's 'critique of money and money-oriented societies,' a critique that has been made in defence of an arguably parasitic, self-indulgent élite, whose dominance and pleasure resulted in and depended upon the brutalization, the abject misery, of the masses of people.[17] It is as if the majority of *Timon*'s critics themselves comprise a beleaguered aristocracy, fearful of the disruptive, subversive, levelling power of money and markets, which, as Timon laments, can 'bless th'accurs'd, / Make the hoar leprosy ador'd, place thieves, / And give them title, knee and approbation / With senators on the bench' (4.3.35–8).

Academic Anti-capitalism

Earlier I noted that all societies are stratified, or ranked; inequality is, shall we say, in the nature of things. Capitalism, as Fernand Braudel reminds us, 'does not invent hierarchies, any more than it invented the

---

As Pettet concludes, by the time Shakespeare writes *Timon*, he 'appears to realize that the new anti-feudal forces of commercialism, money, and self-interest are in the ascendant' (329).

17 On the poverty and economic inequality of pre-industrial Europe, see studies by Cipolla, Clay, and Berger. On the brutality of Elizabethan and Jacobean England, see Barker.

market, or production, or consumption' (75). If inequality is a given, it might seem a toss-up as to which institutionalization of inequality is better – or worse. Yet critics often seem eager to assume that the inequality characteristic of pre-capitalist or pre-industrial societies was or is better than the inequality characteristic of capitalist ones. This is not an argument, but a postulate, and one that is not restricted to contemporary materialist critics on the left.

Indeed, capitalism is routinely demonized in critical discourse.[18] So pervasive is the demonization that Marjorie Perloff has called it a 'pious cliché,' one that is 'repeated again and again in critical texts that claim to have no particular bias'; in contemporary criticism, '"late monopoly" or "consumer" capitalism is ipso facto an evil to be opposed by all right-thinking artists and humanists' (130). But as Michael Bristol points out, such 'sentiments are not of recent emergence'; scholars have long desired 'to be counted as separate from and oppositional towards the imperatives of the market, commodity exchange, and industrial discipline' (35). Despite differences of pitch and moment, anti-capitalism unites critics of the right and the left, as Hugh Grady suggests in pointing out the 'limited but striking convergence of interests and ideas between the American New Critics and the Frankfurt School' (154). In the mid-1940s, John Crowe Ransom published Theodor W. Adorno's work in the *Kenyon Review* because he found much to agree with in Adorno's 'Theses upon Art and Religion Today.' As Grady explains, both Ransom and Adorno 'found in art a possible weapon against the levelling and sterilizing processes of capitalist modernization, and both believed fiercely in the need to preserve art's autonomy, not in order to escape from social reality but in order to preserve the alternatives to it contained within the forms of art' (156).

It should not, therefore, surprise that in 1947 Kenneth Muir, in his chapter '*Timon of Athens* and the Cash-Nexus,' can argue that 'Marx ... was a Shakespearian' (57), or at least the kind of Shakespeare who wrote *Timon of Athens*. Nor should it surprise that in 1994 Christopher Kendrick can insist that 'Upon Appleton House' 'register[s]' a revolutionary moment in the development of capitalist inequality, after which 'there can be no question of returning to, or of salvaging the comparative humanity of, some previous settlement' (14). Whether 'some previous settlement' offers 'comparative humanity' to the people operating in

18 For different perspectives on the pejorative use of capitalism, see Peter L. Berger, and Dennis Wrong.

the entire structure of production[19] is debatable; but it is not debatable for Kendrick. I would argue, in contrast, that the 'comparative humanity' of feudal production as opposed to capitalist production depends on whom one is concerned about.[20] Let me concede, as indeed I already have, that capitalism involves a de-socialization of labour. I concede, as Bauman argues, that what labour rebels against in the transition from feudal to capitalist society and in the development of its class consciousness is not the extraction of surplus value, or even its management and distribution, but capitalism's assault 'upon the autonomy of the producer' (18). Under the previous settlement, labourers were left alone to produce because 'the old power was geared to the task of creaming off the surplus product; it was never confronted, at least on an important scale ... with the need to organise the production itself' (Bauman 46).

Let me concede that the tenant farmer in 1500 wielded more autonomy in production than does the computer assembler in 1998. But by any material standard – income, disposable income, education, housing, clothing, life expectancy, and so on – the computer assembler is vastly better off than the tenant farmer.[21] 'Autonomy' versus 'material

---

19 Kendrick is not speaking of labourers only; the 'humanity' of the 'previous settlement' extends to all involved, from landlord to labourer.

20 Such patronizing would not be tolerated by these same scholars if it were directed at, say, African-Americans. What exactly is the difference between the assertion – heard occasionally even today in the southern United States – that African-Americans 'were better off as slaves' and the assertion made by literary critics like Kendrick that early modern labourers were better off when they were *bound* to a master and a manor in a system of unequal reciprocity? Note that in the passage quoted from *Capital* (above, n2) Marx uses 'slave' and 'serf' as virtual equivalents.

21 On this issue see, for example, Cipolla, who points out that in 1950 expenditure on food represented 22 per cent of total expenditure in the United States and 31 per cent in the United Kingdom (23). In contrast, in sixteenth-century Europe '60 to 80 percent of the expenditure of the mass of the population went on food,' which was of poor quality and quantity (23). After spending the vast proportion of their income on food, 'the mass of the people had little left for their wants, no matter how elementary they were. In preindustrial Europe, the purchase of a garment or of the cloth for a garment remained a luxury the common people could only afford a few times in their lives. One of the main preoccupations of hospital administration was to ensure that the clothes of the deceased "should not be usurped but should be given to lawful inheritors." During epidemics of plague, the town authorities had to struggle to confiscate the clothes of the dead and to burn them: people waited for others to die so as to take over their clothes – which generally had the effect of spreading the epidemic' (25). See also Berger 32–48.

well-being': such a trade-off, if indeed it is one, is not to be countenanced by the academic. For us, autonomy is a principal virtue and goal, not to be despoiled by materialism and never to be sacrificed merely for material gain, which is why Stanley Fish can take 'the relationship between academics and their Volvos ... [as] emblematic of a basic academic practice, the practice of translating into the language of higher motives desires and satisfactions one is unable or unwilling to acknowledge' (103). Above all, states Fish, this 'basic academic practice' requires that 'whenever you either want something or get something, manage it in such a way as to deny or disguise its material pleasures' (103).

Other people, people who labour, for instance, may be less inclined than critics to 'deny ... material pleasures' – a tract home, with built-in appliances; a power boat; a dirt bike; three, four, even five televisions; fast food; cases of cheap beer. Yet critics deny not only our own material pleasures, which – let us be plain – are numerous, but also those of people who have few other pleasures, as, for example, the life of the mind. We focus – and insist that they focus – on their alienation from the means of production and regale them with lectures that their pleasures, the stuff they buy with the wages of their alienation, are measures of their oppression or co-optation, of their failure, not their success. We refuse to consider that exchanging autonomy on the job for material pleasures is, or at least might be, a reasonable choice. As Carolyn Kay Steedman observes in her working-class autobiography *Landscape for a Good Woman*, 'within the framework of conventional political understanding, the desire for a New Look skirt cannot be seen as a political want, let alone a proper one' (121).[22]

Fish thinks that academics' disdain for stuff is *'purposeful,'* since this 'disdain ... is itself a sign of a dedication to higher, if invisible, values' (104, 105). Fish is, perhaps, too generous. Another purpose, I suggest, is also clear: prejudging the issue of inequality and romanticizing

---

22 Steedman challenges 'the structures of political thought that have labelled this wanting as wrong' (23), a position taken up by other writers from working-class backgrounds, including Gloria Anzaldúa and bell hooks, and, of course, myself in this essay. When Steedman defends her mother's longings for things she never would obtain, or when Anzaldúa writes of her frustration in explaining to 'white middle-class women that it's okay for us to want to own "possessions"' (85), each suggests that the disdain of material well-being characteristic of academic radicalism is a disdain born of privilege and reflects (upper) middle-class bias, a point made as well by Pamela Fox in a fine essay on working-class narratives.

feudalism – the obsession with alienation and the stubborn unwillingness, via the demonization of stuff, even to consider that capitalism
is an effective way to better the material life of people – reveals our
concern to be principally with ourselves, our lifestyles, and our values.
To the extent that they threaten autonomy, alienation and consumerism
threaten us, and therefore we project our anxiety about modes of capitalist production onto the working class. We fight capitalism not in our
own name, not in our own interests, but selflessly, in the interests of
the oppressed.[23]

This is mystification on a massive scale. I contend that the profession's
anti-capitalism is consistent with our self-interest. As academics working in educational institutions, we constitute a powerful status group,
not unlike early modern aristocrats, competing for prestige rather than
money;[24] and whether or not we acknowledge it consciously, it is in our
interests to oppose the development of market institutions. The market

23 This is true even of discussions of intellectual autonomy that differentiate among
    segments of intellectual labour and that focus on the protection of intellectuals'
    own interests, such as John Guillory's 'Literary Critics as Intellectuals.' Guillory
    concludes that these interests 'depend especially upon promoting the recognition
    that intellectual autonomy – and therefore intellectuality – is always potentially
    at stake in work autonomy, which is at stake in every sector of intellectual labor,
    and of labor in general' (141). Guillory cannot resist this gesture – the sentence
    must allow 'intellectuality' to trickle down finally to 'labor in general' – despite his
    own admission earlier in the essay that it is possible to conceive of 'a constitutive
    distinction between intellectual and manual labor, a distinction that for good
    historical reasons implicates intellectual labor in the system of economic exploitation'
    (110). Given that responsibility for economic exploitation, Guillory wonders 'how the
    fact of intellectual labor becomes the condition for the innate tendency to progressive
    or even leftist politics that is assumed to characterize intellectuals' (110–11). Guillory
    defers a good question indefinitely by turning immediately to 'the discourse of
    intellectuals *about themselves*,' a constraint allowing intellectuals to be defined 'as
    a political and not a socieconomic [sic] identity' (111), thus clearing away that
    'constitutive distinction' and preparing the stage for his final return to an intellectual
    labour that is liberating rather than exploitative, a good to be desired and fought for
    'in every sector of intellectual labor, and of labor in general' (141).
24 Fish notes that the 'commodities for which academics yearn [are] attention, applause,
    fame, and ultimately, adulation of a kind usually reserved for the icons of popular
    culture' (103). In the parodic 'who-done-it,' *Murder at the MLA*, D.J.H. Jones captures
    the profession's competition for prestige, which compares nicely with Elias's
    description of competitive behaviour among the aristocracy: 'The whole system was
    full of tensions. It was shot through with the countless rivalries of people trying to
    preserve their position by marking it off from those below while at the same time
    improving it by reducing the demarcation from those above' (Elias 76).

threatens us as a status group in at least two ways. The market's allo-
cation of power and privilege according to economic success challenges
the terms and structure of our reward system, the ways in which we
distribute power and privilege. As Weber remarks, a 'status order would
be threatened at its very root if mere economic acquisition and naked
economic power still bearing the stigma of its extra-status origin could
bestow upon anyone who has won them the same or even greater honor
as the vested interests claim for themselves' (2: 936). In the academy,
'mere economic acquisition and naked economic power' will not do;
a security guard, for example, cannot win the lottery, decide that she
would like to teach Shakespeare, and buy the position. One becomes
a professor by acquiring proper credentials after years of study, by
proving oneself worthy in an arena vastly different from the economic;
and today, artists or – even more tellingly, entrepreneurs – must usually
possess the appropriate 'terminal degree' to work in a university.

The market is a highly subversive and volatile arena, in which money,
economic success – however achieved, whether 'by sweaty effort or by
cheating or perhaps by plain luck,' as Berger playfully observes (53) –
speaks loudest about the distribution of privilege, as much or more so
than birth or talent or intelligence. As Marx observes in *Capital*, citing *Timon of Athens* for support: 'Just as in money every qualitative difference
between commodities is extinguished, so too for its part, as a radical
leveller, it extinguishes all distinctions ... But money is itself a commodity, an external object capable of becoming the private property of any
individual. Thus the social power becomes the private power of private
persons. Ancient society therefore denounced it as tending to destroy
the economic and moral order ...' (229–30). Precisely. Those interested in
preserving aristocratic or intellectual privilege do well to resist capitalist
development because, in short, it gives the vulgar a voice, a voice they
exercise in the market. The market, therefore, threatens us again and
perhaps more seriously over the issue of judgment and value.

Space does not permit me to develop this point. It shall suffice
to observe that a number of scholars now agree that the Romantic
aesthetic, the aesthetic of disinterest that governs literary judgment
to this day, flowers in response to pressure from the developing literary marketplace, a market that, like all markets, allows the vulgar
a voice in the determination of value.[25] It is this voice that writers

25 See, for example, Jonathan Bate; Robert Sayre and Michael Löwy; Guillory, *Cultural
Capital*; John Carey; Eric Gans; and Martha Woodmansee.

who found themselves unable to compete effectively in the literary marketplace sought to silence. Martha Woodmansee is frank about this: both Schiller and Coleridge write in opposition to those writers promoting, even celebrating, the 'emancipatory and egalitarian' tendencies in the free market for culture (75, 72–86, 111–45). According to Woodmansee, the attempt to 'sever the value of a work from its capacity to appeal to a public' is directly related to literature's becoming 'subject to the laws of a market economy' and reflects a 'mounting crisis in the relation of serious writers to the reading public' (31, 32, 118). What the serious writers offered, the reading public did not buy; therefore, what the reading public did buy was redefined as unworthy. By rescuing 'art from determination by the market' (33), the serious writers simultaneously rescue themselves and their reputations from determination by the cultural choices of the people.

In this way, anti-capitalism among writers and academics is clearly bound up with anti-populism, with a fear of the people and their voices, their judgments. To the extent that anti-populism is a subtext of anti-capitalism, the mystification inherent in (upper) middle-class academics' trumpeting of the virtues of pre-capitalist economics and social organization is intensified. To be blunt: critics oppose capitalism in the name of the people but do so in order to protect their own prerogative of judgment over the people, to de-legitimize the voices of the people, voices expressed in the marketplace for literature and culture.

Conclusion

Understanding stratification in the Renaissance is difficult and problematic. How could it be otherwise? Not only is this a period of class formation but it is also one during which class begins to emerge both as a principle of stratification and as a concept. Too often, I think, we literary critics do not acknowledge as problematic the categories or terms of our discourse, such as 'class system' and its relationship to status and culture, or 'capitalism' and its relationship to industrialization and bureaucratization. Perhaps this theoretical slackness results from our having given our allegiance for the most part to a theoretical framework that assigns class and capitalism a negative moral value, absolving us of obligations to complicate our understandings of them. Or perhaps more generally it results from a lack of imagination endemic to interdisciplinary work in literary study; we turn immediately to Marx and Freud, and thus need not even demonize competitors like Weber, Durkheim, or William James, because only what is acknowledged to exist can be demonized.

I give much credit to that functional or institutional argument because I know well the allure of lines of least resistance. But our failure to distinguish between class and status as concepts, as modes of stratification with differing systems of meanings, results primarily, I propose, from the power of our own contemporary political allegiances, including an unwillingness to confront our own awkward relationship to capitalism and to the people, and an unwillingness more generally to confront the seriousness of the Weberian challenge to Marx and the Marxian tradition. For it is a serious challenge indeed: confronting Weber and confronting the meanings of inequality rooted in status differentiation means confronting ourselves and the ideology, rooted in the Marxian tradition, by which, whether partially or fully, many of us order our lives as privileged intellectuals. And ideology, as James Kavanagh reminds us, *is* a 'system of representations that offer the subject an imaginary, compelling, sense of reality in which crucial contradictions of self and social order appear resolved' (145).

WORKS CITED

Anzaldúa, Gloria. *Borderlands / La Frontera: The New Mestiza*. San Francisco: Spinsters/Aunt Lute, 1987.

Ariès, Philippe. *Centuries of Childhood: A Social History of Family Life*. Trans. Robert Baldick. New York: Knopf, 1962.

Barker, Francis. 'Treasures of Culture: *Titus Andronicus* and Death by Hanging.' *The Production of English Renaissance Culture*. Ed. David Lee Miller, Sharon O'Dair, and Harold Weber. 221–61.

Bate, Jonathan. *Shakespearean Constitutions: Politics, Theatre, Criticism, 1730–1830*. Oxford, New York, and Toronto: Oxford UP, 1989.

Bauman, Zygmunt. *Memories of Class: The Pre-History and After-Life of Class*. London: Routledge & Kegan Paul, 1982.

Berger, Peter L. *The Capitalist Revolution: Fifty Propositions about Prosperity, Equality, and Liberty*. New York: Basic Books, 1986.

Beynon, Huw. 'Class and Historical Explanation.' *Social Orders and Social Classes in Europe since 1500: Studies in Social Stratification*. Ed. M.L. Bush. London and New York: Longman, 1992. 230–49.

Braudel, Fernand. *Afterthoughts on Material Civilization and Capitalism*. Baltimore and London: Johns Hopkins UP, 1977.

Bristol, Michael D. *Shakespeare's America, America's Shakespeare*. London and New York: Routledge, 1990.

Burke, Kenneth. '*Timon of Athens* and Misanthropic Gold.' *Language as Symbolic Action: Essays on Life, Literature, and Method*. Berkeley and Los Angeles: U of California P; Cambridge: Cambridge UP, 1966. 115–24.

Bush, M.L. *The English Aristocracy: A Comparative Synthesis*. Manchester: Manchester UP, 1984.

Carey, John. *The Intellectuals and the Masses: Pride and Prejudice among the Literary Intelligentsia, 1880–1939*. London: Faber and Faber, 1992.

Charney, Maurice. '*Coriolanus* and *Timon of Athens*.' *Shakespeare: A Bibliographic Guide, New Edition*. Ed. Stanley Wells. Oxford: Clarendon P, 1990. 295–320.

Chorost, Michael. 'Biological Finance in Shakespeare's *Timon of Athens*.' *English Literary Renaissance* 21.3 (1991): 349–70.

Cipolla, Carlo M. *Before the Industrial Revolution: European Society and Economy, 1000–1700*. 1976. Trans. Christopher Woodall. 3rd ed. New York and London: Norton, 1993.

Clay, C.G.A. *Economic Expansion and Social Change: England 1500–1700*. Vol. 1. Cambridge: Cambridge UP, 1984.

Cohen, Walter. '*The Merchant of Venice* and the Possibilities of Historical Criticism.' *ELH* 49.4 (1982): 765–89.

Cressy, David. 'Describing the Social Order of Elizabethan and Stuart England.' *Literature and History* 3 (1976): 29–44.

Dahrendorf, Ralf. *Class and Class Conflict in Industrial Society*. Stanford: Stanford UP, 1959.

Draper, John W. 'The Theme of *Timon of Athens*.' *Modern Language Review* 29 (1934): 20–31.

Elias, Norbert. *The Court Society*. Trans. Edmund Jephcott. 1969. Oxford: Basil Blackwell; New York: Pantheon, 1983.

Fish, Stanley. 'The Unbearable Ugliness of Volvos.' *English Inside and Out: The Places of Literary Criticism*. Ed. Susan Gubar and Jonathan Kamholtz. New York and London: Routledge, 1993. 102–8.

Fox, Pamela. 'De/Re-fusing the Reproduction-Resistance Circuit of Cultural Studies: A Methodology for Reading Working-Class Narrative.' *Cultural Critique* 28 (Fall 1994): 53–74.

Gans, Eric. *Originary Thinking: Elements of a Generative Anthropology*. Stanford: Stanford UP, 1993.

Giddens, Anthony. *The Class Structure of the Advanced Societies*. New York: Harper and Row, 1973.

Giddens, Anthony, and David Held. *Classes, Power, and Conflict: Classical and Contemporary Debates*. Berkeley and Los Angeles: U of California P, 1982.

Grady, Hugh. *The Modernist Shakespeare: Critical Texts in a Material World.*
Oxford, New York, and Toronto: Oxford UP, 1991.

Greenblatt, Stephen. 'Murdering Peasants: Status, Genre, and the Representation
of Rebellion.' *Representing the English Renaissance.* Ed. Stephen Greenblatt.
Berkeley, Los Angeles, and London: U of California P, 1988. 1–29.

Guillory, John. *Cultural Capital: The Problem of Literary Canon Formation.* Chicago
and London: U of Chicago P, 1993.

– 'Literary Critics as Intellectuals: Class Analysis and the Crisis of the
Humanities.' *Rethinking Class: Literary Studies and Social Formations.* Ed. Wai
Chee Dimock and Michael T. Gilmore. New York: Columbia UP, 1994.
107–49.

Hall, John R. 'The Capital(s) of Cultures: A Nonholistic Approach to Status
Situations, Class, Gender, and Ethnicity.' *Cultivating Differences: Symbolic
Boundaries and the Making of Inequality.* Ed. Michèle Lamont and Marcel
Fournier. Chicago and London: U of Chicago P, 1992. 257–85.

hooks, bell. *Yearning: Race, Gender, and Cultural Politics.* Boston: South End P,
1990.

Jameson, Fredric. *The Syntax of History.* Vol. 2 of *The Ideologies of Theory:
Essays, 1971–1986.* Theory and History of Literature 49. Minneapolis: U of
Minnesota P; Markham, ON: Fitzhenry & Whiteside, 1988.

Jardine, Lisa. *Still Harping on Daughters: Women and Drama in the Age of
Shakespeare.* Sussex: Harvester; Totowa, NJ: Barnes & Noble, 1983.

Jones, D.J.H. *Murder at the MLA.* Athens, GA: U of Georgia P, 1993.

Kahn, Coppélia. '"Magic of Bounty": *Timon of Athens*, Jacobean Patronage, and
Maternal Power.' *Shakespeare Quarterly* 38.1 (1987): 34–57.

Kavanagh, James H. 'Shakespeare in Ideology.' *Alternative Shakespeares.* Ed.
John Drakakis. London and New York: Methuen; Routledge, 1985. 144–65.

Kendrick, Christopher. 'Agons of the Manor: "Upon Appleton House" and
Agrarian Capitalism.' *The Production of English Renaissance Culture.* Ed.
David Lee Miller, Sharon O'Dair, and Harold Weber. 13–55.

Lachmann, Richard. *From Manor to Market: Structural Change in England,
1536–1640.* Madison and London: U of Wisconsin P, 1987.

Marx, Karl. *Capital: A Critique of Political Economy.* Trans. Ben Fowkes. Vol. 1.
New York: Vintage, 1977.

Miller, David Lee, Sharon O'Dair, and Harold Weber, eds. *The Production of
English Renaissance Culture.* Ithaca and London: Cornell UP, 1994.

Miola, Robert S. 'Timon in Shakespeare's Athens.' *Shakespeare Quarterly* 31.1
(1980): 21–30.

Moisan, Thomas. '"Knock me here soundly": Comic Misprision and Class
Consciousness in Shakespeare.' *Shakespeare Quarterly* 42.3 (1991): 276–90.

Muir, Kenneth. *The Singularity of Shakespeare and Other Essays*. Liverpool: Liverpool UP, 1977. 56–75.

Oliver, H.J. Introduction. *Timon of Athens*. 1959. Ed. H.J. Oliver. London: Routledge, Chapman, and Hall, 1969. xiii–lii.

Perloff, Marjorie. 'An Intellectual Impasse.' *Salmagundi: A Quarterly Journal of the Humanities and Social Sciences* 72 (Fall 1986): 125–30.

Pettet, E.C. '*Timon of Athens*: The Disruption of Feudal Morality.' *Review of English Studies* 23.92 (1947): 321–36.

Sayre, Robert, and Michael Löwy. 'Figures of Romantic Anticapitalism.' *Spirits of Fire: English Romantic Writers and Contemporary Historical Methods*. Ed. G.A. Rosso and Daniel P. Watkins. Cranbury, NJ, London, and Mississauga, ON: Associated U Presses, 1990. 23–68.

Shakespeare, William. *As You Like It*. Ed. Agnes Latham. London and New York: Methuen, 1975.

– *King Lear*. Ed. Kenneth Muir. 8th ed. London and New York: Methuen, 1972.

– *Othello*. Ed. M.R. Ridley. 7th ed. London and New York: Methuen, 1958.

– *Timon of Athens*. 1959. Ed. H.J. Oliver. London: Routledge, Chapman, and Hall, 1969.

Smith, Thomas. *De Republica Anglorum*. Ed. Mary Dewar. Cambridge: Cambridge UP, 1982.

Steedman, Carolyn Kay. *Landscape for a Good Woman: A Story of Two Lives*. 1986. New Brunswick, NJ: Rutgers UP, 1987.

Veblen, Thorstein. *The Theory of the Leisure Class*. 1899. New York: Augustus M. Kelley, 1975.

Wallerstein, Immanuel. *The Modern World-System: Capitalist Agriculture and the Origins of the European World-Economy in the Sixteenth Century*. Studies in Social Discontinuity. New York and London: Academic P, 1974.

Weber, Max. *Economy and Society: An Outline of Interpretive Sociology*. Ed. Guenther Roth and Claus Wittich. 3 vols. Vols. 1 and 2. New York: Bedminster, 1968.

Woodmansee, Martha. *The Author, Art, and the Market: Rereading the History of Aesthetics*. New York and Chichester, West Sussex: Columbia UP, 1994.

Wrightson, Keith. 'The Social Order of Early Modern England: Three Approaches.' *The World We Have Gained: Histories of Population and Social Structure*. Ed. Lloyd Bonfield, Richard M. Smith, and Keith Wrightson. Oxford and New York: Basil Blackwell, 1986. 177–202.

Wrong, Dennis. 'Disaggregating the Idea of Capitalism.' *Theory, Culture, and Society* 9.1 (1992): 147–58.

Afterword

MARTA STRAZNICKY

If one accepts, as Jane Gallop has suggested, that anthologies of criticism are a sort of 'collective subject' that mark the discourse of knowledge in ways that are symptomatic of their historical and institutional positions (7), then the present collection of essays indicates that, after two decades of diversifying the methods and objectives of historicism, contemporary criticism of Renaissance literature is fully prepared to regard pluralism as a strength rather than an impediment to its intellectual undertaking. As an event in the history of Renaissance criticism, this collection marks a shift from earlier attempts to gather the many varieties of critical practice under headings with emphatically heuristic claims: *The Historical Renaissance, The Matter of Difference*, or *Queering the Renaissance* to take just three important examples. To be sure, other anthologies insisted more on the common project of *rewriting* or *reconfiguring* familiar terrain than on singleness of approach, but none has so obviously renounced the claim to shared methodological or political ground as does this volume. Perhaps more significant, though, than the desire to celebrate discontinuities is the fact that they are seen as evidence of a field in a continuously transitional state, resonating productively between a 'paradigm shift,' whose broadly historicist objectives a critical mass of Renaissance scholars now share, and the establishment of a 'normal science' representing the stable outcome of the revolutionary work of the past two decades. But however exciting a discontinuous critical enterprise may be for researchers, it has some significant drawbacks for teachers, drawbacks that might in fact be preventing historicism from becoming a meaningful practice for non-specialists and hence assuming the privileges of 'normal science' within and beyond educational institutions.

Although I venture this thought most immediately in response to the essays collected here, it is also something that emerges from the frustrations of teaching students who resist or fail to grasp the premises of historicist criticism, who are forever converting the past into the present without any sense of the mediating discourses that enable them to do so. And while they are keenly interested in, say, early modern hygiene or shaming rituals, and perfectly capable of understanding how traditionally non-literary discourses and practices intersect with the Renaissance text, they appear to have difficulty sustaining such work outside the lecture hall or seminar room. It seems to me that this gap between guided and independent study is a side effect of the separation – in both personal and institutional terms – between our research and teaching activities. This separation has by and large prevented us from formulating the new paradigm of research in Renaissance literary studies in ways that are meaningful for non-specialists, and from devising new pedagogical strategies that teach historicist analysis rather than adding to students' stock of 'themes' in literature. There are admittedly formidable institutional (read economic) pressures that keep us from devoting non-teaching time to course development or pedagogical experimentation, or even to the preliminary work of thinking through effective ways of conducting historical analysis in the literature classroom. The institutional reward for top-notch research is, after all, release from teaching duties. But should we not, perhaps, in this as in other areas of the profession go against the institutional grain? Could it be that our failure to engage collectively in pedagogical matters has in fact enabled New Criticism – which still dominates classroom practice – to remain, however submerged it might be, at the centre of literary studies?

Most of us who teach the new knowledge about Renaissance literature would probably agree that there is, *still*, a sharp and powerful distinction between the objectives of our courses (for example, to teach a contextualized Shakespeare, to introduce neglected writings from the period, or to reveal a fractured cultural field) and the message students get from their books, both in terms of content and material substance. For instance, photocopied selections from Renaissance women writers set beside the formidable Norton Shakespeare signify in ways that exceed any attempt to make the differences themselves into instructional material, and when students turn to 'secondary' sources for help in preparing their papers they are, from my experience at any rate, more likely to use criticism and literary histories published before rather than after 1980, the year that is commonly taken as a watershed in Renaissance studies. The difficulty of getting our students to think in the same terms as those that inform the new scholarship in our field is not, as some might argue, owing to a jargon-laden critical discourse or to the extraordinary demands of historicist enquiry. It is due, I think, to the simple fact that there aren't enough material aids – editions, reference works, survey-type literary histories, etc. – designed to help students develop the skills of historicist analysis. Specialized books on nationalism, patronage, censorship, rhetoric, or sexuality might be consulted for 'information' on particular topics but will not, and obviously do not aim to, help students acquire general competence in reading Renaissance literature, nor will they be consulted by the student who is scanning library shelves in search of some basic guidance to a remote and alien literary period. However much we ourselves might find a discontinuous critical field stimulating and liberating, not to mention professionally rewarding, it has prevented us from doing the work of consolidation – from focusing on continuities rather than discontinuities – that is essential if historicist analysis is to become the new knowledge of non-specialists.

By way of illustration let me briefly compare two books that consolidate the field of sixteenth-century English literature before and after 1980: C.S. Lewis's *English Literature in the Sixteenth-Century* (1954) and Gary Waller's *English Poetry of the Sixteenth Century* (2nd ed., 1993). Lewis famously divides sixteenth-century non-dramatic literature into 'Drab' and 'Golden,' terms he claims are descriptive rather than evaluative, and devises a narrative of linear progression leading from a time when 'poetry has little richness either of sound or images' to the point when 'men have at last learned to write' (65). The critical biases underlying Lewis's survey are displayed in small phrases such as these and are so obvious (to us) as to require little commentary. But while we may find them and many of his analyses useless if not infuriating (for example, the assertion that Marlowe's 'sole business' in *Hero and Leander* was 'to make holiday from all facts and all morals in a world of imagined deliciousness' [486]), it is undeniable that in the breadth of his survey and in his responsiveness to historical circumstances Lewis continues, for a variety of purposes, to repay reading. His chronological table is a case in point. Perhaps the most obviously outdated aspect of Lewis's entire project is captured here in the division between 'Public Events' pertaining broadly to the realm of the political, and 'Private Events' under which literary developments are listed. These categories

generate distinctions that might be unintelligible to contemporary scholars: the founding of the East India Company in 1600, for example, is a
public event while the opening of the Fortune Theatre in the same year
is deemed private. But even if we would want to quarrel with Lewis's
categories, it is also true that he provides any number of fascinating
juxtapositions, each of which could spark its own historicist enquiry. In
1587, we learn, the Pope proclaims a crusade against England while, in
London, Marlowe's *Tamburlaine* is being staged. In 1593 the '"Great
plenty and cheapness of grain" leads to repeal of the agrarian law
of 1563,' and Nashe's *Summer's Last Will and Testament*, which deals
explicitly with agrarian economics, is performed privately for Arch-
bishop Whitgift. In short, Lewis's chronological table – and the same is
true for the book as a whole – continues to be both informative and
provocative even though the critical movement to which it is linked has
been superseded. It does so, I think, because of the capaciousness of
Lewis's analytical categories and because of the broad range of events
– political, personal, educational, economic, cultural – that is seen as
correlative to, if not mutually constitutive of, the literature. In other
words, Lewis has his eye on literary and cultural continuities.

Gary Waller's *English Poetry of the Sixteenth Century* is the only critical survey of this period that is informed by recent developments in
Renaissance studies, particularly the concern with ideology as a factor
in literary production. In the introduction, Waller positions the book as
representative of contemporary methodologies in Renaissance scholarship: 'New Historicism, Cultural Materialism, and feminism' (7). These
approaches, he goes on to elaborate, converge in the belief that 'a consideration of literary and related texts is inseparable from the locations
and forms by which power and desire flow through society's dominant
institutions,' and his survey of sixteenth-century poetry takes as its
chief objective the demonstration of this principle. In reality, though,
Waller restricts his attention to the impact of the court – as *the* dominant
institution in sixteenth-century society – on the writing of literature,
particularly the court lyric. This telescoping of what is initially about
as broad a statement as one could imagine of the common concerns in
Renaissance scholarship today – 'power and desire' – produces an account of sixteenth-century poetry that closes more avenues for analysis
than it opens. Shakespeare's poetry, for instance, is an 'apprenticeship'
in literary forms 'directly controlled by the Court' (207). The poverty
of such an approach to, say, *Venus and Adonis* is evident in Waller's
own analysis, his one paragraph on the poem being little more than a

series of aesthetic judgments that are near echoes of Lewis: 'Alongside Marlowe's luxuriant, fluid masterpiece, Shakespeare's is rather static, with too much argument and insufficient sensuality to make it pleasurable reading' (207–8). It seems that when a piece of poetry does not capture the cultural struggles in which the court was engaged Waller has very little to say about it. Surprisingly, he also has very little material under 'Historical/Cultural Events' in his chronological table. The only notable event for 1593 (compare Lewis, above) is 'Theatres closed by the plague'; and an event one might expect to warrant detailed attention in a historicist study of literature and power, the Essex rebellion of 1599, is simply that, the 'Essex rebellion' (288). Compare Lewis: 'Spanish fleet sent to aid the Irish but dissipated by bad weather. Elizabeth boxes Essex's ears and sends him as Ld. Deputy to Ireland; his unauthorized return and imprisonment' (592). If a chronological table is meant to enhance students' awareness of historical events, events that are not necessarily taken up in the critical discussion, then one would expect, especially of a historicist critic, as full and detailed entries as practicable. Waller's 'history,' literary and political alike, is inexplicably restricted and, for this reason, restricting to independent study.

Waller's method of reading – for him a 'very exciting one' (11) – does more to mystify literary interpretation than anything Lewis wrote: 'We are looking for the "unconscious" of the texts we read, not just the hidden meanings but the suppressed or repressed meanings' (Waller 12). Doing so produces a 'careful reader' (13), who *'must* focus not merely on what a text seems to say, or what its author seems to want to be heard to say, nor even on what it does not say, but on what it cannot say, either at all or only with difficulty' (13, emphasis added). Much as I am inclined to share with Waller the aim of alerting students to what is not on the page, and thus teaching them to become aware that literature is written out of and in dialogue with a kaleidoscopic cultural field, I also worry about the authoritarian pedagogical approach this all too easily entails. How does one teach students to figure out what a text has repressed?

Waller provides little theoretical reflection on this matter, and his critical account of sixteenth-century poetry enacts what I think is a narrowly conceived answer: students learn by watching professors put into interpretive action the historical knowledge they have gained in places that are either not accessible to or not easily exploited by students (in specialized history books, in periodical literature, at conferences, from discussions with colleagues, and so on). Accordingly, the second section of Waller's introduction is called 'The Court' and it spells out not so much the characteristics of this institution in the sixteenth century as what aspects of its operations are useful for a 'careful' reading of the period's poetry. The bulk of the book *demonstrates* how the court attempted – often unsuccessfully – to appropriate poetry as a means of maintaining its political dominance. I don't wish to take issue with Waller's argument, or even with his decision to restrict the scope of the book to courtly forms; his is a lively, informative account of the political engagements of much that is considered mainstream Renaissance literature. In this, Waller's book represents a major branch of the new knowledge that historicist methodologies have produced. What I do wish to contest, however, is the book's claim to being a general account of *English Poetry of the Sixteenth Century*, let alone the consolidation of the past twenty years' work in Renaissance studies, and its program for literary interpretation. In scope and approach it is far too narrow, even though a survey is attempted, and its methodology relies too heavily on prior historical knowledge to be useful pedagogically. In both regards Waller's book is symptomatic of historicism's vulnerability to pedagogical authoritarianism and the fragmentation of knowledge.

I should perhaps emphasize that I am mounting this critique of Waller from the point of view of an educator concerned to see the paradigm shift in Renaissance studies reach its final, crucial stage of institutionalization, and I consider this stage crucial because however broadly practised a poststructuralist historicism may be among researchers it will never gain societal credibility until its uses and pleasures are made available to non-specialists. In order for this to occur we need to have, to draw once more on Thomas Kuhn's history of scientific revolutions, 'textbooks' representing the new knowledge – discontinuous as it might in fact be – in broadly coherent and comprehensive terms. As poststructuralist critics and teachers we are rightly sceptical of unifying modes of thought; but until we endeavour to make meaningful and useful *connections* between our disparate findings, and until those connections are conveyed in editions, reference materials, and wide-ranging literary surveys, historicist criticism will not have become 'normal science': it will continue to be something we perform before our students rather than something we can reasonably expect them to learn to do.

More important, we need a new pedagogy that will enable our students to conduct historicist analyses of literature with minimal dependence on extraneous historical knowledge. If we believe, with Louis Montrose, that texts are 'historically determined and determining modes of cultural work,' (15) then we have already committed ourselves to a program of pedagogical reform. Much as we are inclined to feel indebted to New Criticism for sensitizing us to the complexities of literary expression, the methods of close reading cannot in and of themselves sensitize our students to the historical resonance of literature. The historicity of literature must be demonstrable from within the domain of the literary, broadly conceived. I have no doubt that we are all, in the local circumstances of our different academic settings, curricula, and courses, making the necessary adjustments to New Critical methodology, but we have invested little energy in systematizing our practices in order to make them available to the broader teaching community and, more important, to give them the appearance of institutional credibility.

Furthermore, as Brook Thomas has written, the commonplace opposition between close reading and historicist analysis, or even the notion that one is supplementary to the other, is a false and damaging division, enshrining rather than helping to eradicate the conception of historicism as an *option* in the study of literature (243). The idea that historicism merely takes us *further* than close reading undermines the rationale for historicist enquiry itself, which as I understand it is not to read further but to read *differently*, and to do so from the outset. Logically, students need to learn what a metaphor is before they can comment on its political function; but there's no reason why we should trust Cleanth Brooks or Robert Penn Warren to teach them about metaphor. In such handbooks of New Criticism as *Understanding Poetry* far more is taught than figures of speech: in the literary selections themselves, in the rhetorical categories and their ordering, in decisions about which material is sufficiently 'explained' through simple glossing rather than probing interrogative analysis (for example, the image of the cuckoo in Shakespeare's song of Winter at the end of *Love's Labour's Lost* [86]), and in the substance of the study questions, Brooks and Warren are indoctrinating students into New Critical modes of thought. By the time students arrive in the historicist classroom they may have learned to spot a metaphor, but they have also naturalized certain conceptions about what is and what isn't worth reading, what issues and questions are legitimate in literary study, and what the objectives of criticism ought to be. And I think they continue in these beliefs not only because some of their instructors teach the New Critical methodology straight, but also because we ourselves tend to treat 'close reading' as the prerequisite to rather than the precursor of historicist analysis. What is needed is a thoroughgoing revision of close reading as it is practised in the classroom, with a view to incorporating the shared assumptions, methods, and objectives of the past twenty years' work in Renaissance criticism. Discontinuities in specific research goals notwithstanding, I believe there is a continuous critical agenda at work in Renaissance studies today that could, with collective effort, lead to a transformative, rather than additive, pedagogical apparatus.

With the exception of a few remarks made in passing or relegated to footnotes, the essays in the present volume do not address pedagogical issues. In this they are not only continuous with one another but also with much of the academic community that professes Renaissance literature at the post-secondary level: scholarly journals set aside special issues for articles on pedagogical matters; sessions at professional meetings rarely combine research papers with reflections on or accounts of teaching practices; the academic calendar often marks a division between research and teaching activities; and performance appraisals generally consider the two separately. These institutional markers of division, however, are not at all reflective of our work. Few would deny the rich, if unexpected, cross-fertilization that occurs between teaching and research, and few would hesitate to disabuse a student or journalist of the notion that academic research is irrelevant to the 'real' world. In fact, much of the argument for a politically engaged literary criticism, a criticism with consequences, is founded on the belief that the classroom is a site for enacting the meaningful social action to which many of our research programs are committed. Focusing for a time on the continuities rather than discontinuities of the historicist project, and doing so with a view to institutionalizing our methodologies, may, in light of this belief, be the most consequential undertaking of all.

WORKS CITED

Brooks, Cleanth, and Robert Penn Warren. *Understanding Poetry.* 4th ed. New York: Holt, Rinehart and Winston, 1976.
Crewe, Jonathan, ed. *Reconfiguring the Renaissance: Essays in Critical Materialism.* Lewisburg, PA: Bucknell UP, 1992.
Dubrow, Heather, and Richard Strier, eds. *The Historical Renaissance: New Essays on Tudor and Stuart Literature and Culture.* Chicago and London: U of Chicago P, 1988.
Ferguson, Margaret W., Maureen Quilligan, and Nancy J. Vickers, eds. *Rewriting the Renaissance: The Discourses of Sexual Difference in Early Modern Europe.* Chicago and London: U of Chicago P, 1986.

Gallop, Jane. *Around 1981: Academic Feminist Literary Theory.* New York: Routledge, 1992.

Goldberg, Jonathan, ed. *Queering the Renaissance.* Durham, NC: Duke UP, 1994.

Kuhn, Thomas S. *The Structure of Scientific Revolutions.* 2nd ed. Chicago: U of Chicago P, 1970.

Lewis, C.S. *English Literature in the Sixteenth Century Excluding Drama.* Oxford: Clarendon P, 1954.

Montrose, Louis A. 'Professing the Renaissance: The Poetics and Politics of Culture.' *The New Historicism.* Ed. H. Aram Veeser. Routledge, 1989. 15–36.

Thomas, Brook. 'Bringing about Critical Awareness through History in General Education Literature Courses.' *Reorientations: Critical Theories and Pedagogies.* Ed. Bruce Henricksen and Thais E. Morgan. Urbana: U of Illinois P, 1990. 219–47.

Waller, Gary F. *English Poetry of the Sixteenth Century.* 2nd ed. London: Longman, 1993.

Wayne, Valerie, ed. *The Matter of Difference: Materialist Feminist Criticism of Shakespeare.* Ithaca, NY: Cornell UP, 1991.

Contributors

Katherine Osler Acheson teaches in the Department of English at the University of Waterloo. She is responsible for *The Diary of Anne Clifford, 1616–1619: A Critical Edition* (New York: Garland, 1995) and is author of articles on Michael Ondaatje, Renaissance drama by women, and John Milton.

Sylvia Brown is Assistant Professor in the Department of English at the University of Alberta. Her edition of the mothers' legacies of Dorothy Leigh, Elizabeth Jocelin, and Elizabeth Richardson will be published by Sutton in 1999. She is also at work on a critical study of women and godly culture in seventeenth-century England.

Viviana Comensoli is Professor and Graduate Officer in the Department of English at Wilfrid Laurier University. She has published essays on Renaissance drama and culture, and is the author of *'Household Business': Domestic Plays of Early Modern England* (U of Toronto P, 1996), and co-editor of *Enacting Gender on the English Renaissance Stage* (U of Illinois P, 1998).

Elizabeth Hanson is Associate Professor of English at Queen's University. She is the author of *Discovering the Subject in Renaissance England* (Cambridge UP, 1998), and of articles on Renaissance torture, *Othello* and early modern bureaucracy, Renaissance women's sonnet sequences, and John Milton. She is currently working on a book on Jacobean city comedy and the epistemology of economic life in early modern England.

Nate Johnson recently completed his dissertation at Cornell University on pollution and purification in the early modern English canon.

Karen Newman is University Professor and Professor of Comparative Literature and English at Brown University. She is the author of *Shakespeare's Rhetoric of Comic Character* (Methuen, 1985), *Fashioning Femininity and English Renaissance Drama* (Chicago UP, 1991), *Fetal Positions* (Stanford UP, 1996), and numerous articles on early modern culture and on literary theory. She is at work on a book on cultural production in early modern London and Paris.

Sharon O'Dair is Associate Professor of English at the University of Alabama, where she teaches in the Hudson Strode Program in Renaissance Studies. She is co-editor of *The Production of English Renaissance Culture* (Cornell UP, 1994) and the author of essays on Shakespeare, literary theory, and the profession. The present essay is part of a manuscript she is completing, entitled 'Bottom Lines: Class, Critics, Shakespeare.'

Tracey Sedinger is Assistant Professor of English at the University of Northern Colorado. She has recently completed her doctorate at the State University of New York at Buffalo, with a dissertation entitled 'Epistemology of the Crossdresser: Sexual Politics in Early Modern England.' Her article on crossdressing in *As You Like It* has recently appeared in *Shakespeare Quarterly*. She is currently working on a book tentatively entitled 'An Essence That's Not Seen: Sexual Difference in Early Modern Scopic Regimes.'

Paul Stevens is Associate Professor and Head of the Department of English at Queen's University. He has published widely on Renaissance literature and culture, and is the author of *Imagination and the Presence of Shakespeare in 'Paradise Lost'* (U of Wisconsin P, 1985). He is at work on a book-length study of Scripture and the rhetoric of early modern colonialism, provisionally entitled 'The Plantation of the World.'

Marta Straznicky is Associate Professor of English at Queen's University. She has published widely on Renaissance comedy and Renaissance women writers. Currently she is researching radio adaptations of Shakespeare by the Canadian Broadcasting Corporation, and is completing a book on women's closet drama in early modern England.

Barry Taylor is a Senior Lecturer in Literary and Cultural Studies at Staffordshire University. He is the author of *Vagrant Writing: Social and Semiotic Disorders in the English Renaissance* (U of Toronto P and Harvester Wheatsheaf, 1991), and of articles on contemporary popular fiction and cultural theory. He is currently working on Spenser's *Faerie Queene* as part of a study of configurations of the masculine body in early modern England.

Linda Woodbridge is Professor of English at Pennsylvania State University. Her publications include *The Scythe of Saturn: Shakespeare and Magical Thinking* (U of Illinois P, 1994); *True Rites and Maimed Rites: Ritual and Anti-Ritual in Shakespeare and His Age*, co-edited with Edward Berry (U of Illinois P, 1992); *Shakespeare: A Selective Bibliography of Criticism* (Locust Hill Press, 1988); *Women and the English Renaissance: Literature and the Nature of Womankind, 1540–1620* (U of Illinois P, 1984); and numerous articles. She is currently working on early modern texts about homelessness.

Susan Zimmerman is Associate Professor of English at Queens College, City University of New York, and Book Review Editor of *Shakespeare Studies*. Her publications include the collections *Shakespeare's Tragedies* (Macmillan, 1998), and *Erotic Politics: Desire on the Renaissance Stage* (Routledge, 1992), as well as textual studies of early modern drama. Her current project is a study of the eroticized body in Jacobean tragedy.

Index